*What I Can't
Bear Losing*

What I Can't Bear Losing

Gerald Stern

ESSAYS BY GERALD STERN

TRINITY UNIVERSITY PRESS
SAN ANTONIO

Trinity University Press strives to produce its books using methods and materials in an environmentally sensitive manner. We favor working with manufacturers that practice sustainable management of all natural resources, produce paper using recycled stock, and manage forests with the best possible practices for people, biodiversity, and sustainability.

This book is printed on Rolland Enviro Natural, recycled from 100% postconsumer waste.

Published by Trinity University Press
San Antonio, Texas 78212

Copyright © 2004, 2009 by Gerald Stern

Originally published by W.W. Norton & Company, Inc., 2004

Cover design by Nicole Hayward
Book design by BookMatters, Berkeley

⊗ The paper used in this publication meets the minimum requirements of the American National Standard for Information Sciences—Permanence of Paper for Printed Library Materials, ANSI Z39.48-1992.

Library of Congress Cataloging-in-Publication Data

Stern, Gerald, 1925-
    What I can't bear losing / essays by Gerald Stern.
        p. cm.

    Summary: "In this collection of personal essays, which includes seven new pieces, Stern speaks on subjects closest to his heart—family, justice, Jewishness, ecstasy, loss, and love. He ranges from literary discussions to anecdotes and gives readers a glimpse of the poetic process"—Provided by publisher.

    ISBN 978-1-59534-054-2 (pbk. : alk. paper) 1. Stern, Gerald, 1925–
    2. Poets, American—20th century—Biography. I. Title.
    PS3569.T3888Z477 2009
    811'.54—dc22   [B]   2009014782

13   12   11   10   09   —   5   4   3   2   1

For Anne Marie Macari. Always.

Contents

Introduction

It is not easy finding some type of unity among a group of essays disparate in time and theme and even nature. Some of them were written in the early 1980s at the bidding of Arthur Vogelsang, the brilliant editor of *American Poetry Review*, and represent, for the most part, a politico-cultural-literary-personal fusion to parallel the poems I was writing at the time; a few were written for specific occasions; and the greater part I wrote in a burst in the late 1990s and represent, as I said in the introduction to the cloth edition of this book, autobiographical essays whose subjects generally concern events that happened in my second and third decade, in Pittsburgh, New York, and Paris. To this I have added seven new essays, some personal and some literary, and I have restructured the book, dividing it into "personal" and "literary" essays, although, in the manner of disordered tentacles, the one constantly—and relentlessly—invades the other.

I think of myself as a political writer although, rightly or wrongly, I am forever not in the company of ideology. It may be that, though I am very harsh at times, my true mode is forbearance and, finally, I am ready to forgive, if not forget—though not always—which means I can carry a grudge, and stick to a grievance, even to the grave if need be. Frick, Kissinger, Pius, and the like—never! Eli Siegel, one powerful and forgotten poet, said, "Let fat men in black coats live a little." I am with him. So that in my essay called "Salesman" I

not only tolerate poor Dave, who is selling Thermoguard replace-
ment windows and doors, I half-love and half-pity him, though the
"pity" is modified by a certain respect, and even wonder. "Who
made me the judge and why am I so scornful and intolerant and why
was I in such a rage for so many years?" I ask. "I was horrified at my
own anger and didn't know how to apologize," I say, later in the
essay. But now I do, and I know how to make distinctions between
one dupery, one diddling, and another, to appreciate which one is
mortal. I have used the words "forbearance" and "forgiveness" and,
although forbearance *contains* a certain amount of forgiveness, it also
implies "leniency" and "tolerance" and "pity"—even "avoidance,"
all of these aspects of *distance,* something—whatever the issue—I
cannot embrace, or even endure. The struggle between compas-
sion and justice, one dear friend says of this essay, and of my work
in general. But justice is enough; it has many—changing—faces, and
compassion is one of them—otherwise we get into Gnostic non-
sense; the logic that has little to do with actual living. Life itself.
Life as the repository of fullness, what the Taoists called emptiness.
Life, finally, as adequate; very ungnostic.

In my first introduction I said I was surprised by the emphasis on
things Jewish. That brings to mind a short poem I wrote twenty or
thirty years ago, or really part 4 of a poem called "Four Sad Poems
on the Delaware," a "description" of four plants I saw on my daily
walk on the towpath of the Delaware Canal, the flowering dog-
wood, the wild columbine, the mayapple, and the black locust:

> This is a locust tree, dying of love,
> waiting one more time for its flowers to come,
> regretting its life on the stupid river,
> growing more and more Jewish as its limbs weaken.

The black locust, not to be confused with the honey locust, is an asymmetrical, short-lived, "ugly" tree, used, by the East Coast farmers, for fence posts and such, but which bears a blossom, maybe every other year, that is the most heavenly odor that exists in the whole kingdom of plants. The tree is treated with contempt, often called a weed, and cut down as a matter of course to make room for better plants, maples, say. The property that I "owned" at the time was covered with black locusts, and I had to fight my local carpenter and landscaper to save them. They were, they are, for me, Jewish trees, may something forgive me, but I am reminded of yet another poem where I discuss the "three sides of Judaism"—unless there are four, or even six, so no one needs to get excited. Is the Judaism I speak of in the forgiveness, in the justice, in the relentlessness, in the affection, in the humor? Well, it's the "third side," and if I had to I could name ten others.

The humor is broad, and it's sometimes black, and it's sometimes mean and outrageous, though my quill represses me. Like many athletes, comedians, and surgeons, I suffer from Tourette's syndrome, which, in my case, takes the form of utter invasion of the beloved other, even including (mildly) biting him (or her) or kissing (him and her). At a reading a year or two ago at Poets House in New York, I chided Bill Murray who was standing near me—for not knowing enough about Punxsutawney, Pennsylvania, home of the famous groundhog, a city I had spent more than a few days in since my cousin Jack Grossman owned the best restaurant in town. Jack, formerly a city detective, was reputed to have been the toughest cop in Pittsburgh. You could see the murderous history in his eyes and in the welts on his face, but by this time he wore ostrich shoes and had a bit of a stomach. After my reading, Bill, echoing one of my poems, ran up and bit me on the shoulder, leaving teeth marks, and demonstrating that he had Tourette's too. The women there were furious that he chose to bite me instead of them. Tourette's is maybe one of the sources of my humor, as it is—maybe—of my quick thinking, my sudden shifts and—certainly—my tic. Though I hate it when, after a reading, some idiot or other tells me I should have been a stand-up comedian, this when there are not many dry eyes left in the audience. It's the nervous mixture, the going back and forth between modes, the tic itself, all Jewish. Side seven.

I think my new essays are in sync with my old ones. One of the new ones, "The Morosco," written in the early 1980s and only changed a very little, indeed precedes most of the others. If I haven't changed that much, it's probably because I began the whole business of writing them, all of them, when I was already into my fifties, with a fairly cohesive point of view. I wrote somewhere that I was a poet—and, I might add, essayist—who wrote for the second half of life. That's generally a difficult thing in America, where new blood is more or less young blood. Who needs old blood? It's usually half-water or half-alcohol anyway. (Though mine is half ichor, let Diet Pepsi be damned.) I like the idea of having something to say *later*. I like the decades rolling along, pulling one more small and sun-damaged sheet off the calendar. What I really like, even if it's corny, is the image of myself as a bald Chinese poet in the fifteenth century, standing on a cliff top looking at the sky. There are some clouds below on one side and hints of a pine forest below on the other. His hut, bamboo roof and all, is in the midst of the pine forest. He is wearing a loose robe and is holding a long stick in his left hand. There is a sash around his waist. And there is a mountain, a kind of smudge, towering in the distance. He is thinking of his wife and the poem he composed for her. The subject was separation. The grief. He remembers the T'ang era and wishes it was he who broke away from the elegance. He weeps over the poem of the grass hovel,

"Not even a tattered blanket to sleep on," "No coals in the house." And he wonders what he should do when the rain starts. He tries to remember the name of his last superior—at the office of metallurgy and naval procurement—but, for the life of him, he can't. He is in a good place.

Suddenly, he—I mean I—remember an event from my forty-fifth year. I had at the time written only one book and was teaching at a community college because the pay was astonishingly bad. It was New Jersey and the state legislature had just passed a law sanctioning and encouraging the formation of unions among public employees. Public Law 303. I was the president of the union and its chief negotiator. The first year I got a 27 percent increase in salary for the faculty. The second year, with the aid of my team, I presented management with an eighty-page proposal. They were shocked and responded with an insulting counterproposal. Par for the course, except that my team got me so riled up, so angry, that I refused to sit down and negotiate unless they removed their counterproposal altogether. I was dealing with the president of the college and the business manager, both friends of mine, and they had coffee, wine, juice, and sandwiches waiting for us. When Trenton (the state capital) got word of this they rushed up the two state heads, union and management (in a car together), to explain the law and talk sense into me. I refused to budge, and after an arduous day of talk, management removed the counterproposal. My team knew that I'd give in to anything, out of courtesy, kindness, and embarrassment—unless I was truly angered by lying and stupidity. And they did the legwork.

I sometimes wonder if that anger is the key to my writing, the source for it, and, if it comes from the desire to point out the imbalance, the injustice, to set things right. If that desire is what moves my heart—and rouses my voice. My Chinese poet must have lost his anger somewhere on that mountain. He is, surprisingly, no longer in exile, even if he is alone. He may even have forgotten the very name of his absurd outpost, where he slaved away all those years, caught up in ritual, politics, and repetitive acts, although he certainly remembers the larger things. He may call that outpost, that region, *the lower world*, but he doesn't do that with contempt. Indeed, he is amused by the simultaneity of the literal and the figurative, how a mountain both is and isn't more than a mountain, and he doesn't give a hoot if the Romantic sublime is in fashion or not. Even when I started out, I imagined a place apart, that I had finished with the labor of writing, that lifetime pursuit, and was sitting somewhere watching and waiting, a park bench outside the main library preferably, flakes of snow dropping on my hat, since it wasn't—for me—a mountain. Are the essays, and the poems for that matter, only for the lower world? Don't I still love both places, and don't the essays address them both? What did it mean to retire? Why do fools ask me if I'm still writing? Where does that crazy Yiddish-speaking Chinaman hide his ballpoint and his string of notebooks? What's next on his list?

PERSONAL
ESSAYS

SUNDAYS

SUNDAYS, WHERE I GREW UP, were bad enough for their bleakness and oppression, but Sunday was also the day when the battles between my mother and father took place, since it was the only time that my father slept in. Normally, six days a week, he'd be up and out by seven o'clock or seven-thirty and my mother would sleep in till eleven or so. The battles lasted for a good hour and a half, say, from ten to twelve, and were punctuated by his sighing and banging dresser drawers in their crowded little bedroom and her talking low and sometimes wailing in her frustration and desperation. The lingua franca was English, though there were some things that could be said only in Yiddish. They kept the door closed—in fact the battles always started with my mother carefully closing the door and clearing her throat, as if to clear her mind and get up her nerve. Closing their door was a useless and ridiculous measure, for their voices were loud and the apartment was small. It was called four rooms but it really was three and, by my calculations, it was not much more than five hundred square feet. I slept in the living room, on a couch, no place for my books and clothes, and wrote and did my homework, from time to time, on a rickety secretary that sported a small picture of myself, age eleven or so, that I had to either face or slip into one of the tiny drawers when I picked up a pencil, my knees lifting the piece of fake walnut that extended into my stomach, the table of choice thus going uphill, indicating either a great slide into truth or a sudden leap from hope.

When they opened the bedroom door, it was as if a two-headed dragon had come out, spitting fire. They never threw plates—that would have been too loving. It ended usually with my father putting on his hat and coat and venturing out, slamming the front door, his stomach empty, his throat engorged, off to the solace of upper Fifth Avenue and the wholesale houses, open on Sunday.

I always had a sense that they were fighting, as it were, for their lives, to regain their honor and dignity, remarkably the way characters in a Greek play argued, only they—the Greeks—had a double, even a triple, audience, if you counted the other actors, the chorus, and the spectators. The Greeks always had the option, which they constantly used, of seeking justice and understanding from the profound multilayered intercutting of listeners. My parents were desperate for listeners and in the wringing of their hands and in the grimness and sneers and appeals to unseen witnesses, they expressed, in grotesquerie, their limitations. Alas, they had only one listener and he was silently begging them to stop arguing and he was holding his ears and clenching and unclenching his fists at the secretary, or the bookshelf he had built in the little hole in the wall that went for a closet, housing his first buys, his Steinbeck, his Hemingway, his Yeats.

What is amazing is what wasn't said between them, how neither would address the sadness and the need of the other. But, of course, that's not amazing. Ordinarily the fights—whatever the nominal causes were—centered around his desire for a family life, for attention, even affection. He never directly recognized her depression and loneliness. He would have been content with black bread and schmaltz herring, let the psychology go. He raged inwardly, sometimes he managed a *wei ist mir* as he bent over the laundry, which got as far as the hall closet, still half-wrapped in its ripped-open brown paper, sheets and towels ironed, underwear and socks in a loose pile. She, on the other hand, was jarred back into a wakeful, dutiful, unnerving state, those Sunday mornings; normally she would eat her eggs and toast about noon, pull her long facial hairs by the light of an upended shadeless little lamp, and talk for an hour to her friend Pauline. I remember asking her—in her mid-eighties—about those Sunday morning fights and how she insisted they were only about one thing, my father doing favors for his family, his nephews in particular, all fifty of them, getting them jobs, buying them clothes. We didn't mention, there in hideous Florida, how I sneaked off, as a boy, to her older brother's apartment, next building over, with small envelopes stuffed with cash, my Uncle Simon who was unemployed most of the thirties and, at forty or so, at the height of his powers, went from door to door collecting dimes for Prudential or Metropolitan Life. I tried to give her the chance to talk about her own childhood; her relationship with her father, the heartless blue-eyed scholar; my sister Sylvia's death; her breakdown the week after Sylvia's death; the curse of once being a beauty; her hatred of housekeeping; her loneliness; her failed attempts in her mid-forties, born thirty years too soon, to create a life for herself outside the home by going to college and starting a career; or her melancholy, sarcasm, and stubbornness, but she refused to respond. Once, maybe in her late eighties or early nineties, talking about her father, the chicken-killer, she blurted out, to our mutual amazement, "He never kissed me once," but loyalty forbade her from going any farther.

If as a boy I took sides, it was my father's. I saw him as unappreciated, uncared for, and treated unjustly. Sometimes I went with him to the Avenue and spent time with him and his cronies in the wholesale houses, listening to them talk business and politics, or eating a roast beef sandwich at the long counter at Goldstein's, the rye bread soft from the cooked juices, the meat piled on thick. I'll never forget him explaining to me, driving home on the Boulevard of the Allies, how the Ethiopians would surely conquer the invading Italians—the year was 1935—because of their elephants and blow guns. We knew nothing about Count Ciano, Mussolini's son-in-law, and the beautiful silent explosions his bombs made over Addis-Ababa. We even thought the Spanish Loyalists would win and the Jews of Europe would escape. My mother, who read the *Pittsburgh Sun-Telegraph* from cover to cover, word for word, methodically tore up each page after she was finished. She started to get dressed about five and was ready to go out to dinner by six or six-thirty, by which time my father and I would have returned home. No sign of that morning's rancor remained. The three of us usually went to a restaurant where we waited in line for an hour or so before we were seated. The House by the Side of the Road was our favorite—the best chicken in four counties, and all you could eat—burned to the ground, everything lost, one night. I, however, preferred the times we ate at home, those Sundays, gorging on hot dogs and baked beans, listening to Jack Benny, Eddie Cantor, and Kay Kayser, playing ping-pong on the scarred dinette table.

My own unwillingness to face off with the women in my life probably stems from those Sundays, and my hatred of Sundays stems as much from that as it does from the repression, rigidity, and emptiness of growing up in that filthy, law-abiding city.

God knows who took it but there's a snapshot of me, taken I'm sure on a Sunday, for it's gray and empty and I'm wearing a suit and tie and I have a less than triumphant smile on my face. My hair is wavy and I remember now that I rubbed fingertips of brilliantine through it and combed and brushed it, the part on the left side. I had several brushes with soft bristles, from the toilet kits I was given on my bar mitzvah, complete "sets," with the items enclosed in little wooden boxes, the whole thing in a heavy leather case with a zipper on three sides. I don't think they were plastic. Du Pont had not gotten there yet. I was fourteen or fifteen, already into my diet and exercise phase, tall, muscular, and dark-skinned. Most of all, earnest.

What I did was get up early, even though it was Sunday, and shower, shine my shoes, and put on a suit, white shirt, and tie, even though I had no place to go. I left the house quietly and walked up the main street of my neighborhood, sometimes ending up at my favorite pharmacy where I sat at the counter with a cup of coffee and maybe a Western magazine, the pages new, thick, with a certain pulpy smell that was my drug of choice then. There were very few people out; the fruit stores and groceries were not yet opened though there were already little crowds at the two or three bakeries, one of them—Rosenbloom's—smelling of fresh rolls in front and rats in the back where the dirty work was done in the garbage cans, the telltale smell, astonishing in the small cement backyard and the steep hill that rose abruptly behind it. I returned to my house at nine or nine-thirty, just in time for the sweet music and the despair of that third-floor life.

It was a Jewish neighborhood, so there was some life there Sunday morning, but we were nonetheless affected by the overwhelming oppression of the Calvinist Sabbath, vividly reflected in the state's blue laws, where nothing that expressed pleasure was allowed to openly manifest itself, where movies, bars, gas stations, and stores of all kinds were tightly closed. I can't remember exactly, but I think the ballparks were closed and we didn't play ball ourselves in our local field, the ruts all memorized to give us a tremendous home-team advantage, the wire fence forced open in one or two places to make our entrance onto the field easier. It may be that we played a little in the afternoon, so we could keep the morning holy. The main library was open for a few hours in the afternoon but I think the adjacent museum was closed. At two or four in the afternoon there was an organ recital in the ornate ancient Carnegie Hall, and I sometimes sat down in a balcony seat (I was sixteen or seventeen) to listen with the few others—all old men and ladies with pink faces—who attended. I always hated the organ—so I said—and the reason I gave was that it was church music and therefore offensive to a freethinking and desperately loyal Jew, but I'm not sure if that was the reason or if, after all, I really disliked it. Carnegie Hall was such a magnificent building, marble wherever you looked, selected and cut certainly by the Poles and Slovaks in any one of the many quarries Andrew Carnegie kept running along the three slag-ridden oily rivers he owned in western Pennsylvania, Vermont, PA, Caralla, PA, and such.

I don't know when the Pittsburgh Symphony Orchestra started playing Sunday afternoons in addition to Friday evenings, but when I was in my twenties it certainly did. It was an activity that the privileged enjoyed, so it was more permissible on Sunday, for the privileged were allowed their golf and tennis and even—God save us—their martinis and gin and tonics in their country clubs, which were not, God save us again, in the country, not counting Jews, who were excluded, and African Americans—who weren't even considered—and Hunkies, our Pittsburgh word for East Europeans of all sorts—who had their own clubs, albeit there wasn't much room for golf or tennis, the hills were so steep. Certainly the pool halls were closed. Morry's, where we hung out, played eight-ball and nine-ball for money, occasionally straight pool, exchanged information, told jokes, and lied about girls, all under the excellent tutelage of Morry, who had a wooden leg, which he sort of hoisted when he made a shot, who had a polished moustache and chewed gum incessantly. Somewhere in the world downstairs (we were on the second floor) and far away from that iniquitous nest, he had a teenage daughter whom he loved dearly and protected endlessly against the boy-monsters in his care. He also owned a tiny watch-repair shop across the street and I would often see him in the window with a glass in his eye and his face all screwed up. It was rumored that he belonged to the KKK, though I was sure he was a Jew.

Walking wasn't a sin in those days and, still with suit on, the years after I stopped accompanying my father to the wholesale section, I walked for hours on end, through Schenley Park, past the Phipps conservatory, past Carnegie Tech, down Forbes Avenue (then Forbes Street) as far down as Soho, sometimes across the Brady Street bridge to the South Side, sometimes to the Hill itself. I was already given to studying houses, those three-story red-brick ones, with the front stoop and the elegant stone, cement—or ancient wood—around the windows, and the front doors of wood and glass, some single, some double. I stared in the windows and I walked into the backyard, as I still do today, and I reconstructed family life, particularly if it was a decomposed dwelling, that family life when all was fresh and new and hopeful, maybe fifty or a hundred years before. I loved walking over the bridges—there were dozens of them—and I loved looking at the houses almost on stilts climbing up the hills.

I took long walks on other days too, Fridays, Saturdays, but on Sundays there were no distractions, no bookstores, no burlesque houses. I can't express the joy I felt walking the hills in some unfamiliar neighborhood, climbing the cobblestone streets—sometimes wood instead of stone—till my thighs and calves themselves turned to stone, and lingering in the alleys so I could get a sense of what the intimate life of families was in the meager yards behind their houses: toys, half a car on blocks, an overturned aluminum chair, clothes on the line; or taking the streetcars that I adored through every part of the city and stopping to wander through the local streets as if I were in a foreign country; or, on some Sundays, running by myself around an abandoned grassy race track in Schenley Park, called the oval, until it got dark; and walking the two miles or so back to my house.

I was talking recently to a woman who spent her first ten years in the Appalachian Mountains in western Virginia. She is of Scotch-Irish ancestry and a daughter of that group that leapfrogged over first the English, then the Germans, so they could settle where the soil was thin and the rocks abundant, and the life hard, similar to the Scotch-Irish who came across Pennsylvania and made their homes in the reaches of Somerset and Pittsburgh where they could scrabble a little so God the demon would notice them. She said that on Sunday she went to church twice a day and wasn't allowed to play cards. I'm sure she wasn't allowed to dance, read—except for the Bible—listen to music, play instruments, or swim either. The temptation is to compare the Jewish and the Calvinist day of rest, a day of celebration and a day of gloom, yet both days, both Sabbaths, are suffused in negation; there's no denying it. The Jewish Sabbath is a day of rest and abstention from work. It is also a day of study and of taking delight in the senses, gustatory and sexual. It is a day of sanctification and holiness, and preempts all other holy days, and it is a memorial of the creation of the world and of the exodus from Egypt as well as a memorial to the pact between God and the Hebrews, the covenant. It is because God "rested and was refreshed" on the seventh day that subsequent Jewish law defined thirty-nine separate types of action that constitute an infringement of the Sabbath. I can see black-coated rebs and Presbyters arguing the Sabbath far into the night (of what day?) and comparing both outrages and technicalities. Ah, they would learn from each other.

The Christians got their Sabbath originally from the Jewish one, but it was changed to Sunday to differentiate it and because that was the day of the Resurrection, although the Sabbath was altered, certainly by the Protestants, certainly especially by the Calvinists, into a day almost of mourning, and it is that mourning I remember, in which not only is every pleasure denied but punishment is positively engaged, even enjoyed. The causes can be found (partly) in theological theory, most especially the idea of total depravity, or original sin, and the notion of predestination, as well as in cultural history and economic conditions. I spent a year in Scotland and I deeply love the Scots, but I don't know enough about the Scottish character in the days preceding John Knox—or the centuries—to know what changes ensued when Presbyterianism became established there. I read with joy Robbie Burns's great poem attacking the Presbyters and I remember two men, Wee Frees, walking by my friend Beth McDonald in the country outside of Glasgow one Sunday morning while she was in the act of fiercely painting—of all things—the same Wee Frees, who had visited her the Sunday before in the same spot. The men's faces were murderous, and only in Jerusalem, walking with a woman in jeans, blouse, and sandals on some fundamentalist side street, did I encounter such looks.

I experienced head on the Calvinist Sabbath, but I didn't yet know about such things as double predestination and the outrage in the Garden. I just suffered their *effects*. Nor did I know much about the late-nineteenth- and early-twentieth-century religious justification of murderous economic profit and endless economic abuse by the panderers of wealth unlimited, who built their system on greed, hypocrisy, exploitation, and self-congratulation. Calvinism, in its heyday, taught that mankind was essentially doomed because of Adam's disobedience and is by itself incapable of goodness, nor could any of its "works" have any merit—as far as the election to eternal life—and all are in a state of ruin meriting only damnation; yet some men (and women) are undeservedly rescued from this helpless and hopeless condition through God's love. The reason some are saved and others are lost is beyond comprehension; it has to do with divine choice and that alone, and it is absurd to inquire into God's will. The word for this is "predestination." Simply, God's freedom seems to deny or override man's freedom (or responsibility), since God is *completely* free of any fate or external necessity— which would mean that the Christian gospel of love and forgiveness represents only an optimistic hope in the face of unknown odds and that God will save or damn without regard to what anyone thought was just, under the circumstances. Why anyone would believe in such a God is hard for me to understand, unless such a person was convinced of the doctrine's truth and believed that any forgiveness was only a gift, or fudged it a bit the way we fudge the reality of death. Anyhow, modern Protestantism, by contrast, emphasizes the dual and concurrent contributions of God *and* man, and all through the five hundred or so years of its existence, Calvinism compromised God's "sovereignty," or at least his willfulness, in one way or another with its emphasis on repentance, forgiveness, and reconciliation. Catholicism at least was more pleasurable. After an hour or so of morning duty the Sabbath was given over to family gatherings and walks, no guilt attached. The very existence of the Protestant Sabbath was a protest against Catholic "paganism" and "hedonism."

The Calvinist Sabbath was merely the state of the religion seen purely—or in extremis—and if it was dour on Thursday it was even more dour on Sunday. Certainly the Sabbath was not an exquisite foretaste of eternity, where mankind eats three meals a day instead of two and lounges forever on clean pillows, maybe velvet ones, and recites poetry easily in every language. I'm shocked by how little Jesus is listened to, here and elsewhere. He did go so far as to deliberately violate the Sabbath, according to the Gospel of Mark, but he did so, it is clear, as a protest against mere form. True, to disconnect from Judaism, Paul and others chided early Christians who abided by the laws of Sabbath, but that is another matter altogether. Jesus would presumably protest *Christian* law, as he did Jewish. I, for my part, had two Sabbaths and that wasn't so bad a thing. It would be nice having seven—or six, one day of "work."

Walking around in my suit and tie, I was constantly reminded of the sharp lines in Pittsburgh, the demarcation, the segregation—of the rich as well as the poor. I was just beginning my reading—some of it locked behind glass—of the economic history, and I was horrified by the arrogance and righteousness of the owners and managers and their defenders. At fifteen. They assumed that they were "the elected," as it were, to eternal life, because they accumulated such wealth. Not only that, but those who weren't elected—amply demonstrated because of their poverty—were damned, even, I suppose, if they were Catholic, which most of them were, forget about the Jews, nicely damned by everyone. It was a combining of social Darwinism with Calvinism (natural selection and the survival of the fittest), one presumably the mirror of the other, which meant the elimination of the unfit and the condemnation of the poor on pseudo-moral and biological grounds. They were blamed for their own poverty, the poor. As always, only more so.

The best, certainly the most famous, writing on the subject is the article *Wealth*, by Andrew Carnegie. He states the "survival of the fittest" idea in plain, clear terms. It was based on competitive individualism and its three pillars were economy, thrift, and stewardship. God gave wealth to a few to be used in the best manner to produce the most beneficial results for the community. It was the Gospel of Wealth, of course, as opposed to the Gospel of Poverty, or the Christian Gospel, at least the Gospel of Jesus. For Carnegie, and others, it was a justification for the grossly unequal distribution of wealth, or a gross defense of greed, and in its name the most outrageous things were said. Would you believe "No man can be obedient to God without becoming wealthy" or "the wealthy man was the victim of circumstances over which he had no control" or "it is only to the man of morality that wealth comes, for Godliness is in league with riches"? I don't know when it ended—with the Great Depression or World War II? I know I was stopped and questioned several times by Pittsburgh's Finest in my wanderings. The law was against loitering, though it may as well have been against idleness and sloth. You had to have three dollars in your pocket.

On Sunday I thought of these things and I thought I was living in a world of total hypocrisy when I didn't think it was total madness and I winced—at fifteen—at religious perversion. Bad enough the religion, but the perversion worse, I thought. Nor did I believe for a minute that the elect (an hour at church maybe, where they were adored and envied) denied themselves anything on that day, nor suffered at all as the bucks came rolling in.

The bars closed at 12:00 A.M.—Saturday night—as if a whole city
had to be treated like fourteen-year-olds, as if the punishment had
to start exactly on time, 12:01, beginning of the true night, as if the
streetcars and taxis would turn into pumpkins if the mice weren't
back in time, as if the religious rules of one group—a minority cer-
tainly—were to direct the civil authority, as if one could go to sleep
at such an early hour, especially on spring and summer nights when
the moon sometimes broke through the filth and the rivers them-
selves shone.

But there is always a *riposte* and we had the clubs, which could
legally stay open till 2:00 A.M. or all night. There was the Legion
and the Moose but most especially the ethnic clubs. I belonged
to three, the Italian Club on Mt. Washington, the Serbian Club
in Duquesne, and the Post-War Literary Club, neither ethnic nor
literary, on the second floor of a building on Atwood Street, in
Oakland, between Forbes and Fifth. Generally the rooms were
barn-size, there was a long bar at one end, tables to sit down at,
a kitchen, and a small dance floor in the middle. And they were
graced by either a huge jukebox or a small band, playing dance
music from both sides of the Atlantic, polkas especially. And they
were Catholic. I'm sure they're still there, most of them. There were
also, I might add, the whorehouses in Homestead and the North
Side, where both sides of the street were lined up with cars starting
about midnight, and the police kept order. The whorehouses were
illegal but the gatekeepers were paid off, and I don't remember the
mayor ever coming through with a curved ax in his hands and a
retinue of photographers at his heels. Inside, in the more elaborate
ones, you could even get a drink, although there might be a good

deal of water in it and the price wasn't quite the same as in the Serbian Club. These were the row houses I loved so well, Pittsburgh style, a little different from the Philadelphia and Baltimore ones. I imagine that at the turn of the last century, and earlier, the German and Irish wives scrubbed the marble steps till they gleamed, as they did in Baltimore and Amsterdam.

One of the women took a fancy to me, and I used to visit her in her corner apartment on the first floor of one of the row houses where she lived with her little girl. We saw each other for several months and there was harmony between us because the sex wasn't an issue in terms of seduction and power-grabbing. She was taking a few college courses and when she put her glasses on and began to study I found her endearing, which was part of my hopeless adolescent romanticism, but she started to resent my endless questions and when she discovered I was writing a novel about her she grew furious and threw me out. Her name, like mine, was Jerry. I was nineteen.

Some of the more gluttonous religious caterpillars started their Sabbath on Saturday sunset and some kept it till late at night on Sunday. There was no unified standard as there is in Judaism, sundown to sundown. But the tail end you could still feel and I'm sure many of the prayerful went to bed on Sunday night still in a righteous condition. In our neighborhood—in our world—there were weddings on Sunday night at any of five or so synagogues and we went almost every week. There had to be at least one wedding and we went from shul to shul. I was in my late teens when we did this. I always shaved, shined my shoes, put on a suit, necktie, and white shirt, slicked back my hair, and gargled with some burning liquid. We had to put up with the ceremony, which was always boring, but it was important that we be seen there. There was a *huppah* or not, according to the orthodoxy of the bride. Upstairs, or downstairs, there was food, drink, dancing, and beautiful girls, all open and giving because it was a wedding and because we might be related, cousins or whatnot. Many guests were from other cities. We didn't get caught because we *acted* as if we belonged there and, who knows, we could be from the other side, the groom's, the bride's. I quickly gathered the necessary details, made friends with one of the older women, worked up a defense in case anyone should recognize me, and adopted a persona and a history for the evening: I was from Steubenville, Ohio, or Detroit, or the Bronx. I even did Russian dances, *kazatskas*. There were four or five of us crashers.

One time, at the wedding of one of my cousins, where I was *legitimately* invited, one of the faux guests—whom I recognized—was caught in the act, kicked out and almost beaten up, certainly humiliated. He looked at me knowingly and appealed to me with his eyes. But I couldn't do anything. I was even indignant, now that I was on the other side, but I did feel some sympathy and restrained my cousin's friends, a rough group.

I stayed till the last dances, always got a bit tipsy, ate like a king, kugels and cakes you can't imagine, and as likely as not accompanied someone home, or to her hotel if she was from out of town. At one wedding, it was my cousin Michael's and the synagogue was the Tree of Life, I met the sister or friend or cousin of his bride and we hit it off immediately. She was from Ohio somewhere and her parents, especially the father, kept a close eye on her. I took her to the Webster Hall Hotel where she was staying, a University of Pittsburgh dorm now, and we practically consumed each other in the back seat of the taxi. She had her own room, but her mother and father guarded her too well. Furthermore, she had marriage on *her* mind and asked me the telltale questions—what my profession was going to be, what my father's business was, how I felt about Ohio. My God, I was twenty at the most and my secret plans were to go either to Mexico or France, write poetry, and get in touch with the past. I hope she found what she wanted—I did. And though Sunday was always melancholy for me, I came to understand it was because of those two wonderful decades between 1925 and 1945, and I did everything I could, and I do everything I can, to understand them and undo them, even as, in memory, I love them.

THE BEACON

Foo's name was Sidney Santman though I could as easily say that Sidney Santman's name was Foo. We were friends during the war, part of a forlorn group of young men with various kinds of deformities and deficiencies that made us unfit for military service, though much of that had to do with the needs of the local draft board and even the demands of the government, which, from time to time, relaxed some of its restrictions, it was so short of manpower. I was one of them, doomed—or saved—because of bad eyesight, not even qualified for "limited" service, though I was able to play football well enough and run the mile and even, it turned out, when I was finally drafted—five months after we dropped the bombs—I was able to knock a few people down in the small ring, with the oversized gloves we wore, and helmets, at the Virginia camp where I was stationed at the end of my tenure.

I don't know why Foo was 4F. The doctors kept you out for the oddest things. I had a feeling that in his case it was asthma. Many years later, 1980 probably, I ran into Foo in a deli in Pittsburgh and we hugged and talked. I was shocked to see that he had fingers missing from one of his hands and retained only the index and the thumb. It was an accident in a machine shop he owned. That would have certainly kept him out, but by that time we had no more wars to go to.

During World War II he managed a small settlement house in the part of Squirrel Hill south of Forbes, mostly Jewish. He spent much of his time at his oversized desk writing letters to his friends in the service, and the battle at Anzio and the slaughter was much on our minds. We used to meet about nine o'clock—two or three of us—usually there were no clients then, play some basketball, take a shower, and then walk the three or four blocks up the hill to the Beacon Pharmacy, where we'd eat sundaes or pie and coffee before we walked home. Foo always bought a *Post-Gazette*, a morning paper (it is Pittsburgh's only remaining paper) from a small black newsboy on the corner. It was a ritual that they would play the Dozens every night and Foo would generally give him a quarter or fifty cents, good money then. The Dozens is a street ritual where the two contestants insult each other's families, particularly mothers, a macabre game of one-upmanship that was practiced in the African American community on the Hill, and Foo, who still lived there, was very adept at the game. They—Foo and the newsboy, maybe fourteen years old—threw the verbal slings back and forth. ("Yo' mutha' ain't got no drawers." "Yo' mutha' got 'em, but she don't wear 'em." "Yo' mutha' like a slaughterhouse, she either full o' shit or full o' blood." "You ain't got no mutha', you got two bald-headed daddies." "I seen yo' mutha' down at the police station where all the dicks hang out.")

The game usually ended in a shouting match and hugging, but one night Foo seemed especially hard, or the newsboy especially sensitive, for the boy began to cry and, through his tears, continue to shout insults at Foo. Foo tried giving him a dollar, but he followed us (Foo and me) up the street, tears pouring down his face, shouting, "You big fat mutha' fucka'." Money wouldn't pacify him; he followed us past the Orthodox synagogue on our right, even past the deli where Foo and I ran into each other again thirty-seven years later—before going back to his papers. Foo looked nervously around him—I'm sure he was terrified of meeting one of his board members on the way, half-shocked, half-amused. We arrived at the Beacon Pharmacy a little subdued and pensive—and remorseful—and had our fruit salad sundaes in silence before he boarded a street-car to take him home the old route. Down Forbes Street to the Hill, Webster Avenue, Logan Street, Wylie Avenue, where I was born, a huge Jewish enclave once, as well as black, Syrian, Irish, and Italian, mostly black by 1930, killed by the planners after the war.

The sidewalk in front of the Beacon Pharmacy was double, maybe quadruple in width, a kind of plaza where people could gather, what went for a square in our neighborhood. When I was a junior in high school—in 1941—there was a series of fights, battles really, between the Jews of my neighborhood—high school students mostly—and the Eastern and Southern Europeans—Poles, Slovaks, Italians—of near neighborhoods, also mostly students. And one afternoon there was a huge confrontation in front of the drugstore. There were two, three hundred people there; how it started, how they got there, how the word was spread, I don't know. There were some pushes and shoves, some fringe fisticuffs, some ugly insults, but the police arrived in force to break up the crowd and send every-one home. It was literally an invasion of our streets, our living space, by outsiders from other parts of the city coming to intimidate and assault the Jews. Cars couldn't get through, or trucks or streetcars, till the police arrived. There were some knives and clubs, in addi-tion to fists, and there would have been a lot of bloodshed if the police hadn't come.

I don't think America was officially at war yet—it was spring or early fall. There was incredible hatred and violence, and anti-

Semitism was rampant. In our case, the confrontations, the incidents, were ironically partly based on physiography—hills, rivers, and bridges—and the structure of high schools. There was geographical propinquity, but total economic, social, religious, and ethnic separation. The Jews and the non-Jews were both first or second generation, but the Jews were shopkeepers, salesmen, store managers, artisans, electricians, plumbers, and a few pharmacists, dentists, lawyers, accountants, and doctors; whereas the Eastern and Southern Europeans mostly worked in the mills or on the railroads. The children of the one were at least half college-bound or readied for some "adventure," the children of the other were more doomed, as it were, to work the same jobs as their parents, and half of them left school when they reached the compulsory age, often after the tenth grade. They—their families—brought the hatred and contempt for Jews over with them—from the Ukraine, Poland, Lithuania, Romania, Russia, Czechoslovakia—and combined this with the frustration and resentment they felt at their economic plight, which they also blamed on the Jews. Who had absolutely nothing to do with J&L, U.S. Steel, Pittsburgh Plate Glass, Alcoa, Gulf, Westinghouse, Mellon Bank, the Pennsylvania Railroad, or the other "oppressive" employers. They neither were owners nor managers. Indeed, in my generation, Jewish college students never studied engineering because the doors were closed to them in the large industrial firms.

The hatred didn't stop in the least during the war. In fact, it increased. One night a close friend and I—it was two, three years after the abortive riot—were leaving the Beacon Pharmacy after our usual repast. It was late September 1943; I know this because I was starting my sophomore year the very next day. The front door of the pharmacy was blocked by three strangers, people I'd never seen, in their early to mid-twenties. We were so engrossed in our conversation, sports, women, literature, the war, that we hardly noticed them. My friend's name was Bill Kahn—not the famous Billy Conn who almost knocked out Joe Louis in 1940. He was tall and athletic and a star on the University of Pittsburgh's basketball team until he suffered a severe injury that prevented him, at the time, from lifting anything or making any sudden movements. I politely and unsuspectingly excused myself and tried to get by the three strangers but they continued to block the door. "Take off your glasses, you fucking kike" was the response. As if it were a courtly challenge I started to remove my glasses with my left hand but one of them suddenly sucker-punched me, a sharp ring on his finger, in the left eye. I staggered back, dazed from the blow, toward the rear of the store where the pharmacist was standing in his nice white uniform, holding my hand against my bleeding eye, but he was no help. "I don't want any trouble in here," was what he said, so I groped my way back to the front, supporting myself on the glass cases to my left, full of powders and perfumes, past the startled diners on my right, sitting on their stools at the long soda fountain. My friend Bill couldn't do anything to help me; he would be back in the hospital if he so much as lifted a finger.

I opened the door, my glasses lost somewhere, blood coming out of my eye, and there, across the little plaza were the three of them, sneering and laughing, a little crowd gathering. I was able to find my assailant somehow, with one eye closed and the bad vision I had anyhow, and lift him up like a stick or a wet cloth and begin banging his head on the front bumper of a car, detached from the car's body as it was then, curved and sharp on top. He was unconscious in a few minutes and would have been dead in a few more, and it took the usual five or so to get me off him. I didn't for a second think of what I was doing but I came close to killing him. I felt neither righteous nor horrified, not even saddened, more than anything a little amazed at what I did. I certainly didn't feel like a hero—I just felt something happened to me that could have happened to anyone who approached that front door.

A half-century later I would remember the event as typical of the ten or fifteen years of stupidity, bigotry, violence, hatred we lived through. I'm not in the least proud of it, just a little ashamed and embarrassed, not only for myself but for the others in that cement plaza, most of all for the druggist who "didn't want trouble." My assailant's friends half carried him onto a streetcar, going toward Homestead, a number 60. Famous Homestead, scene of the steel strike, the lockout, Frick's use of the Pinkertons, the war between the strikers and the state militia, the permanent scars.

Bill Kahn's father was Ziggy Kahn, the director of the Irene Kaufman Settlement House on the Hill, the extraordinary athlete who played football opposite Jim Thorpe. Ziggy found out in an hour who it was who hit me; it turned out he was a professional boxer and because his hands were considered weapons he was barred from further boxing.

Within a few weeks my eye was better and I was reading Plato, Montaigne, Joyce, and the late plays of Shakespeare again. There was a little more violence in the next year or so, street fights, head banging, some hand wringing. There would be racial violence in Detroit and other places soon enough, but I want to save the reader. I hate to say this, but what used to be the Beacon Pharmacy is now an Eckerd and there is a Rite-Aid and a CVS down the road. Nor does Eckerd have toasted cheese sandwiches and fruit salad sundaes. Not even a soda fountain.

I remember walking by that troublesome corner one time in the winter of 1944–45. My guess is it was February 1945, and the great thaw had just begun and the world was wet and dark and dreary. Coming the other way was a friend of mine, Marvin Hadburg, limping in half-opened galoshes, a grin, as always, on his face. I don't know what was wrong with him that he was 4F so many years. But in the winter of '44, as the Allied troops suddenly bogged down in the face of the huge German offensive—their last—he was called up, sent for ridiculously brief training to Fort Benning, Georgia, and shipped after six weeks to Belgium and the Battle of the Bulge. He lasted a week or so, was hospitalized with badly frozen feet, and was discharged less than three months after he was drafted, a cripple for life. His father owned a small store in one of the towns around Pittsburgh, I think it was Munhall—next to Homestead—and Marvin worked there, straightening stock, selling underwear, saying good morning in Polish.

I saw Bill Kahn one time when I came back to Pittsburgh to teach at Pitt in 1980, but the fight never came up. Those were growing pains, weren't they? They'll never come up again, right? My own children were spared that foolishness. They grew up more or less civilized. What a horror that I had to interrupt my reading and arguing to bang a head on a car, and not only one time, mind you; my father and mother used to look me over if I got home first to see what was bleeding or swollen or broken. I was a ridiculous hero—like all of them, I guess. The photos of the time showed the young men with huge muscles, at moments of great physical concentration, absolutely embarrassing now to look at.

And what became of the young African American who sold *Post-Gazettes*, seventy or so years of age by now? What did he go through in the 1960s? What did he settle for eventually? Does he remember the crazy man, Foo, who played the Dozens with him, the fat white man? Who acted like a baby, who thought it was for love? And Foo's quiet friend with the thick glasses who tried to restrain him, but laughed like a fiend sometimes and hugged him—the boy—so many years, so many decades ago.

REMORSE

THIS HAPPENED IN 1945, between the end of World War II
hostilities and January of 1946, when I was finally drafted after years
of visiting the central post office, third floor, every six months,
guest of my local draft board, 4F each time, unfit for military ser-
vice, unwanted by the Allied powers, I who knew all the verses of
"Let's Remember Pearl Harbor," my eyeballs curved a little too
much.

My downstairs neighbor, already in his thirties and married to
a beautiful sharp-tongued English girl, the mother of a small noisy
baby, was the son of an Army-Navy store tycoon, with long dark
stores all over western Pennsylvania, West Virginia, and Ohio.
Stores that sold surplus and fake-surplus military goods, from
T-shirts and canteens to tanks. They were named the Honus Wag-
ner Stores, after that bowlegged, toothless, hooked-nose German,
the greatest baseball player in history, who drove the ball so fault-
lessly into the deep fences it was just my fate to miss, although I
had Arkie Vaughn and the Pirates of the late thirties, including the
Waner brothers, Gus Suhr, and Al Todd.

My neighbor—my friend—didn't seem to have a nine-to-five
job; he was around at odd times during the day, but I'm sure he was
engaged in some activity for the family business that permitted him
to earn the pretty pennies he was making. He had a car and a truck,

and the car was significantly more expensive than those of his fellow sufferers on that block. He certainly was living there—with his English bride—only temporarily, for housing was extremely scarce in the immediate postwar period. They would be moving on as soon as possible. I know my parents were paid a premium when they moved out.

One day as I was walking down the heartless staircase onto the cement stoop I ran into him with a large set of keys in his hand, rushing out on an errand. He was driving off in his truck to the huge barn in the country he used as a warehouse to store his army surplus goods and he asked if I'd like to go with him. I was perfectly free—I was probably going off to the library, or on one of my long unplanned walks, so I climbed up into his truck on top of God knows what blankets, paintbrushes, hammers, and beer bottles, and off we went grinding gears the way you did then, lurching a little till the engine revved up, inhaling the delicious smell of gas, oil, old rags, and exhaust. I hardly knew him; he was thin, quiet, and impatient. He treated his wife to silence and was deferential in an unexpected way to my father and mother, who sat on his closed-in porch at night sometimes, playing with the baby. I would love to remember their names. If my mother were still alive she would recall them immediately, for they were more a part of her life than they were of mine. I do recall he had a certain preppy air about him—he was arrogant, lazy, uninterested, complacent. I don't think before this trip we had exchanged thirty words.

I am sure it was late August, or early September just before college resumed. I was going into my last year and since the war was over and my friends were coming home I made my adjustments and was content not to have gone; I had no idea that in four or five months I would suddenly be drafted and sent off to Fort Dix the

very day of my examination, just as I was embarking on a new read-
ing program, with lists of books—novels, poetry, history, biogra-
phy, philosophy—waiting to be read, some new shirts waiting to be
worn, one or two lovely women waiting in the wings I thought—
full of ambition and dreams. I was in some respects quite innocent,
but not more than any comparable figure, say, from Cleveland or
Detroit. I studied political issues with a vengeance, but I probably
didn't have access to the right journals. I don't know if it would
have mattered though, I was so fixed—if you asked me—on para-
disial themes, whether they came from Hebrew scripture or leftover
socialist pap or my own trusting hopeful nature. I was as angry and
horrified as the next one when the news of the concentration camps
arrived, but it didn't radically change me—at least not immediately;
and I was perfectly numb—though suspicious—over the two bombs.
As the news trickled in from the East Coast that we humans were,
after all, totally depraved children of Augustine and had picked
more pears than we could eat, I found it hard to accept, even though
I had been reading Reinhold Niebuhr for over a year.

Even three years later when I crossed the Allegheny Mountains
in a streamlined Greyhound—for $8.75—and was in closer hear-
ing to the new sound, I didn't quite get it. The 1950s were already
happening, but we didn't know it. Winston Churchill was about
to make his "iron curtain" speech in Fulton, Missouri; Truman
dismissed Henry Wallace as secretary of commerce because he pre-
ferred cooperation rather than confrontation with the Soviet Union;
prices doubled. In a little while there would be the Taft-Hartley
Anti-Labor Act, the Marshall Plan, loyalty oaths, the Korean War,
the Kinsey reports, the Berlin Blockade, NATO, McCarthyism.
Plus the McCarran Act, color television, the imprisonment of Alger
Hiss, the execution of the Rosenbergs, *Catcher in the Rye*, Levit-

town, bomb shelters, the hydrogen bomb, the treaty with Franco, the revelations about lung cancer, *Brown vs. Board of Education*, the Salk vaccine, the Negro bus boycott in Alabama, and sit-ins and segregation reprisals. Ingemar Johansson would beat Floyd Paterson, paratroopers were dispatched to Little Rock, Roger Bannister ran the four-minute mile, the Newport Jazz Festival was created, General Douglas MacArthur was fired, Allen Ginsberg read *Howl* publicly, Miltown was invented, the *Tonight Show* got started, the Russians invaded Budapest, the Edsel came and went, Fidel Castro ousted Batista, Khrushchev visited New York, Disneyland opened, and the $64,000 TV hoax shocked the nation. There would be an increased concentration of economic power, General Motors would destroy the transportation systems of a hundred cities, the airplane would replace the oceangoing vessel, the financial and military powers would be allowed free rein, the hopes of the 1940s would be shredded, and everyone would put on a thin tie and take a step to the right, or buy more soap to wash more diapers and take a few more steps to the right.

We drove up the main street of our neighborhood—it was Squirrel Hill—past three movie houses, an always empty Chinese restaurant, a Jewish deli, some classy women's dress shops, bakeries, post office, banks, shoe stores, an Orthodox synagogue, and stopped for a red light at a busy corner, Forbes and Shady. A woman I knew was waiting there for a streetcar, probably a number 60, on its way to East Liberty where shops and offices were lined up across the street from the Mellon Church, so-called because the bastard put it there to dominate the street (Penn Avenue) and prevent the section from competing too much and taking business away from downtown, which he more or less owned. She was dressed up and wearing a hat, the standard costume for

a woman shopping or visiting her dentist. I was twenty then and
assumed she was in her mid-thirties. She had an older sister and
the two of them went—as I did—on Sunday nights sometimes to
the YMHA on Belfield Avenue to dance to records in a dark-
ened and slightly bedecked gym. Entrance fee was a quarter. I
thought of her as a very pleasant, slightly pretty, and already faded
woman, and I thought of the two of them as flowers of a sort,
maybe because there were two other sisters—a decade or so older—
that were friends and near relatives, professional women who
got married in their forties and fifties, named Rose and Violet, a
dark brunette and a blonde, and in my mind I slightly conflated
the two pairs. It wasn't that I dismissed or was put off by "older"
women. The fact is that at that time I was sleeping with two such
women, one I remember, my mother's age (then forty-five), and
one slightly older; something out of my incestuous dreams cer-
tainly, the one a nurse and part-time prostitute who took a liking
to me, the other a hostess at a restaurant I ate lunch at, wise, funny,
and beautiful. They both had children my age.

My friend—it's beginning to dawn on me right now that his
name was Mel—I even remember his last name, which I'll leave out
in consideration of his family. "Melvin," it turns out, means friend
and counselor in Old Teutonic. What irony! I have no idea what
the Hebrew name is, possibly Moses, but there were a lot of Mels
in the decade immediately preceding mine. Maethelwine was his
name in Old English. At any rate, Mel reached across me, opened
the heavy door, and invited the woman in, offering to drive her
wherever she was going. I got out and she slid over the gunny sacks
and beer bottles to the middle of the seat. Beyond the reek of oil
was the stench of cigarettes and the empty packs—Luckies or Cam-
els, without doubt. She had a nice sense of humor about the irony

of her dress in that truck and demurely crossed her legs. She was, I now remember, no more than five feet tall.

A woman beside him—of all things accepting one of his Luckies (oh, Lord of Sex)—Mel was alive to the possibilities. He made a quick stop at the State Store, a half-block away, and bought a quart of Jack Daniels or Jim Beam and began sipping—from the bag—and offering her sips, which she smilingly accepted. No word of East Liberty or the dentist. By the time we got to the barn she was quite drunk and he was close to it. I'm sure I was offered a taste a number of times, but I hadn't as yet touched the stuff and wasn't about to start then. I realized, in a second, that we were in a horrible situation, even a banal one, two men, a woman, a filthy truck, a bottle of whiskey, not to mention the bizarre nature of the relationships. She and I hardly knew each other, yet she climbed up into the truck because she recognized me, knew me from the dances, saw me— probably—as dependable, respectable, a neighbor, even as a member of the extended Jewish tribe on those treeless streets and alleys. I worked at a large gas station on the main street, I rode the streetcars, I may have gone to the same synagogue as she, we must have seen each other at more than one of the bakeries or delis, or we must have run into each other at the drugstore where we sat down in the back room eating toasted cheese sandwiches and milkshakes.

Mel, Melvin, she didn't know, but he was, after all, with me, and therefore probably a friend. I hardly knew him myself but she didn't know that. If he grew up in one of the streets in the neighborhood I didn't know it; I didn't even know if he went to the same high school, or who his friends were. I never saw men his age visiting him, or parents or relatives for that matter. He was a good ten years older than me and belonged to a different world. Our visitor evidently found him a little charming, even intimidating, with his rich-boy airs, the way he looked at you, the way he lit his cigarette, some boring actor or other second- or third-hand.

The interstates hadn't been built yet so you got to the country through towns, occasional boulevards, two-lane bridges, old highways. I think the barn was in the north, maybe still in Allegheny County, off Route 8 or 28. It was enormous, a bank barn, at the bottom of a hill, no other buildings in sight. There was no house. It was a cool day for that time of year, totally quiet, except for the insects, and the rich smell of freshly cut grass was everywhere, the sweetest smell in the world. The barn was wood and the red paint had lost its luster; it was almost built as a warehouse, which it was, and not a shelter for animals and their food.

Mel parked the truck at the top of a hill, maybe thirty, forty yards from the barn, and in his eagerness he didn't take a minute to look out at the site, so much more beautiful now with the noisy motor off and the sounds and smells beginning to overtake us, but half-dragged her, still smiling but truly drunk now, down the hill into the barn—and closed the door. He may have been there fifteen minutes. I, in the meantime, was left with the stinking rags, the overfull ashtray, and my own thoughts. I climbed down and waited outside the truck, picking the humming stems, I'm sure, to distract and occupy me. I wasn't thinking straight. I should never have come here; I should never have let him bring her to the barn; I shouldn't have let her get in the truck in the first place or, at the very least, I should have insisted on a destination. I myself was being used by that prick, but more important, she was being humiliated, put in danger, violated.

I thought of forcing my way into the barn but I was embarrassed, confused, compromised, cowardly, operating by some foolish fraternity code, some primitive male piece of shit, no older sisters in my life to teach me the why-fors, nothing except what seeped in without me looking, like oil through a rag, or what I knew forever, it seemed, of decency, respect, delicacy, veneration, squashed by the prick's hand, although I was transferring the blame a little too easily, wasn't I? I who was in the truck, I the pimp.

Too much mea culpa I see, but what I see now in a trice was slower then in coming. I lived for a long time with my guilt, cowardice, and stupidity. And I worried about her and longed to talk to her for weeks after. But what would I say? And what did she remember? And wasn't it better not to compromise her again? And finally and overwhelmingly, wasn't I complicit? I did see her several times in the few months before I went off to New Jersey, Mississippi, Maryland, and D.C. to save our faltering Republic, but nothing of the incident was ever mentioned, nor did our particular relationship seem to alter at all, so I left well enough alone. Though I never for once treated the event lightly or just absorbed it as so much libido-ridden horseplay, whatever the apologists of our century and centuries past and centuries to come say, or have said, or will say.

When Maethelwine, my friend and counselor, came out of the barn with a smirk of sorts on his face, it was clear that it was my turn, though I don't know if any words were exchanged. She was lying in a bed of hay, disheveled and inert. The trucks and jeeps and boxes of uniforms were covered shadows in the dim, cobwebbed light. "Kiss me, Jerry," she said. I was grateful that she was alive, conscious, alert enough to know who I was. I lay down beside her on the hay, pulled her skirt down and kissed her, as she asked. Whatever desire I might have felt for her under different circumstances I don't know, but here it was pity, and the common bond that links one of us to another. She fell asleep in my arms and I had to nudge her more than a few times to wake her. I didn't want her to pass out and deal not only with that but with Mel's reaction to the situation. I felt him suddenly to be a danger and I was consciously protecting her against him. I was awake and defensive, as I should have been earlier.

On the ride back she fell asleep again in my arms, breathing heavily. It took only a half-hour, the country was so close then. I remember clearly that Melvin wanted to let her out where we picked her up, at the streetcar stop. When I told him we had to take her home and up the steps to her apartment, he understood immediately that he didn't have a choice and had better do what I said. The circumstances of returning her home, opening the door, alerting the sister, whatever we did I don't remember that now. Maybe mercifully.

He and I never talked to each other about what happened in the barn. It was a common practice—my God, how old—to ply someone with alcohol and take advantage. Or drugs. Not to mention the other charms. And there are cases and cases within cases, and modulations, and permutations. And jokes, and excuses, and poems. And it was just my luck to be implicated in the most profane, unsubtle, uncomplicated case I know. It stinks of the balcony at the Loews, of the locked door at the head of the stairs, of the twenty-dollar motel, of the Ford v8. But in every one of those places there were—there are—souls, and abused souls.

Melvin used to wink at me knowingly when he saw me on the steps. But I never responded. He was particularly nervous when I was in his wife's company. She was, as I said, an English beauty with a wild tongue, the kind of woman I loved. Words flowed between us, and jokes and puns and references. Maethelwine, with his rusted jeeps and his long khaki overcoats, could never understand. The only reason she and I never had an affair was we didn't think of it. Or we were too busy loving each other with language. Afterward, I regretted it terribly. It would have been my first affair and she *was* an older woman, and beautiful—and funny—and I know she was taken with me, and I've always been a sucker for children, the younger the better, and it would have been such joy making those horns sprout— oh, I would have watered and polished them endlessly!

Years later rape was finally honestly and publicly talked about. Nor was there any question in this case. Melvin was not just a cad— he was a bastard; and the moment he saw his prey, he attacked. He had no concern for her; I doubt that he remembered her name let alone anything else about her. Young men and middle-aged men grow crazy with lust, but lust, though it entered in, was a minor part of what happened. As far as the question "What's the big deal?" as far as "There's worse cases than that" and "It happens every Saturday night in a thousand living rooms, motels, and vans"—those are just excuses and rationalizations. She was abused and exploited. She was raped. I may have been outraged—when I thought about it—because I was outwitted, because I was forced into an uncomfortable situation, because I had to make hard choices, because I shared the guilt, because I was roped in. And I was furious because I didn't see things more clearly, because I didn't have more courage, because I didn't beat Maethelwine's brains in when I had the chance; and I hope in hindsight I'm not liberating and dignifying myself at his expense—and hers.

Melvin and his war bride got divorced a year or two after this—so my mother told me years ago. I am sure he was a ne'er-do-well, a bad student who went from school to school, that he was in accidents, that his father bought his way through life, that very few people loved him. I could tell all this at a glance, wizard that I am. I hope his lovely wife took him for everything he had. I'm sure she did. I hope he learned the meaning of remorse, but I doubt it.

FIRST RITES

I WAS SIXTEEN OR SEVENTEEN when I first heard of summer camps where the rich and semi-rich sent their sons and daughters to live in cabins, swim in lakes, play tennis in mountain retreats, and live by marvelous codes. I did know that there were places in the country for the deprived and underprivileged and that my poor cousins went there for a week or two at a time, but they never interested me. My thoughts were only of the Jersey shore and the Atlantic Ocean. I learned in the early 1940s that you could go as a counselor to one of the camps and earn good money in salary and tips and have a kind of vacation besides, in fact enough to pay for tuition at college, given the economics of the time. Since there was a shortage of eligible men because of the war, and since I was "unfit for military service," I had a great advantage.

For three or four years, until they lowered the bar and I was finally drafted, I went to camps in Massachusetts and Maine as a specialist in one area or another, swimming and wilderness treks, for example. I was extremely cunning at writing letters of application to the small list of camps I selected from a reference book at the library. I was able to make about three hundred dollars in salary and an additional two hundred or so in tips for a seven- or eight-week period. Food and lodging were free and I even found ways of living without the burdensome responsibility of overseeing campers directly. Tuition at the University of Pittsburgh was ten dollars a credit at the time, and since thirty credits constituted two semesters, it cost me three hundred a year, which left two hundred for books and incidentals, a radically different money-to-value system than existed only a few years later, when students were trapped by colleges, governments, and businesses into being slaves for ten or twenty years.

In the summer of 1945 I went to a camp in Lenox, Massachusetts, as a waterfront specialist, canoes and swimming—I even had a Red Cross certificate. It was a wilderness camp where New Jersey and New York boys, raised in great comfort and even a little luxury, learned the art of simplicity, as Thoreau taught it, by sleeping on lumpy mattresses and putting up with various kinds of pain. I was reading Dickens at the time, and as soon as I was free from work I surrendered to one tome or another in some simple space where I could not be found. There was no television yet, there may have been one radio and one telephone in the whole camp, but the boys thrived. I think they may have been allowed to send their laundry out and eat cooked food, but that's as far as it went.

The head counselor was a New York City high school English teacher, rather stern and reserved, but smart—and endlessly pedantic. The whole camp gathered on Saturday night around a fire deep in the woods where he lectured in brilliant imitation of one or another religio or politico of the time, and even the counselors were forced to give short talks, sort of pep talks around the fire, their fronts roasting, their backs freezing from the night's cold.

Sunday night there were either movies (some silent), boxing, drama, or more talk. We either gathered in the round or faced the small stage at one end. The "theater" was an old chicken coop or small barn, with a dirt floor, and we sat on rough benches. The drama counselor was a New York bohemian, originally from Michigan, maybe thirty years old, with wire-rimmed glasses and a contemptuous air. He tolerated me and my hard-driven innocence, but he looked down on almost everyone else, particularly on the head counselor and his upbeat mode. He gathered campers at inconvenient times in the early morning or late afternoon for rehearsals where he railed at them and gestured and bellowed like some lunatic out of one of the state zoos. He particularly detested the parents and gave lectures on guilt and responsibility, every bit as onerous as the puffed-up head counselor. They were opposite sides of the same coin. I don't remember which plays he was doing, but they surely reflected his own bias and his hatred of anything that was a deviation from his bohemian idealism, which meant almost everything that was commonly shared, from songs to cars to canned beans to the war.

The parents made one or two visits during the summer, always on Sundays, and they stayed through the evening to see the play or movie or boxing matches. Sometime at the end of July the drama counselor put on a play for the campers and their parents, all crowded together on the uncomfortable benches, the loud cricket-song penetrating the thin walls and open windows. I can't for a minute remember what the play was, but in that dim wilderness, in the middle of the forest, in a small barn with a dirt floor, he interrupted the play to announce that the war was over and Japan, like Germany before it, had surrendered unconditionally. From nowhere the bottles appeared and the kissing started, and the dancing and laughing and shouting. It went on for a good half-hour before someone had the sense to call the newspaper or the sheriff or just turn the one radio on to discover that the war *wasn't* over and our sneering drama counselor had just pulled an Orson Welles by re-creating—in his own way—the *War of the Worlds* broadcast of 1938 that brought fame to Welles. He was out of there in a half-hour and probably spent the night on the floor of the train station, unless they had a bench in the bleak waiting room. The parents were comforted, they were probably served tea, and they made their way home in their forlorn vehicles, lights bouncing down the rough dirt road. I was appointed drama counselor the next day and had the job of reenergizing the dramatically lost campers. This I did in addition to my waterfront duties but I'm sure I was recompensed for it.

The war did end that summer, the two bombs were dropped, and the word "mushroom" gathered new meaning. The English teacher was horrified and told us that life as we knew it was changed forever and we were most likely doomed. We were already sleeping under blankets, the end of August, when we said goodbye to each other and boarded trains for the south. In New York, I had to transfer to a train bound for Pittsburgh but I decided to spend a day or two in the city, visit some bookstores, and, hopefully, look up the drama counselor whose phone number I had written down before he left camp. He answered the phone when I called, and invited me to come to his apartment though I couldn't tell whether or not he was pleased. I stayed at the Sloan House on Thirty-fourth Street.

He lived on Horatio Street, north of Twelfth in the West Village, up three or four flights. I remember the main room was very large and the ceiling high and it was almost empty. Boxes and cushions for furniture and the same boxes—they were crates—for book cases. And he was there with a couple of friends sitting against the wall, smoking and drinking beer. The empty bottles were piled up in a garbage can and there were some scattered on the floor. The door was painted a rich blue—I had never seen a blue door before— and the walls were patched, scarred, cracked, and splattered. There probably was a table and chairs, but I don't remember them. I was in love immediately, stricken, lost, bedazzled, and God knows if I would ever recover. The conversation was witty, enigmatic, knowing, and totally unbeknownst to me in its references. The others caught my innocence and toyed with me in a friendly way, asking me a lot of questions. I wanted nothing more than to be one of them, or at least to be accepted. They could have been writers or actors or bums, but they were united by a common bond. It was the first time I had been to the Village.

I'm sure I thoroughly understood what the ridiculous hero was doing when he stepped in front of the curtain that summer, and if he abused, single-handedly, everyone there, and if he shamelessly copied the greater actor and the greater director in order to amass credit, what he did required such faux-courage, blindness, self-deception, and anger that he had to be taken at his word, and taken seriously, which was all he really wanted. I know I understood the artistic "idea" when I was fifteen but I don't remember any examples in my life to that point. In my own case, it wasn't just purple hair, smoke, and broken-down chairs. Nor showing contempt. I was too puritanical for that and too serious, and committed. Now that it's gone, and all we have is parody, I honor at least the memory.

HÔTEL DU CENTRE

ON THE GROUND FLOOR of the Hôtel du Centre was a small square room with a sink and stove at one end, a sofa at the other, and a table and chairs in the middle. Certainly a bed and bath beyond but nothing more. A kind of apartment where the owner and her husband lived: she, a beautiful pale-skinned Norman with short black hair, always in the same tight sweater; he, much older than she, with gray stubble and crooked yellow teeth, a Pole with a thick, unctuous accent both in French and English. He worked as a waiter in a nearby restaurant and was much diminished and more humble at his workplace than he was at the hotel; she changed the coarse sheets, replaced the threadbare towels, sort of ripped and spotted tea towels, more rag than towel, and dusted a little with a dry mop she shook out the window. The hotel was on the rue de la Boucherie, a block from the river, more or less facing the river side of Notre Dame. There were six stories, two rooms to a floor, as I remember, and a toilet, a WC in the hall, the kind you squatted over, feet on the metal rests. I forget the hands—straps maybe, or metal handles. When you pulled the overhead handle to flush, you leapt out.

I was on the first floor (European counting). Next door to me there was another American. He painted grotesque sexual horses and hated me for moving in. He moved out, in self-assigned dis-grace, when Sylvia, a lovely Hungarian in her early thirties, waved

43

and started to talk to us from the stoned-in yard but made it clear it was me she was interested in and not the grotesque horse-man. Sylvia didn't live there but was the best friend of a Serbian woman who occupied a small building in the yard. The four of us, Sylvia and me, the Serbian and her boyfriend Peter, another Serb, took long walks in the evening on the quai St. Michel, arguing love and politics. The two Serbs, their arms around each other, Sylvia and I hand-in-hand. Peter, from his Augustinian perspective, thought we Americans didn't understand evil, which, of course, Europeans did. We who butchered each other at arm's length in the nineteenth century, we who dropped the two bombs. Sylvia wore a hip-length brown wool cardigan and had short brown curly hair and talked English with a heavy accent. She made me lunch one day in her small apartment near rue de l'Opéra—she was kept by a French businessman who visited her once, twice a week. She served a couple of dishes that were unflinchingly Jewish, and when I acknowledged I was right at home she was horrified—that a Jewish girl would be found out to be so brazen—and wanted to marry me rather than sleep with me from then on. Those were the choices then.

The second, third, and fourth floors (European) were occupied by ten or so Romanians, living off the fruit of UNESCO. They got their checks once a month and spent them at once, drinking and weeping for the good fascist times, reciting poetry and eating karnatzlich. On the top floor was a French prostitute and her mother in one room and an American couple, Howard and Maryann, in the other.

I can't remember the name of either my landlady or her Polish husband. She came to my room at the same time each day, late in the morning, to dust, to shake the bedclothes, and very quickly we talked a little, became friends, and, after a while, lovers. She came from a small village in Normandy and I loved to call her "my Norman" and tell her about the Conquest. I don't know how or where she met her husband but it seemed to me a classic mismatch and I didn't have any hesitancy or remorse over giving him horns. In fact, every time I was in his presence I tweaked and polished those horns and gave them shape by endless trimming and cutting, which he only felt a little. Christian Poles, unlike Jewish Poles, were welcomed in France, and seen, certainly in the early days, as courageous warriors in the struggle against German dominance and Nazism; and became, as far as the Jews were concerned, easy allies with the German and French police after the occupation. I can't be sure about *this* Pole but he had a way of saying my name—half sneer, half ingratiation—that set my alarm off. He certainly did have a reason to hate me—later—but his *mode* was there from the beginning, when he first gave me my room key and recited the house rules. "Meester Shterrn," he called me, with a knowledge, an understanding, he assumed we both shared. I must admit that I detested him on sight, which I insist had nothing to do with my relationship with his wife. I am not that vile. I hated his small feet, his skinny thighs, his filthy undershirt, his crooked mouth, his red eyes, his unscrubbed teeth. I hated the small-rimmed fedora he put on when he left his dungeon and went off to work. And I hated his mincing manner while at work, and that fake, self-deprecating smile of his when he moved between his tables, for I and my friends did occasionally visit the small Russian restaurant where he worked.

His *wife* owned the hotel, not him, and she made that clear in a number of ways. She expressed no fear of him, contradicted him in public, and behaved, in general, like the madam and not the maid, whatever work she was doing. She had great passion and went about the affair quite deliberately. It was an act of her choice and not something that overwhelmed or surprised her. I don't mean to say she was calculating—I mean that when she decided to sleep with me she wasn't coy or maidenly. She acted with knowledge and generosity, and though it perforce had to be secret, given the circumstances, she acted with caution but never with fear or shame. I remember her and our time together vividly, everything but her name, which infuriates me. It was the simplicity—the innocence—of our love-making that touched me—even shocked me. Its base in affection and its respect for the other's separateness.

The year was 1950. It was Holy Year, as I discovered later when I went to Italy and was deafened by the bells. I was twenty-five, she was in her early forties. I was taken then by older women, often in their fifties. My mother, in 1950, would have been fifty on the nose, so there's no question of the Oedipal connection. I knew it then but was not bothered by it in the least.

When she came to see me, right after her husband went to work at the Russian restaurant, she was barely into the room before she was pulling her sweater over her head. She had exactly three pieces of clothing, not counting her slippers, and she was in bed almost before I had a chance to push away from my volume of Milton and the dear bluebook I was writing my epic in. She was trying to learn English, so I read to her from Cummings and Stevens while we lay there for a half-hour or so, and she nodded gravely as if she even understood one word, I was such a shit. I had a tiny stove in my room, with one burner and a fierce flame, and we made cocoa every day, or she did—it was the one domestic thing we did together—and drank it from large cups, I'm sure cracked and handleless, I'm sure we held with both hands, our knees, each of us, pressed together demurely. There was some ridiculously quaint legend on the cocoa can, a grandmother, a cat, a braided rug, a wife dreamily pouring hot water into her husband's mug, certainly in red, brown, and yellow, colors of Proust's Europe.

We never spent time together out of the room. In all that time—three months—we never met at a café, kissing each other, oh, on the cheeks, first one then the other, as if we were friends, not lovers, keeping things disguised, delighted say, with a new pair of shoes, a book. I never took her to an afternoon movie, across the river maybe, walking out into the late sun, having a glass of wine, some *choucroute garnie* or a nice *jambon* before we kissed goodbye. I never bought her a gift, not even a flower, for God's sake. Four months maybe! Not one walk on the river. Nor do I remember now if she had children. Certainly there were none at the hotel. There may have been one with the *maman* in the country. I hope so. If she is alive today she would be—what?—ninety-two, ninety-three years old.

I like to think—that is, I liked to think—that the husband didn't know. But there's always a clue, something to sniff, in a closet, in a glance, that gives it away. Especially if the husband is despicable and unworthy and knows it. One evening we had an early dinner at the Russian restaurant and returned to the hotel to get ready for the party that Howard and Maryann were planning in their room on the fifth floor. I think the prostitute and her mother graciously offered their room as well, for the space was small for the fifteen or so people that would be showing up. By nine o'clock I was dizzy and had sharp pains in my stomach. A half-hour later I was throwing up and fainting in the WC. Eventually I was crawling on my hands and knees over the stone and brick in the hallway, breathing in the centuries of dust and dirt. I was sweating profusely and couldn't even take in water. I could hear the happy noises drift down the courtyard from the party upstairs and my regret was I wasn't with the

Romanians, the Americans, Sylvia, and the Yugoslavians, plus the few stragglers that showed up. Maryann came down after a while and sat on the edge of my bed. She wiped my forehead with a cold towel and covered me a little so I wouldn't shiver so much. We both agreed it was the *bœuf bourguignon* which we had eaten, or most of us, but only mine apparently had a special invisible sauce that produced certain effects on rats and wandering rogues. I should have gone to the hospital or at least to a doctor, but I was still young enough to be immortal. I'm sure a couple of the Romanians had medical training—for all I know, one of them had been a distinguished doctor in Fascist Romania.

I didn't have the strength to go upstairs nor did Maryann or anyone else visit me again that night. I was a little bitter that Sylvia didn't come down, though I wasn't sure she was there. I guess I wanted visitors to come streaming in, sick as I was, to show concern and offer advice that I would surely reject. Most of all I missed my sweet Norman, she who would surely help me. But aside from the fact that I couldn't even walk, how could I get in touch with her? And how would I explain that the poisoner, the murderer, was sitting down beside her reading a Polish newspaper and grumbling over some soup he had taken from his restaurant, chunks of fatty meat, carrots, and potatoes swimming to the surface, surely wiping his mouth with the soiled napkin he kept for his own use. What would she say to him—I'm going upstairs to visit with Meester Shtern, I understand he is sick and dry-heaving from the poison you sprinkled on his *bœuf bourguignon*? I want to make him some tea, with a cube or two of sugar, from the strong flame on his little stove. Then I want to kiss him lightly on the forehead, cheeks, and lips to calm him down so he can go to sleep. Later I want to slip his hand under my tight sweater so he can feel my breast and the brown nipple that is rising for him. I'm planning to stay all night. I'll sit on that rickety wooden chair and when he dozes off I'll take my three items of clothes off and slip in beside him. Fate might still give him some power and maybe about the first dawn I'll mount him gently, taking care that I don't disturb his wrenched stomach muscles, exhausted from the convulsions, or his beautiful thighs worn out from squatting and crawling. Don't worry too much. I'll be back in time to make you some café au lait and pour it into your bowl so you can dip your stale *bâtard* into it, *mon bâtard*. And when you go to work at 10:45 I'll climb the stone steps again and bring him a bit of hot croissant and a large cup of coffee with milk. I'll be back in the afternoon, two, three o'clock, when you return for your afternoon nap, *mon idiot*. And how curious he must have been, and how inquisitively he must have looked at the laughing staggering visitors who came down the last set of stairs, two, three, in the morning.

I was sick for at least another day, maybe two, and did have the chance to see my sweet landlady and she did bring me some soup and bread, sans meat, sans fat bubbles. I never told her that her husband poisoned and almost killed me, since I didn't want to alarm her and anyhow I had no proof. But I know she knew something was going on and she expressed concern—and anger. But not verbally, needless to say. I never went back to that restaurant. I saw the husband a few more times, mainly when I was paying my rent at his cracked oilcloth table. I have relegated him to Hell, along with a few Germans, Ukrainians, and the like. I don't want to think about that Hell too much, it is so populated, it stinks so much, it is full of such ignorance and stupidity. Stay there forever, *mon bâtard*.

My plan was to go to Italy for a while. I was living off the World War II G.I. Bill, which gave me—as a student—seventy-five dollars a month, half of which I saved every month, prices were so low. I was studying for my *doctorat d'université,* a kind of second-class doctorate, but it didn't matter since I never went to classes. I just collected my check once a month at the American Embassy. I was going to go with Sylvia but I decided to go alone at the last minute. I wanted to walk by myself—which I did—across the northern half through that incredible string of cities ending up in Venice. My Norman certainly would have walked with me. Sleeping in the fields with me, listening to the dogs barking early in the morning, eating warm tomatoes off the vine, mortadella sandwiches, wine. Occasionally going to a hotel for the luxury of a bath and a soft mattress. I walked from Venice to Bologna but took a train to Florence. I washed and drank at public wells, which was certainly not a wise thing to do, and when I got to Florence I felt ill again and lay down to sleep in the Boboli gardens, waking up after an hour or so completely cured, I thought. I was on my way to the youth hostel, on the outskirts of Florence then, and stopped first at a bank to change money. Standing at the *caisse,* whatever it's called in Italian, I suddenly passed out and fell to the floor. I woke up a few minutes later—I think it was only a few minutes—surrounded by an inquisitive crowd. A twenty-five-year-old American, dressed in army pants, a T-shirt, boots, and an army sweater was lying on the marble floor of a busy bank, a small backpack at his side with two seventy-five-dollar checks and an American passport in the side pocket of the pack, which my inquisitors were busily studying when I woke up. Somehow that fall cured me, and I was able to get up, get my Italian money, and walk to the hostel. I was weak—probably dehydrated—for a day or two, but I was better—no pain, no dizziness, a huge appetite.

I thought of my friend in Paris. The daily visits seemed like a heaven I had left forever. But I would see her for a week or so when

I came back, before my train ride to Antwerp to board a Dutch ship for my return to America and my fiancée, for I kept the room, which cost me about twenty-five dollars a month. I finally abandoned my Norman, but I had no other choice. I probably should have confronted the *bâtard*. I am amazed how we make contracts with each other and loyally keep them, no matter how restricted they are. I am grateful for what we did together. I am grateful I remembered it.

Vow of Silence

I AM ONE OF THE STUBBORN ROMANTICS who still honor the Republic of Spain and owned—and lost—an old 78 that contained the ancient songs of the Lincoln Brigade; and Pablo Casals I loved and honored beyond any other, so when I heard from my friends in Paris that he was going to break his vow of silence against the Franco regime in Spain and play again in Prades, a little city in the French Pyrenees, I claimed a seat in the 1949 black Citroën with the front-end transmission (*traction avant*) and the look of a 1946 Ford. My seat, really my space, was in the back middle. Dick Hazley, my friend from Pittsburgh, was to my left and Kurt Schneider, a medical student and effete poet from Michigan, was to my right. The car belonged to Dick Foster, also from Pittsburgh, who ended up a corporate geologist, and he did the driving. Jack Gilbert was in the passenger seat. We always kept the same seats; no one thought of changing, nor did Foster ever ask any of us to share the driving, nor did we offer. I think I didn't have a license then, certainly not a French or an international one. I don't know about the others, except I know that Jack didn't drive and, for that matter, doesn't to this day.

I have been studying a map of France to see which route we took to get there. I am amazed that not only can I not remember the route, but where we stayed overnight, either going there or coming back, or if we did. What I do remember is the dynamics of the car, the love and hate we bestowed upon each other, the stay in Prades itself, and the stop we made in Avignon on the way back. Usually I remember such things as the temperature, the specific color of the ocean, which shoes I was wearing, what we had for breakfast and on which day. My friends hate me for my memory. But in this case my mind is mostly empty of the dear irrelevancies. We might have gone through Dijon, for all I know; we certainly went through Nîmes and Montpellier. There were no auto-routes yet. Gilbert, who has a terrible memory, says that he was already in Prades and, anyhow, he wasn't driving. Foster doesn't remember the route but he does remember, keenly, sitting on the grass beside the Columbia Records trailer listening to them record and overhearing Casals instruct the technicians that a "sour" flute note was acceptable and it wasn't necessary to play the piece over since it happened "naturally." He was allowing for imperfections, like God, say, who could never have gotten a job at that company. Jean-Pierre Rampal was the flautist. Hazley is dead, *hélas,* he would have remembered everything, and Schneider, who had a sour soul, is nowhere I can reach·him, even if I wanted to.

Prades is a market town in the Pyrénées Orientales and has a population of about five thousand. It is almost entirely surrounded by mountains and the river that runs through it is called the Têt. About thirty miles west of Perpignan and a part of French Catalonia, it is the same country, as it were, as Spanish Catalonia, with its capital in Barcelona. Casals came as a refugee when France reluctantly opened its borders at the end of the Spanish civil war, along with over six hundred thousand others, many if not most of them Catalans, and he spent many grueling years overseeing relief operations for the destitute. Indeed, for ten years Casals's primary energy was directed as much to writing pleading letters and distributing food, clothes, and medicine as it was to music, and his bedroom at the Grand Hôtel in Prades was the headquarters. During World War II, he was pressured by the Germans and "invited" to play in Berlin as Hitler's guest, but he resisted. When the war was over he innocently and naively assumed that the Americans, the French, and the English would extend their fight against fascism to Franco and the Falangists and was bitterly disappointed when they didn't. He particularly had hope in the English whom he specially loved, and it was during his first postwar tour of Britain, in 1945, and his subsequent triumphal tour of France, that he took his vow of silence, refusing at first to play in any country that recognized Franco's legitimacy, and a little later in any country whatsoever. It wasn't that he seriously believed his boycott could reverse the inactivity of the West, but he would not give the democracies the comfort of displacing their own guilt—even in a small way—by bestowing honors and accolades on him. Nor could he do it as a matter of conscience. Nor could he do it out of loyalty to the forgotten ones. Probably it was that the war was over and the West was exhausted, or that they shifted interest or that the battle was suddenly against communism and Franco would prove a useful ally or that there were deals made (certainly that) during the war. And why would the powers that cut up Czechoslovakia in nice little slices for the insatiable Germans or refused refuge to the beleaguered Jews care anyhow in their righteous cowardice?

I think I got wind of the Prades festival in an article in the *Herald Tribune*. At any rate, it seemed as if all my friends knew about it and there was excitement in the air about making the pilgrimage. We talked about it as Casals ending his vow, but in some way it was about a continuation of his own private playing—dozens of the world's greatest musicians and hundreds of music lovers gathered in *his* back yard. He must have seen it that way, a decision to play "out loud," as it were, different from shining his shoes and going to Chicago or Milan. Prades was crowded, but it was not uncomfortable. We got rooms and ate in restaurants. I remember the flowers on the jagged mountain and the clean air and the fresh fish we ate. And the practice sessions and the recording sessions. And walking into little St. Peters every night, and sitting with the press corps fifteen feet away from him—on the right. And watching him sit on a large box in front of the altar and play Bach's *Unaccompanied Cello Suites* or conduct his friends in the *Brandenburg Concertos*. In the church and out, I felt that I was in a protected and joyous place. It was quiet and civilized and purposeful. And I was not just an observer—I had a place, we all did. And for once, no one I met was rude or arrogant. If Blake were there, if he were envisioning us, we would all be sitting in a pair of huge hands—God's or Milton's—and we would be small creatures, large-eyed and illuminated.

The day we left Prades we left about noon, and we had the same places in the car. We made our way northeast, then east, along the Mediterranean, for we were determined to take a swim and lie in the sand before we returned to Paris. By this time we had divided into two antagonistic groups: Hazley and I on one side and Gilbert, Schneider, and Foster on the other. One way of looking at it was through aesthetics, another was through class—and the two overlapped. From our view, the other group was snobbish, arrogant, elitist; from their view we were vulgar. Schneider, for example, couldn't accept the fact that I was a poet. I was too burly, too profane. I don't know who belonged on which end of the ladder. Poor Gilbert, who sided with them, hardly could put one foot on the lowest rung, but he bravely climbed up. In a way, he was more naïve than snobbish; he was the innocent. And it wasn't really class—it was class presumption, an American phenomenon. Gilbert's father was an exterminator and a circus performer, just as Hazley's father was a plumber. Mine was a salesman. Schneider's and Foster's were more suspicious.

The three of them—the enemy—really two, since Foster was driving—buried their faces in guidebooks as we drove through the lavender. There were *Guides Bleus* and *Baedekers;* I don't think that Fodor had found his way yet. Each town we approached, each Roman ruin, each ancient church, they looked up from their books and made pronunciamentos. "The first well was dug in 833"; "there were heated baths in 724"; "all the Arabs were exiled in 1501"; "there used to be a square where the small forest is." Hazley and I looked at each other in wonder—and amusement. They were inconceivably academic, and they were cheating. "Ah, the Camargue! Neither tree, nor shade, nor a soul. Its exotic wildlife unique in Europe, its wildest reaches inaccessible by car. Ah, its birds!" "And Arles! The Romanesque Eglise St. Trophime. Its superbly preserved twelfth-century sculptures on the entry façade; its transept dating from the eleventh century; and its first-century (B.C.E.) theatre." "And Van Gogh's house, destroyed by Allied bombs in 1944. You can stand in the empty space on Place Lamartine." "And the ear, dedicated to Gauguin."

We arrived in Avignon in the heat of the afternoon, the end of June. The talk in the car was of the Pope's Palace in exile (Babylonian captivity). I learned from the dedicated scholars surrounding me that seven exiled popes ruled there between 1309 and 1377, after fleeing from the corruption and confusion of Rome, that the most famous of these was probably either Benedict XII, a puritan, or Clement VI, a luxuriant; and that Avignon was a center of French power and influence. I also learned about the tapestries, the frescoes, the richly decorated ceilings, and the Chapelle Clémentine, where the College of Cardinals once gathered to elect the new pope, and decided at once that I abhorred the place and didn't want to visit it. Hazley came to the same conclusion and we arranged to meet the others outside the palace when it closed.

Now we were free and we practically leapt for joy. Down one street, up another we went, eating, drinking, talking to strangers, making fun of the scholars. Just off the Cours de la République on the rue Victor Hugo—one such thoroughfare—there was a narrow street going down a very steep hill with a sign on the side of the building in faded letters saying "Off Duty to American Military Personnel," left over obviously from the war. At the bottom of this street, facing a little square, was a small, dark bar with a beaded curtain for a door. If it was a hundred degrees outside, it was twenty-five degrees cooler inside. There was a zinc bar, a bartender, a few bottles, a beautiful young woman sitting at one table, and a young man, her boyfriend, at the other. She had a little girl with her, three, four years old. She was dark, and thin. She kept raising her skirt, almost over her head, saying—over and over—"*il fait chaud.*" I went upstairs with her first, then Hazley. She attributed her lack of interest to the heat and urged me to come back in the winter. I remember drinking a beer afterward and exchanging pleasantries. I had little trouble with the accent for I had learned my French in Montpellier. I remember how pleasant and polite her boyfriend and the bartender were.

We made about two hundred kilometers that night before we found a place to sleep. The scholars reminisced about the furniture and paintings. I, for my part, would have been interested if we had been discussing the centuries of violent and corrupt politics of that place, but it was only beauty they wanted. The sin of separation. Our very foray (Hazley and I) was a plaint against that "beauty." We were merciless that night. We countered every aesthetic observation with another detail of our adventure. Gilbert, whom I'm in touch with, tells me that I taunted Schneider and explained that his name meant "tailor" in Yiddish. He says, fifty years later, that he should have gone with Hazley and me. I don't remember much more about the trip, when we got back to Paris, how we separated, who paid for the gas.

I returned to Prades in the mid-1990s, on a side trip from Barcelona, in a rented car, with a wolfish woman. Everything was exactly as I remembered it, except what was different. The overwhelming sense was that you were surrounded by water, even though it was almost summer. It was partly the river, and partly the snow-capped hills, and it was partly the water rushing down the marble sidewalks. The mountains were close, and the square itself was perfectly simple, a few stores, a hotel, and pollarded plane trees. La Mairie was the same and it was the same WC—with new fixtures and a freshly varnished door. There was a video store now, a patisserie, a photo shop, a brasserie (L'Europe), a bank, a boutique, a pharmacy, a bar, a charcuterie, some closed-up shutters. There were men my age—with sticks—sitting under the trees and small cars parked everywhere.

The church was larger than I remembered. And it was more elegant, with marble floors and carved pews and gold leaf. Everyone inside seemed to be holding something, a cross, a stick, a trident, a sword, a cello bow, whether it was Aquinas hiding in a dark chapel, or an obscure pope inside a hideous painting, or a saint of some sort rolling his eyes. And there were fresh lilies on the altar. I sat down—

as I recollect—in the very same seat—same bench, as I did in 1950, twenty feet away, with the critics and reporters. I don't remember where my friends sat, or if they got in. Gilbert, in a letter, tells me that what he did was go to the rehearsals, which leads me to draw certain conclusions. It was such a pleasure sitting there. It was absolutely still, a little light coming through the colored windows, the organ in back, the journey of Christ in ivory.

I don't think I had ever heard the *Brandenburg Concertos* or the *Unaccompanied Cello Suites* before that time, nor could I believe my good luck or contain my joy. I was what, seven yards away from one who was probably the greatest instrumentalist of the twentieth century, who not only had the most powerful, most tender sounds that ever were played on the cello, but who reinvented the instrument and its uses for our time. Among Casals's devotees it is well known how—when he was thirteen—he discovered the six suites Bach wrote for unaccompanied cello in a secondhand music shop on a cramped street near the harbor in Barcelona. How for twelve years he studied and worked at them every day and it was not till he was twenty-five that he had the courage to play one of them in public. Nor had anyone ever played one through at a public performance before, as far as we know, maybe a dance here or there. They were considered too dull, too technical, exercises merely. It was an amazing—I want to say God-given—fact that the revived interest in Bach in the nineteenth century coincided with—or made connections with—Casals's reinvention of the cello, technically and emotionally, as a vehicle, a medium, to hear Bach. Generally, it was away from stiffness and formality, toward freedom. One of his students observed that "there was no law of the cello he would not break if he thought the music required it." But it was a moral as well as an artistic liberation. "You hear when a note is false the same way you feel when you do something wrong in life." Which makes the technical, the fingering and bowing, something other than a physical or formal issue; just as sound itself, just as *the* sound itself, is not, as such, a technical but an emotional and philosophic issue as well, a marriage of at least two.

I don't know what the postmodernist view of Casals is. Perhaps he is considered sentimental, or personal; emotional, romantic. Perhaps indulgent. To his earliest critics, those rooted in the early nineteenth century, he was not pure. I suspect that at the end of his life he came upon the same criticisms, but differently based, and thus the snake has his own tail in his mouth. And the pedants meet. A friend of mine, a cellist, in her mid-forties, called Casals her hero. She praised him and his playing as original, rough, personal, with deep insight into the music he was playing. She loves his improvisation and compares it to jazz. It's not just about sound, she says, and certainly not about toeing the line—nor is polish, as such, his goal. She says he is sometimes considered old-fashioned and is criticized as taking too many liberties. Those who played with him talked about his depth of feeling, his profound knowledge, the love that came from him.

I suspect that the issue of Spain—and especially Catalonia—was never absent from Casals's mind. He was obsessed by it, trapped by it, yet liberated at the same time. He was certainly the most stubborn of men, and the most loyal. It's as if his whole vision of justice, rectitude, decency, all his beliefs—ethical, religious, political, personal—were centered on the one cause and as if he, as a Catalonian, a musician, a man, had only one place to turn, and as it turned out only one place to live and one gift to give. The arguments for and against ideological art are absolutely beside the point in his case. He was not adopting a "cause" and arranging his art to accommodate it. The cause was as natural as a tree is natural, or a dead man lying under that tree with a bullet in his head or his back. He became a prophet of resistance and a symbol to tens of thousands of his fellow countrymen, and he was willing to endure privation and sacrifice for his ideas. In his acceptance of poverty, at least in the 1940s, he lived like a monk, but he did not confine himself to a hole in the ground but converted his "protest" to dull and backbreaking acts of service and charity, this in his late sixties and seventies. His hatred of Franco and the Falangists was clear and simple. They were anti-democratic and totalitarian. They were allies of the Nazis and fascists, Hitler and Mussolini. Indeed, Germany and Italy, through brutal use of their airpower, had helped in a major way to destroy the Republican cause. Nor was there the least hint of compromise in Casals's position, however the agonizers wavered, reconsidered, and explained.

There is a famous conversation reported between Casals and Albert Schweitzer—it took place in Zurich—in which Schweitzer advised Casals that it is better to create than to protest, to which Casals said, "Why not do both?" and went on to say that the Prades festival had the double character of creation *and* protest. It is possible that the very playing combined them, not that you finger differently when you protest but that the feelings involved, whether they are anger or love or regret or hope or despair—whatever—underlie both actions and they become one and it becomes ridiculous to call them by their mundane names. Only that the fire is there at all times.

Does one play like that because he has practiced day after day, hour after hour, for fifty, sixty years? Does one play like that because Franco and his police have tried to destroy Catalan culture, even the speaking of the language? Or because only by reaching certain perfect sounds can the spirit even know what it has lost—or almost won? Because Europe has descended back into cowardice, into complicity and delusion, after a moment or two of vision? He who has love for his neighbors, and generosity, he who suffers thereby, he does it even when he least knows. Moreover, he was lucky, poor musician, that the artistic and the moral were so absolutely and unquestionably contained in him, the man, Pau Casals. Everything bespoke his unity, his vision. By playing—and by not playing—he was on that edge, he *was* conscience. As far as the joining of political parties and such, he refused to attach himself to any governing body or political group. "Alone," he said, "I possess a moral independence which I would not have if I acted differently. I am not a politician . . . I am an artist who wishes to keep faith with human principles."

It's more than fifty years after the fact that I'm thinking and writing about Prades. I write, as I always do, at the crowded kitchen table overlooking the Delaware and Raritan Canal in Lambertville, New Jersey, not far from the Delaware River, and I'm listening to one of the *Cello Suites*, Casals playing. He is slow and deeply serious yet not solemn. One biographer describes his playing as "simple, smooth and precise." His art certainly lies in that simplicity, although it is only the end result of knowledge, hard work, and sophistication. It's as if he had totally absorbed the piece and can play so effortlessly that he appears to be making new choices as he goes along. I sometimes lie on my sofa to hear him, a perilous place for music, but I am usually in my rocking chair. This morning I heard Misha Mishky play one of the unaccompanied suites and was struck by the difference in pace and tone. The Mishky, I would swear, is twice as fast, a recent version certainly of how Baroque sounded, but for me, though it was lovely, it lacked the depth and tenderness of Casals.

Fifty years is a long time, isn't it? I'm not bemoaning anything, though—I'm just getting ready for the next jubilee. I don't know exactly what he was like as a man. That last quarter of the nineteenth century produced a dozen or so giants, whose shadows hung on a long time. But I have a feeling that Casals was much less pompous than the rest, partly because, whatever fame he achieved in his long life, he always remained a type of peasant, an impoverished Catalonian and a democrat. Exile, not that I would wish it on a dog, as they say in my other language, was probably his great luck. I know I would have minded his conservative views on modern music and art—he criticized Bro Picasso for his distortions and Bro Stravinsky for his. He admired certain modern composers, including Bartók and Enesco, and his orchestra in Barcelona did play from a wide range of composers, but he was against egocentrism, eccentricity, irony, experiment, and unconventional forms unless they were grounded in "general laws," and he disliked dissonance just as he loved melody. His radicalism had to do with his instrument and its physical and spiritual enlargement and it had to do with a new realization of Bach and Bach's own radicalism, enough for one life.

Me, I'd like to go through Prades one more time, on my way maybe to Carcassone to see the Roman and Visigoth walls; and I'd like to sit in the same place, for I'm a stickler for such things. The second time I was there I noticed above the altar the large figure of Peter wearing a red miter and a dress and blessing us with two fingers since he was the first pope—sort of. He is seated under a canopy borne by angels, a fitting background for Casals, sitting in his wooden chair. My friend Willis Barnstone, the first Jew I know of to translate the New Testament, emphasizes Peter's confusion and impetuousness, but I rather like that he jumped naked from the boat when Jesus filled the empty net with fish and that he snored in the garden, since I am a snorer myself. In my notes I describe climbing the hill above the town past the perfect plane trees till after a while it seemed twenty degrees cooler. Through the valley I heard a rooster crow though I swear by Peter that I had not betrayed anyone; and there were lilac and black locust in bloom, filling the air with their fragrance. The snow seemed right in front of me and the swollen streams were both visible and audible. Though the next morning we were back in the car and I was longing for his cello.

ANDY

I FIRST MET ANDY WARHOL at a Carnegie Biennial in Pittsburgh in the late 1940s. He was a classmate of Philip Pearlstein and Pat Miller, who would later become Pat Stern, and the three of them came through the front door and up the marble stairs together. I knew Phil from high school and he introduced me to the other two, Andy and Pat, but a little reluctantly in Pat's case since he was apparently in the process, long and slow at the time, of inducing her to remove her clothes and "model" for him. He saw that I was attracted to her and warned her against me since "I hung out at pool halls, flunked courses, and got into fights," which attracted her to me immediately. Of course I had changed since high school but Phil didn't know that. I was by this time a self-declared poet, arrogant beyond belief, reading and writing a good ten hours a day.

Andy, whose name was Warhola then, was thin, quiet, and friendly. He was the youngest in his class since most of them, certainly the men, were veterans of the war and were going back to school, or starting over, in their early twenties. He was well liked and seen as a superb draftsman and colorist. I don't know how many words we exchanged with each other, precious few I think, though we were in each other's presence a number of times, at picnics, in drugstores, in living rooms, at parties. My single favorite memory of Andy is of him sitting with his legs almost wrapped around each other, with an ice cream cone in his hand and a smile on his face. He was, even then, an observer, detached, a little ironic, but a participant nonetheless, and not superior but interested. We talked about him, even then, as a "voyeur," but in a general sense and without reference necessarily to his sexual habits. I remember having a lot of affection for him and for the group of which he was a part. I have always had a soft spot for art students, their bohemianism, their group loyalty, their commitment to an idea, the very clothes and colors and smells that permeated their lives, almost a kind of envy that we poets could not have that, that we had only dull pencils and paper and a few books, that the overriding romantic idea was not a constant unless we deliberately introduced it, as I did with my sacred items, books, rugs, special paper, bowls, clocks, photos, pens, plants, statues. And the computer—my God—it only further debased the poet as he joined the company of scholars, secretaries, and petty businessmen and made his or her position, tenuous as it was, only more so as he stared at the screen and moved his rodent around.

I can't remember anything about that biennial, except that it was either altogether, or mostly, abstract stuff, probably some Rothko, some Guston, some Rheinhardt, maybe Pollack, Kline, or Gottlieb—certainly some lesser-knowns, and we went from painting to painting rubbing our chins, desperate to understand, nodding our heads, positioning our bodies, the way you do. At the time, I wore expensive double-breasted suits, which I got from the credit store my father managed on Liberty Avenue or on upper Fifth Avenue from one of the wholesale houses. And white on white shirts, with elaborate cufflinks, pointed shoes, and a rich tie. I was familiar with the bohemian ideal of dress but I was instinctively opting for the idea of the dandy, easy enough since my clothes were free. By the early 1950s I would abandon that idea for the costume, the clothes, that have stood me in good stead for the last half-century, corduroys, sweaters, boots, old fedoras. When Pat met me she thought I was rich. She certainly knew before long that I was disdainful of the slow-minded and was a kind of dictionary of partial knowledge—though maybe I'm being too hard on myself.

Andy and Phil went to New York City to find work in commercial art when they graduated from Carnegie Tech. Andy, who already had a stunning portfolio, would in a matter of weeks get major assignments in freelance illustration and design in *Glamour, Mademoiselle, Vogue*, and other publications whereas Pearlstein got nowhere. Their teacher at Tech, Balcome Greene, who walked around the quiet college neighborhood with his two aristocratic Russian wolfhounds and an aristocratic wife, used his influence to find them an apartment just off Tompkins Square Park, on St. Mark's, for the summer, and that fall (1949) they found an apartment together on Twenty-first Street in Chelsea. I found out later that Andy, after he and Phil went their separate ways, lived in an apartment on West 103rd, the same street I lived on, a block or so away and probably at the same time. But I didn't know it at the time, nor did we ever see each other.

The biography I used has Andy and Phil making several forays to New York before they left for good in the summer of 1949. It describes them boarding a train "late one evening" and arriving at the Pennsylvania Station "around dawn," certainly a perfect time to arrive, just as the light was pouring into the vast hall. They may have planned to meet on the train but it was I who drove Andy—alone—to the East Liberty train station (no longer in existence) in my father's new 1949 Ford and said goodbye on one of the platforms. He had one of those flimsy cardboard suitcases in one hand

and a painting maybe twenty-four inches by eighteen in the other, which he apparently intended to take with him to New York. He suddenly gave me the painting, in a gesture of friendship or indifference, which he cemented with a quizzical smile, as if to say, "Do you really want such a thing?" He clearly didn't hold it dear or he didn't want to be bothered with it or he was showing his cosmic detachment or he just wanted me to have it and take care of it. I was delighted with the gift, maybe the first painting I ever owned, and treasured it. My only private place in my parents' apartment, I am a little ashamed to say, was a long closet in which I had built bookcases for my fast-growing collection. I nailed the painting to my wall, the right of the door when you entered alongside the pull chain, and it gave me a secret pleasure when I walked into that closet to retrieve my sleek new Auden or my huge Rabelais.

The painting was gray, blue, and white, with a firm black line, a representation of an older woman, extremely well done, glasses on her nose, a kind of wen on her chin. I had met Andy's mother—Julia—once and the painting reminded me of her. It also looked like Andy himself just as the 1974 portrait of Julia at first blush looked shockingly like him, a stouter, older female Andy, the same face. At least I thought so, his own hand at work this time, the painting less mechanical, more expressive, more vulnerable and emotional, than the other things he was doing. Less detached or ironic. Julia was born in 1892 and Andy in 1928, so she would have been approaching sixty in the earlier painting, an older mother, certainly an older mother for the time, particularly in the Slovak or Carpatho-Russian culture she came from; Slavic Andy.

When I left Pittsburgh for New York I gave the painting to my mother to take care of, along with my boxes and my old drawings and poems, and she put it in a bin or locker in the basement, along with her other treasures, which we protected with a padlock. It wasn't that it had any value over and above my own connection with the artist and my attachment to the work itself. It was 1949 and Andy wouldn't be doing his tin cans, dollar bills, and comic-strip characters for another decade. I took a full-time teaching job in the fall of 1956 and Andy Warhol was the farthest thing from my mind. Even when he became a world-famous figure I paid little attention, I was so busy with my own life, trying to stretch the money and find the right words. Nor was I much interested in pop art itself. It was Soutine I loved, and the Apollo of Veii, he of the large eyes and shattered arms, and I rather loathed art that was ephemeral and facetious and mocking. Even when it occupied the whole of what was once Volkwein's Music Store across the river on the Northside, once a separate city called Allegheny, where good Gertrude Stein was born, one of the famous Jews in his series of paintings called *Ten Portraits of Jews of the Twentieth Century*, including Einstein of course, and Freud and Kafka and Buber and the Marx brothers, such a zeal he had for exploitation, such an opportunist he was, the saintly simpleton.

When Andy died in 1987—on my birthday—my mother had been living in Miami for nineteen years, and she would continue to live there till her death in 1993; she was born in 1900, eight years after Julia, probably three hundred miles away. I began obsessing about the painting, a ghost by now, and when I went to Miami a few weeks later for my annual visit I immediately started to ask her about it. She had a huge closet off her bedroom where her things were stored, certainly as large as the dark bin in Pittsburgh. I called him Andy Warhola to identify him and she remembered "the thin, raggedy Polish boy with pimples," whom she had met once. I told her he was not Polish but Slovak, that yes he did have bad skin and that he was a millionaire, the term I used instead of "famous painter" or "underground filmmaker" to draw her attention.

We both went rushing off to the oversize closet to search for the painting. There were heavy leather suitcases covered in dust, a couple of ratty old fur coats, rows of ancient dresses, some with the tags still on them, twenty pair or so of shoes, hat boxes, cartons of old tax returns and photograph albums, some dreary books, a couple of lamps, a broken-down Hoover, and a large unfinished painting of me, age sixteen or seventeen, posing in a chair, my muscular legs painfully crossed, the painting covered with a yellowed sheet, the painter my cousin, Schimmy Grossman, done the four or five months he was an "artist," for which my father gave him probably twenty dollars, some time in 1941 or '42—but no Warhol. We unpacked boxes, we went through thirty years of large stiff pocketbooks with tarnished clasps, we breathed in the dust, some of it gathered into small balls, but Andy's painting wasn't there.

We went back to the living room to take stock, I sitting in my accustomed chair, my mother in hers, both of us sneezing. She was full of remorse and desperately tried to remember how the painting got lost. But it was small, maybe it leaned against a wall and the movers didn't see it. As usual, I found myself consoling *her* for my loss, though she was responsible for it. It wasn't that it was a great painting, it was only a student work; the *value* was partly in the money and partly that it was the early work of a world-famous artist as well as being a link to my own relationship with Andy. I ask myself how I would feel if it was an early Pearlstein I had lost and not that of a cult figure like Andy. Would I have reclaimed it years ago and nailed it to the wall? Do you leave a Pearlstein in a bin?

I sat there thinking that I not only conflated the ghost painting with Julia but I was beginning to include my own mother as a companion piece and I would then have compounded all three of them, though no one had ever painted her; and what it would have been like if Andy had taken a Polaroid of her, and caught her girlish beauty—though she was eighty-seven—and did something with her heavy makeup and her blue hair and her eyes that were full of grief and fear. I made her tea, as I always did, and she cleared her throat by way of forgiving herself and the world its careless and destructive ways, and to show her gratitude.

I was in Iowa City when Andy died and I took his death in stride, more bemused than shocked, and I wondered at the time, with the details of his life so much in the news, why I hadn't ever visited the Factory, why I didn't knock on his door even once, he who was as cunning and resilient as the other Pittsburgher, Andy Carnegie, who also got other people to do his dirty work for him, who also had his own elaborate explanation, and who also put a crown on his own head, like Napoleon. My guess is that when I drove Andy to the train station in 1949 he sat in the front seat looking straight ahead, maybe hugging his knees. He was probably impressed by the car, the gearshift knob, the curved front window. When we said goodbye, there may have been a cursory shaking of the hands, a brief touch, with no pressure from his side. I was doing him the simplest of favors, saving him from taking several streetcars or, God forbid, a cab, which could have cost him three dollars, a sum he couldn't afford—which, ah, makes me think for the first time that he was possibly "paying" me for the ride with the painting. For which I owe him much change and a worthy receipt. Though then, as later, it was hard to know *what* was in his mind. Probably nothing. Probably it just was what it was and had no poignant or metaphysical aspects about it. I thank him though for the painting; I'm sorry I lost it.

PARIS POST

IT BREAKS MY HEART that I can't find a copy of the *Paris Post* anywhere among my boxes and bags, though I know there is one— or two—somewhere, for I never finally destroy anything, my heart is so attached, especially to the blunders, failures, disasters, misunderstandings, of my fault-ridden life.

The *Paris Post* was a tabloid newspaper, maybe a mite smaller than the *Daily News* or the *American Poetry Review*. And it was the only newspaper in English besides the *Herald-Tribune* meant to serve mostly the community of young Americans in Paris circa 1950, artists, intellectuals, students, bums, living mostly on the Left Bank. I was one of them, living off the World War II G.I. Bill, occasionally attending a class at the Sorbonne, writing poems, reading Rimbaud and Milton, going to movies, picking up girls at the Du Pont Café, walking the neighborhoods.

The founder of the *Post* was Marty Fleer, whom I met on the boat going over. It was a Dutch ship, *The Edam*, and went from Hoboken to Antwerp, carrying about twenty passengers in addition to cargo. Marty was skinny, without muscle, his hair was wavy, and his nose met his chin. His girlfriend's name was Mildred and she already was giving some evidence of swelling in the middle. She was black-haired, dark-skinned, and beautiful, and clearly it was an outrage that Marty had the privilege. We consulted about the newspaper during the long trip, walking the decks, strolling like *boulevardiers* with our hands behind us, past the heavy smell of oil and the coiled bull-ropes. For him the purpose of creating the paper was to make money—through ads and eventually sales. I never heard him once mention any journalistic ambitions, political, aesthetic, cultural, and when he roped me in, to help him on the writing side, he not only didn't want to control what I said, he almost showed no interest. As I look at it now, it was utterly peculiar, but it seemed reasonable to me at the time.

The Hôtel du Centre, where I lived, dated from Henri IV, and the steps were worn smooth. The only other Americans in the hotel were Howard Kirchwehm, who spoke French with a Chicago accent, and his wife, Maryann, who was studying Cambodian. He worked in some minor capacity, an elevator operator for the *Herald* and dreamed about getting an editorial position on that paper and living forever in Paris. I arranged with Marty that Howard's name would be on the masthead as editor in exchange for a promise to "produce" all the news and editorials.

The paper didn't actually have an office at the time. It operated from one of the two desks in a small travel agency and consisted, as far as I could tell, of a telephone and a typewriter. We did the first issue in two days. It consisted of a false interview with Salvador Dalí, a report of the first major postwar literary festival (which we created ex nihilo, on the spot), art reviews, drama reviews, reports of art openings, film reviews, and the like, much of which we took verbatim from other sources. And we attached made-up names. I think there was an editorial that Howard wrote on the new art and the new politics, very negative. The only authentic review was of a production of Thornton Wilder's *Our Town* in the American Center on Boulevard Raspail. I saw the play and wrote the review under the name of Yunkel Dohlgyapiet, my grandfather's name in the Ukraine, and mine as well if he hadn't changed it to "Stern," under advisement of a Yiddish-speaking guard at Ellis Island. I praised the performance generally, but attacked in particular the lighting, which was designed by my cousin Israel (Eo) Grossman, an amateur thespian from Pittsburgh. I remember apologizing to Eo thirty or thirty-five years later at a reading in California, where he had spent his life as an elementary school teacher.

As I write about all this I am surprised both by what I remember and what I forget. I often brag about my memory for details, what color some curtains were, exactly where the door to a cellar was, what year a president was born, what year I first went to Florida, but I forget what month my sister died, what my time was in the mile, the name of the hotel we stayed in every year in Atlantic City. And I forget whether the *Paris Post* was a weekly or a monthly or if it just came out from *temps* to *temps*. There was, as I say, no office, no central administrative location, no place to hang out. There was the single shared desk in the travel bureau, Marty's room and a half, smelling of cats and dirty clothes, and my room at the Hôtel du Centre, blessed be the name. Nor did Marty have a telephone in his room, nor were there answering machines then—Marty must have sold ads by using the travel agency phone or knocking on doors. However, he was persistent and successful. Certainly it was the most naked and rudimentary of operations: he was in it for the money, Howard was in it to get his name on the masthead, I—and Dick Hazley helping me—was in it for adventure, joy, madness, hooliganism, theater.

The night before publication we threw names and ideas at each other across my room. We each sat there, me on the edge of the bed, Hazley at my little wooden desk, Howard standing, writing

our articles, vying with each other to see who would finish first.
I know Hazley did the piece on the huge conference and I did the
"interview" with Dalí. I would love to read again the description of
the little restaurant on the dock where we "talked." It was beauti-
ful writing and I may have missed my calling. The questions were
good, even sharp; Dalí had a hard time responding to the issue of
Franco. I remember how interested he was when I told him about
my origins. Spaniards are keenly interested in what happened to
the Jews after they kicked them out, and what the trek south or east
was like. Hazley was particularly good at the little boxed inserts. He
had worked on a college newspaper and had great confidence and
skill. I think we stayed up all night to make the morning deadline.
We didn't have green shades, we didn't type with two fingers, but
we were something.

Howard had gone before breakfast apparently to a nearby kiosk—
probably on Boule-Miche—to buy a copy of the *Post* as soon as
it came out, for he banged on my door at seven in the morning
to bring the terrible news that his name was *not* on the masthead
but that Marty Fleer appeared as owner, publisher, and editor. My
name appeared as drama critic, even though it was "Dohlgyapiet,"
but Howard's name was nowhere. He was white-faced, furious,
betrayed. He had on a half-smile, a grimace, below his sunglasses,
and he was ready to commit murder. "Let's go kill the son-of-a-
bitch," he said. Six foot one or two, powerful, the veins sticking out
of his forearms. He could easily have crippled Marty, crushed him
with one blow. I dressed and went with him as much to protect the
prick as to attack him. He lived three or four blocks away, through a
hopeless warren into which Howard strode, through the front door
of a church I remember, and out the side, me following him.

We knocked hard on Marty's door and after a long pause—clearly

he was considering not answering—there was a friendly birdlike
voice that asked, "Who *is* it?" the indication being, oh sparrow,
that he knew very well who it was, and that the jig was up. "Just a
minute," the sparrow said. Mildred answered the door, looking sad
and weary. She was getting quite large and was breathing through
her mouth. Marty was sitting up in bed three feet away, wearing an
undershirt and boxer shorts, his knees up, a coarse sheet half cover-
ing him, his thick hair disheveled, a kind of board on his lap where
a newspaper (not the *Post*) and a cup of tea rested. His nose, as usual,
touched his chin, and he was all smiles.

Howard was almost speechless—he was Billy Budd and Marty was
near death. I did the talking in a cold, formal, accusing manner. His
answers were simple and all apology and concern and promise. He
was eternally grateful for the work we did, the layout was gorgeous,
he couldn't get along without us, he loved the interview with Salva-
dor Dalí at Dieppe—had we really gone there? He loved Howard's
long article on the coming America and the missed chances and 1950,
that year, as the apex of the seesaw, and what was bound to happen
as America moved from the left to the right, with the new bombs
hovering over us, and he loved the information we had gathered (sto-
len) and the attractive headlines and such. Next time we would need
more pictures and we should develop a little staff who would work
(free) to keep ahead of the many details. And of course, we would
need an office and our own typewriter—maybe two—and files, and
maybe a rug we could pick up in the Arab Quarter. And certainly
Howard's name would be on the masthead next time as editor, and
my name as well, and as soon as we began to make a little money
from ads and sales we would begin paying salaries, albeit small in the
beginning. And the reason Howard's name wasn't there this time
had something to do with French law, since the paper was techni-

cally—but only technically—registered under the woman's name who owned the travel agency and he, Marty, was the "front," and all that would be corrected as soon as possible, and how did we want our coffee and let me move those things (books, eyeglasses, clothes) off the chairs, and was it too early to start thinking of the 1952 elections and how should we handle it in the paper and how was Maryann and was it true I was considering moving to Toulouse and what a loss that would be to him and what did we think they should name the baby if it was a boy, if it was a girl?

Howard and I left our coffees untouched and walked downstairs and more or less out of Marty's life. Somehow he got someone else or several someone elses to write the articles for him, to do the news. I had a lovely time and very few hard feelings. I was going to Italy anyhow in a few weeks. Howard licked his wounds, vowed revenge, and began his search for a job that would keep him connected some-how with Paris, or at least France. He eventually got a position with the State Department as an information officer (spy) and his first assignment was "Indo-China," though he had a hard time getting a security clearance since a doorman at the *Herald*, or a newsboy in Saint-Germain, or a concierge in the Bastille District—I can't remember which—had talked to someone who had once talked to an ex-Communist in Dijon, or some such place. He told me there was going to be a war there but I didn't listen too closely since the Roma-nians upstairs were talking war everyday. Rumor after rumor with those snakes. Dien Bien Phu hadn't happened yet and Ho Chi Min was still talking Jefferson and Lincoln. And little expecting betrayal. At any rate, Maryann's Cambodian would come in handy.

I have seen Howard several times since then; the last thing we did vis-à-vis the *Paris Post* was walk into the travel office—it was empty—and swipe the typewriter from the desk on the balcony.

It was an American brand, but it had the French accents. When I remember now, I'm pretty sure I did it alone. I sold it at Goldenberg's, which in those days was a classic Jewish sit-down restaurant, for I had contact with a Polish architect who had been a prisoner at Auschwitz and was doing black market to keep body and soul together, since the French weren't going to let him practice a trade, the fucking Jew; especially since his mouth was smashed in by the Germans. I always had a little guilt about the *machine à écrire* for it might have been the exclusive possession of the travel agent, and Marty only the borrower. We got a hundred dollars for it and Marty had to replace it to stay in business, I'm sure. It was a petty revenge, but I had to do something.

I came back to Paris about four years later and I was startled to find the *Paris Post* still for sale in the kiosks, and the paper thicker than it had been in 1950. I had gone through graduate school, marriage, a job as a principal at a private school, and a job as a visiting teacher in Glasgow, Scotland, in between. And I had changed my poetry three or four times. I was reading and studying Stevens then and a number of British poets I had bought in bookstores in Glasgow and London. Dylan Thomas was dead and I had discovered Hugh MacDiarmid, the poet and the man. We marched side by side in a May Day parade in 1953 and my heart beat with joy at being a Scot's Socialist. By the time we left Europe to go back to America in 1956, the *Post* had disappeared. It was sold, I was later told by a friend of Marty's and mine, for a huge sum. I remember the figure $500,000, but that hardly seems possible. Whatever it was, Marty had outwitted the world and was sitting back in his underwear in some fancy apartment in Manhattan, his chin a little longer than before, certainly a ten-dollar cigar in his mouth, planning his next move.

BLESSED

I HAVE ALWAYS WANTED to write about my relationship with the police. There are those in the culture who have a daily connection with them and there are those whose only connection revolves around traffic tickets and accidents. I come from a comfortable immigrant culture, obedient, law-abiding, grateful, unquestioning, and destined for a little success in America. I myself was an angel who believed literally in what I was told—at least to a certain age. I don't know if it was the sudden death of my sister—when she was nine and I was eight—or the move to a new neighborhood, in the mid-1930s, in order to escape her memory and presence, that changed me. We had been living in a crowded little settlement, in a small house across the street from a woods in what was then a suburb, and we were the only Jews on the street. The new neighborhood, Squirrel Hill, was all apartment houses, densely populated, and predominantly Jewish. I suddenly had many friends, I hung out on the streets, and there was no more Jew-baiting. No one broke my glasses or pummeled me with snowballs because I killed Christ. And no gang of twelve-year-olds ever left me bleeding—from a nose, a mouth, an eye, an ear—because I was rich and abused Christians, especially Catholics.

As far as the police were concerned, they were benevolent and gracious, and I never could understand why Krazy Kat threw bricks at Occifer Pup. When I was fourteen or fifteen, things changed. The high school I went to, Taylor-Allderdice, and the streets and alleys around it, suddenly found itself the center of a real battle between the Jews—sons and daughters of storekeepers, salesmen, and a few professionals—and the Hunkies, sons and daughters of the millworkers, mostly of eastern and southern European stock. The Hunkies, a pejorative term ridiculously connected with "Hungarian," relieved their frustrations and lack of hope, and coupled it with the anti-Semitism they brought over from Europe, by beating up isolated Jews. After one Jewish boy was permanently paralyzed from one such beating, we fought back by surrounding our enemies when they left school, and inflicted a little damage. The police arrived in force, arrested only the aggressors, and took us off to juvenile court. I remember that the ringleaders, myself foremost, were held overnight, and I remember I made a speech.

I was shocked by the stupidity, deft ignorance, and insensitivity of the police. They apparently had never heard of anti-Semitism, and knew nothing of the conditions at our high school. In my innocence, I had believed the police's own version of themselves, that they were above the fray and interested only in justice; but quicker than you can say Eugene V. Debs or Karl H. Marx, I learned that they not only had the prejudices of their class, including religious, racial, ethnic, geographic, and economic bias, but were themselves a kind of class. This is certainly a no-brainer today, but I'm writing about a fifteen-year-old boy in the '30s and his education. I was a quick learner, though my grades were bad, and my own experience taught me where matters truly lay when I was arrested several times for the same charges, including "inciting to riot" and disturbing the peace.

It's hard for me now—in my seventies—to know when I finished my learning. I was already in my late thirties and early forties during the civil rights and antiwar protests. I had small children and a university teaching job. I made a speech or two and read some poems of protest against the Vietnam War, which came very close to getting me fired; and I organized and led the largest civil rights march in Pennsylvania, which required the cooperation of the local and state police, but by then I knew the rules, and it was easy enough to get them to *protect* the marchers. Also, I and my family were permanently barred from using the local (segregated) swimming pool (Indiana, Pennsylvania) by a retired state trooper with a bad heart who "didn't want any trouble" when a small group of us, black and white, dipped our bodies in the bigoted water, but no one got hurt, and no one got arrested. You never finish learning, but I understood things and was "armed" by the time I was twenty or twenty-one. Maybe the poor and tinted know it when they are half that age. I at least was Caucasian, educated, and had a smart tongue. And I could "escape" anytime I wanted, just by doing nothing.

I was arrested and taken to one station or another a number of times. It happened mainly because I was out there, active, in the way. And I stayed up late. The best single way not to get in trouble is to stay home, bolt the door, and turn on the TV. If a child is bleeding to death on your stoop, for God's sake, let it die. It's the best way. To avoid getting fingerprinted, of course, one shouldn't dress oddly or drive an unusual car or stop to pee against a bush or a wall. When a friend of mine—late 1950s, Philadelphia—parked his rusted-out Chevy a little too close to a hydrant for a policeman's comfort, we measured and won. But the policeman was furious. He kept saying, "You're a dead giveaway," and his face got redder and redder. I don't know if he was referring to the rusty car or to my friend's full beard, not yet in style, but what he was really saying was, "Behave according to a convention I can recognize and approve of; don't be an ingrate, wise guy, intellectual, bohemian, arrogant, irresponsible; pay your goddamn taxes; get your sticker in time, commie bastard homo."

Or am I being excessively hard on him? Wasn't he underpaid, overworked, lonely? Was he having trouble? Was he sick, harassed? If he was defending class interest, was it working class or middle class? What did it have to do with his uniform, his sense of duty? Did he think at all in terms of class? What was his value system? If it was hard work, punctuality, toeing the line, dependability, suspicion of the outsider, one form of Puritanism or another, weren't we perfect game? Even in our lack of respect and fear? Even in our dress? Even that we were not working, but floating about? Free? How old, and persistent, is this love affair?

One time, in Pittsburgh, Dick Hazley and I made arrangements to meet, probably at eleven or eleven-thirty at night, on a certain bridge on Murray Avenue in Squirrel Hill. We had gone earlier to a meeting of the Progressive Party in someone's living room. It was 1948 and Henry Wallace, vice president under Roosevelt, was running for president against Truman and Dewey. I was in my aesthetic and antipolitical phase at the time, so was Hazley, and we went there to get free food and to pick up girls. The one we both wanted preferred Hazley to me, hence our agreement to meet on the bridge afterward, to walk a while and discuss the evening.

Just before Dick arrived, an unmarked car with two detectives stopped beside me and I was arrested—at least they pushed me into the back seat of the car. "Where's the other guy?" they actually asked, and just at that moment Dick came up the hill, whistling, probably from his conquest. He was pushed into the back seat too. When we indignantly protested that we both lived a few blocks away, I think they knew they had made a mistake, but they were determined to go through with it, especially when they learned we were at a meeting of the Progressive Party, nor would they listen to our pleas but berated us for being "communists." It seemed that two sexual predators used that end of the bridge for their forays, and that's why we were stopped. So they claimed, but they said nothing more about it, drove us to old number 11 on Northumberland Street, and kept us overnight. In the morning they let us call our parents, who were extremely angry—at us—and we were released, with no charges but dire, vague warnings. I don't know if a phone call was a nickel or a dime at the time. I voted for Henry Wallace, the first time I voted.

Maybe six months later, Jack Gilbert and I were taking a walk in the section of Squirrel Hill that had huge houses and large lawns, off Shady Avenue, between Forbes and Fifth. It was about midnight; we had finished talking about poetry and, in the presence of these grand homes, we were doing architecture. I think I was delivering a lecture on the Georgian style when suddenly a black wagon pulled up and we were forced inside by Pittsburgh's Finest. Again it was a mistake—someone had reported prowlers. After all, it was late. We were taken to number 11 and, in front of a huge desk out of Kafka, we were questioned by a very heavy sergeant. He paid very little attention to me at first but lectured Jack, whose father he had known, about walking down the streets late at night and thus giving the police trouble. Jack's father, who fell out of an attic window to his death, had been a slack-ropewalker and dog-faced boy in the circus, and later an exterminator. He was a well-known figure about town, and the sergeant was particularly angry at Jack for disgracing his memory this way. By way of pride, he ordered Jack to remain in East Liberty (three blocks away) and not return to Squirrel Hill. Instead of agreeing with this absurd demand, Jack insisted on his right to go anywhere he pleased, and I almost ended up in one of those cells again. What distracted the sergeant was a poem I was carrying around about Jonah and his reluctance. It was in four parts and quite dramatic, as good as most of what was being published then. The sergeant was very distrustful of the poem, questioned me about it, and even held it up to the light. It saved the day and we were discharged, with a warning.

I don't know if I'm getting these events in the right order or even the right year. I think I am. Except for the high school incidents, they were preceded by two arrests (for the same charge) while I was in the army just after World War II, but I'll come to that later. In the late spring of 1949, after I had returned to Pittsburgh from New York City, where I had gotten an M.A. in comparative literature from Columbia University, I rendezvoused with the future Pat Stern, who was a student in the painting and design department at Carnegie Tech, outside the Carnegie Library. On the steps. Her grades had suffered a lot since we met—a year or so earlier—and she was feverishly trying to get through several projects before graduation. She had to get back to her dorm by ten, so we had about an hour together. We were sitting on a park bench under a street lamp faced away from the street—it was Forbes—about fifty yards from the library. Suddenly we were approached by a man who identified himself as a detective and placed us under arrest. (The dear words again.) Pat was startled and confused, and I was alarmed and suspicious. He showed me a badge but was evasive when I asked what the charges were. He and a colleague drove us in an unmarked car to the local police station, where we were held overnight and driven down to the courthouse the next morning. I knew the detectives were from the vice squad, and I knew the vice squad generally preyed on homosexuals, so I was trying to figure out why we were being held. They probably had no luck in the latrines and had to move one step up (or down) the sexual ladder. I knew the charge would be sexual and I assumed we would be accused of committing an "unnatural" act, probably fellatio, which, in legal terminology, is called sodomy. A crime then, when done in public. Probably still so today.

I called my parents as a matter of course, and my father came down to the courthouse. He was furious and embarrassed, and though no charge had been made yet, the nature of it was in the air—you could smell it. I think we had about eighty steps to climb to arrive at the entrance—enough to make us breathless and humble—and while we were walking up we were approached by someone who claimed to be a lawyer, insisted he knew our family, said it was a mistake, and offered to "fix it up." He took the three of us into a side room to sign some papers and asked us for money, five hundred, a thousand, whatever the false fee was in those days. My father was ready to sign but I wouldn't let him. After a few minutes we were called into a small courtroom full of police, social workers, reporters, and a judge. The odd thing, now that I think of it, was that there was no police presence when we were with the lawyer, or even before. We were just left in his custody—or company—without any formal or legal sanction. There were no handcuffs; we could have easily walked out.

Pat was stunned, but her main concern, I found out later, was how to explain her absence from the dorm the night before. She was due to sign in at 10:00 P.M., but she didn't arrive till the next afternoon. She couldn't very well say to her housemother that she was arrested by a detective from the vice squad and held in a cell overnight and charged with sodomy. Nor would it have helped to explain the corruption in the system, neither to the housemother nor the dean of women, not in 1949. The assumption was that she had spent the night with me and hadn't covered her tracks. Indeed, her close friend, Ellie, hedging her bets, said that Pat had spent the night at her house, so we had to accommodate to that lie too. What we came up with was that I got sick—I fainted, or had a heart attack, something like that, and we went to my house. Luckily my mother corroborated the lie. Carnegie Tech, of course, punished Pat. They let her graduate but forbade her from participating in the ceremony. Which infuriated her father.

At the hearing I was lucid, calm, and convincing. I explained that we were sitting under a street lamp twenty feet from the street and that it was not a likely place for us to have oral sex, which was the charge. That we were engaged—Pat and I—and I would not expose her to the indignity of sex in a public place, and that it was clearly a vicious trap involving lying and intimidation. And false, even fake, arrest. My memory is that the detective gave a lame and unconvincing argument.

We were sent to another room, the three of us, and the vile prick who "represented" us kept bouncing in and out. I was reminded by Pat, with whom I checked the events out on the phone, that his name was Martin. She remembered that. Finally Martin told us that the case was being remanded to the grand jury, but not to worry, it was common practice.

On the way out I insisted that we go see our family attorney. My father, who now believed my story, was ashamed and wanted to give Martin the money. However, I persuaded him, and when our attorney found out the facts he thought it was a perfect opportunity to get Martin—whose "work" he knew well—disbarred and the vice-squad detectives fired, maybe jailed. But my father didn't want my name in the newspaper. Our attorney found out in a few minutes that there was no case—that it had not been remanded to the grand jury—it had been thrown out by the magistrate.

For my part, I visited Martin every few days to see how things were going. We were both stringing each other along, only I had the advantage. I didn't confront him then because I was worried that he would interfere in some way with Pat's graduation, by a dumb phone call to the wrong person, for he was not only vicious but a little stupid. As soon as Pat got her diploma—through the mail—I visited Martin for the last time and calmly told him what I knew before I cursed him out. He wasn't embarrassed, indignant, or apologetic. What he said was, "You could at least give me fifty bucks for my time." I refrained from breaking his jaw and left. I was starting to pity him.

In the army you're more or less guilty till you're proven guilty, or on occasion innocent, at least in the lower ranks, which is why I spent months in the guardhouse, at hard labor, waiting for my court-martial. I remember six months, but it could have been shorter. I was in the army between World War II and the Korean War, 1946–47, while America was disarming. After a brief and boring basic training in the Air Corps, I was sent to Holabird Signal Depot in Baltimore, Maryland, a counterintelligence training center, where I would be educated for six months, then sent to Germany as, forgive me, a secret agent in de-Nazification. We took classes all day, lock-picking, jujitsu, German language, history of the Nazi party, and we had Class A passes that let us stay out till midnight. I had been a philosophy major at the University of Pittsburgh, half intellectual, half weight lifter, and it was natural for me to gravitate to the odd—and older—people in my class, namely a former cop from

Chicago we called the Greek and a short fat man in his thirties, with small hands and feet and a stiletto-like knife hidden in a thin pocket of his calfskin boots, reminding me of the knives that were standard accessory of the hightop boots we wore as kids. His name was Hans Spalter and he was a heavily ribboned veteran. The three of us were a team in the constant games we played as part of our training, trailing someone without his knowledge, interrogating professional actors in German as to their supposed whereabouts during the war and the years preceding it, in preparation for what we would be doing in earnest in a few months in occupied Germany. Hans and I were buddies. We went almost every weekend to nearby Washington, D.C., where we slept with two sisters we knew, late thirties and early forties, or went to dances where there were two or three women to every man. Hans was a highly gifted pickpocket. We would walk through a little alley and he would emerge with tens and fives and twenties he had stolen from slightly drunk sailors, who tended to distribute their cash in various pockets. I never knew—at the time—that it was going on.

One time we were hitchhiking to D.C. and were picked up by a guy in a beautiful new Chrysler. It was a warm day, his suitcoat was lying over the seat between us, and Hans, who was in the back seat, naturally stole his wallet. It was a rich leather breast-pocket wallet, with very little money in it. I was angry at Hans, took it back to Holabird the next day with the intention of mailing it to the owner, temporarily put it in my footlocker and promptly forgot about it, what with our busy schedule, my endless reading from the pile of books on my bed, and the endless bad writing I was filling notebooks with.

As part of our training, Hans, the Greek, and I were sent—as a team—to a wretched little bar in the fish and produce market on the

waterfront in order to question, in an unassuming way, the patrons
and customers. The only problem was that it was a regular stop for
the school, and the owner asked us to drink our beer and lay off.
He was tired of Holabird sending its trainees into his bar. When we
were outside, Hans showed us the wallet he had stolen. It belonged
to a Harry Shapiro, there were two dollars in it, and it was made of
cardboard. The Greek, angry and disgusted, left. Hans threw the
wallet and its rotting cards into a sewer, and we took in a movie
and dinner, I and my criminal friend. Hans and I went by streetcar
back to Holabird and, sure enough, some MPs were waiting for us,
questioned us about Shapiro's missing wallet, since the owner of the
bar had obviously gotten in touch with the school, and finally let
us go, since there was no evidence and Shapiro was a well-known
heavy drinker. The next evening, a night and a full day later, the
MPs sheepishly came into our barracks to make the routine check
of our footlockers. There was the beautiful wallet Hans had stolen
on the trip down to D.C., the cards intact. I had forgotten to mail
it to the owner.

There was no guardhouse at Holabird, so Hans and I were
taken to the nearest camp with a guardhouse, which happened to
be Aberdeen Proving Grounds, beautiful in the spring, where the
army was conducting chemical and biological experiments on ani-
mals. We slept, and hung out in the evening, on the second floor,
a kind of cage, and did our dreaming under a couple of bare light-
bulbs. During the day we emptied large garbage cans full of dead
dogs, cats, rats, squirrels, rabbits, and raccoons into cement holes
in the ground. After a day or so I had some ugly words with the
provost-sergeant (I was protesting my job), who ruled like an abso-
lute monarch; as a result I was transferred to a rock pile, where I
worked alone breaking fieldstone with a sledge hammer—for no

purpose—from sunup to sundown, eight or nine o'clock at night, a guard with a carbine always beside me. The provost-sergeant—I forget his name, though I planned his murder for years—drove me to the site in his jeep, picked me up for breakfast, lunch, and supper, which I ate alone in sight of the others, and drove me back at night. I worked for about ten or eleven hours a day, Sundays included. The rock pile was situated in such a way, just below the crest of a hill, that my torturer could come upon me suddenly and if I was loafing the poor guard could be subject to a summary court-martial, so I kept working day after day, week after week, almost peacefully—I was waiting for my own court-martial. I guess the rock chopping was in lieu of bail.

Hans was released after a day or so. I was the only one charged. We worked up a story between us in which I confessed that *I* had taken the wallet in the car on the way to D.C. but that it was part of a "stealth" game influenced by our training at Holabird, and anyway I intended to return it, kept the cards, etc. The Shapiro wallet I said I knew nothing about. It was the best I could do and still get Hans's support. Of course the army lays it on. The charges included grand larceny (Shapiro claimed a couple hundred in his wallet), the 96th article (conduct unbecoming a soldier), impersonating an officer (I had a card on me that said Major Gerald Stern, which a friend had typed up as a joke), and one or two other minor charges. It was a special court-martial, and if I were found guilty I could be sent to Leavenworth, six months on each charge.

The provost-sergeant, who was from rural Virginia, was in his fifties. He had a great paunch, a red face, and a mean scowl. He hated me because I was a Jew, a northerner, educated, and young. I accepted his hatred as natural, and hardly blamed him for it. My own hatred grew slowly. There was also the issue of me being an "odd" guest. The other thirty-five or so were young African Americans, in the guardhouse for drinking, fighting, and AWOL. They quickly sized up the situation and expressed sympathy for me, giving me comic books and chocolate bars when I came back exhausted every night. I was a few years older than them and I was reading the New Testament, a paperback, with a crackled cover. They thought I was a preacher of some sort, and came to me with their problems. I will love them forever.

My counsel—assigned to me—was a smart young lieutenant with a soul. His name was Long, Lieutenant Long. We met regularly to plan my defense. Since I was in the guardhouse for months already, we decided to plead guilty to one minor charge in order to appease the court and claim I was already sufficiently punished. I think it was a warm September when I drove up to Holabird for my trial. The driver, whom I knew, decided not to handcuff me. I was wearing a summer uniform, complete with necktie tucked in between the appropriate buttons instead of the two-piece outfit with a huge "P" sewn to the back of the cloth jacket, or painted on, I forget which. I was perfectly happy, totally unafraid, driving through that lovely countryside. Later, when I read French and German philosophers describe the enlightened or existential moment, I understood where I was on that ride, and later in court.

The courtroom itself was packed, to my surprise. I guess a court-martial was unusual for Holabird. When the charges were made and Lieutenant Long got up to plead, I pulled at his arm and whispered, "not guilty on all charges." I didn't know, even a second before, I was going to say that. I don't remember many of the details of the trial, but I do remember there was a lot of noise and a lot of gaveling when we pled. The court expected the defense we had planned, I'm sure of it, and were going to comply or not comply according to how they felt about me, maybe according to the testimony. I had put myself at risk by my plea, or I had freed myself, I didn't know which.

The trial lasted two days. Shapiro was a very unconvincing witness, especially regarding the two hundred dollars. The little man whose wallet I never returned was terrified. He claimed he never saw us before, and that he probably dropped the wallet somewhere. Spalter, the thief, stuck to the script. He had been in the army since 1939, first the Canadian, then the American. He had been wounded in the attack on Dieppe, was in the Battle of the Bulge, was with the advanced units in Germany. He was born in Austria, spoke perfect German, and hated the Nazis with all his heart. Nor was there a speck of anti-Semitism in him. He just had a small weakness. For my part, I was indeed found not guilty—of all charges—and received a thirty-day furlough the next day.

The prosecutor, a highly intelligent and well-trained captain or major from one of the great southern military academies and, I guess, law school as well—Duke, Virginia—was angry and a little mortified, and the commanding officer of the camp, whose name was also Sterne, only with an "e" at the end, asked me, rather sardonically, how I felt about military justice now. Lieutenant Long urged me to make peace with the prosecutor, to congratulate him and "sir" him to death, which I did, but he remained distant and disappointed, personally piqued. What I believed, what I was certain of, was that the court not only felt I was innocent but knew Hans was guilty, considering his record, his past "accomplishments." I'm sure I appeared like a foolish and gullible provincial intellectual to them, which I was.

Lieutenant Long tried to get me shipped off with the next group, which was going to Japan, but I stubbornly refused since I was trained for work in Germany. Another case of stupidity. At any rate, the wartime draft had just ended and I had the choice of enlisting for two years or being discharged, after five months in my case. Since I opted for out, I was sent to the nearest air base—I had been assigned initially to the Air Corps—which happened to be Andrews Field outside of Washington. They didn't know what to do with me at Andrews; when I told them I came from Holabird, they assumed, in spite of my protests, that I was on a case, "disaffection" probably, someone spreading communist propaganda, and they gave me a small job at the gatehouse that kept me busy ten hours a week, and a private room in the MP barracks. That's how I spent my last few months in the army, except that Spalter came down to visit me and I was lured back to Holabird to "see my friends," slept over, and was arrested, again, in the morning by a Baltimore city policeman, taken downtown, put in a filthy cell, and arraigned the next morning on the larceny charges. It turns out there is no double jeopardy as far as military and civilian arrests are concerned. It turns out I was a fool for going back.

My poor parents, in their little apartment in Pittsburgh, had to find out the name of a lawyer in Baltimore and put up bail. The lawyer they found was on the top floor of a downtown office building. You had to walk up the last flight. I remember he was very tall, had bushy eyebrows, and slightly aging furniture. He agreed to take my case, although he didn't seem to believe my story. He was angry that a Jewish boy would get caught up in such a thing. On the way out of the building I glanced at the board and saw that a friend of mine had an office there, and went up to see him. He had been mayor of Baltimore and was very successful—and connected. His son had been at a camp in New Hampshire and I had literally saved the boy from drowning in a scary accident on one of our trips. (I was the wilderness counselor.) It sounds a little absurd, the whole thing, something out of Henry Fielding, but every word is true. He welcomed me—the father—into his huge and gorgeous office, and when I told him the bare facts he said he would clear it up with a phone call. I had to tell him about the shabby lawyer on the top floor, which put a different light on the matter. It was necessary to go—again—through the pretext of a case, and even to pay for it this time, while my true lawyer was the ex-mayor, who wouldn't take a dime for his service. There was actually a trial, but it lasted about two minutes. Ex-mayor leaped to his feet and said something in Latin, and the judge announced me a free man. Shabby lawyer was astonished. That night I had dinner at the ex-mayor's house and I saw him once or twice more before I left the area. I am deeply indebted to him.

I was discharged a few months later. I spent my remaining time visiting bookstores and libraries, writing incoherent poems and cryptic short stories. I memorized "The Ballad of Reading Gaol" and "The Rubaiyat." I discovered Yeats, then Pound. I carried around a small anthology of poems that fit in my coat pocket.

The army, in its relentless wisdom, has to punish someone when they feel something disruptive has happened. In this case, though they knew Spalter was a thief, or *the* thief, they couldn't prove it, so they got him on another charge, wearing a ribbon he hadn't earned, a battle—they said—he hadn't fought in, among a chestful of other ribbons, other battles, though the war was over and nobody gave a damn, and anyhow he probably did earn it, slicing a few throats with his stiletto. For which he was sent down for six months. He wrote me later but I didn't answer. He had some ideas about political action in the new Germany, and wanted me to join him. But I had had enough.

I feel a little ridiculous recounting these events. It's all minor, a trifle, in the crazy history of arrest and imprisonment. Men putting other men in cages. Punishing them, killing them. Political, racial, otherwise. Hikmet for thirty years, Mandelstam driven to death. My suffering, such as it was, was mostly the result of backwater bohemianism, vile innocence, and a few unlucky accidents. This coupled with stupidity and corruption on the part of the police, and some bigotry and drum taps in the army. I was lucky my family didn't stay in Poland. I was lucky I wasn't poor—and therefore powerless. And I was lucky—I suppose—that the state was hardly interested in my bitter birdcalls. Nor can I keep a grudge. I actually feel blessed. Can you imagine?

BULLET IN MY NECK

I AM SO USED TO having a bullet in my neck that I never think of it, only when the subject comes up and someone—full of doubt or amazement—gingerly reaches a hand out to feel it. It is a memento of the shooting on an empty road on the edge of Newark, New Jersey, when Rosalind Pace and I got lost on the way from Newark airport to a conference of poets in Bethlehem, Pennsylvania. We made the mistake of stopping at a red light and were cornered immediately by two boys, sixteen or so, dressed in starched jeans and jackets and sporting zip guns. Before we could reason with them, or submit, or try to escape, they began shooting through the open windows. The boy on Rosalind's side pointed his gun, a .22, directly in her face, a foot away, but it misfired. The boy on my side emptied his gun, hitting the steering wheel, the window and the dashboard. One bullet grazed my right shoulder, and one hit my chin then buried itself in the left side of my neck, less than a half-inch from the carotid artery.

Everything in such a situation takes on a life of its own, and the few seconds it took me to realize I wasn't going to die seemed like a much longer stretch of time, and though my neck swelled up and blood was pouring out, my only thought was to get out of there as quickly as possible. My memory was that I fell to the floor, pushed the gas pedal down with one hand, and with the other put the gear into drive till Rosalind took over and drove us out of there. All the time I was screaming at her not to lose control, that she had to save our lives. It was Friday night and we were someplace in downtown Newark, and it was 1986 or 1987. No one would give us directions to the hospital; it seemed as if everyone was drunk or high. I kept jumping out of the car to stop cabs, but when they saw the blood they rushed off. Then, by some fluke, we found ourselves driving up a lawn to the back entrance of Beth Israel where, after a crazy alter-cation with a ten-dollar-a-day rent-a-cop with a noisy beeper, we drove over another lawn to the emergency entrance where, thanks to the fake cop, two doctors were waiting to rip my clothes off and save my life. I told the fake cop that if there wasn't someone waiting I would crawl back and kill him, even if it was the last thing I did in this life—I think I said "with my bare hands" for, after all, I was in the midst of a great drama—and that may have awakened him.

The one thing the doctors, the nurses, and police lieutenant, who came later, said over and over was that it was a mistake to stop at the red light. "Why did you stop at the red light?" I was asked. "No one stops at that light!" I felt guilty, as if I myself were the per-petrator. It was as if Newark lived by a different set of rules. Cer-tainly it was a battle zone and probably more intensely so in the mid–1980s than it is now in the twenty-first century, at least at this point, 2002. There is rebuilding and there is talk about rebirth. But the burning and the racial wars and the final flight may have been too much, and New Jersey may have lost its only true city.

Rosalind has written an essay about the event. Some of the differ-ences in our memory are striking, particularly in details, but what interests me is the *emotional* difference, what we make—or made—of the shooting. She remembered the boys as eleven or twelve years old—I thought they were a little older; she remembers the one on her side as wearing a sweatshirt—I remember them both in freshly ironed matching jacket and jeans, almost like uniforms; she remembers us going up a drive, at the hospital, into an *entrance*—I remember us driving across the lawn. We could either be right, or neither, and it makes little difference—it is how we received the event in our lives, how we absorbed it and located it. For her the initial emotional response was a mixture of shock, disbelief, and fear. Later, it was more anger, mixed with guilt, sadness, and frustration. My initial response was also disbelief and fear, though later it was mostly grief—and almost no anger. I don't mean to make an odious comparison; if anything, I am perplexed at my *lack* of anger, and if I comment on my own feelings it is not by way of either denigrating or elevating Rosalind's. I may have been only concealing or converting my anger; furthermore it is a quite decent and quite useful emotion—anger—one which I make use of all the time, and I get furious at soft-spoken cheek-turners who smile lovingly at the slaps, even as their eyes are wet with pain, rage, and disappointment. It just didn't happen for me here. Also, Rosalind's experience was different from mine in two ways: she was driving and therefore felt responsible and she wasn't shot, and I was. It was more than guilt, her pain; it was agony.

I know that I was more "accepting" of the event than she was. I never argued with the circumstances or raged against the gods. Nor, for a second, did I blame her. We *did* make a wrong turn off the highway, we *did* stop at the red light, we *didn't* leave ten minutes earlier—or later. That's that! If anything, I felt lucky. The bullet didn't kill me, the gun on her side misfired. There were angels watching over us and they had a hell of a time leaping from side to side of the car, deflecting and stopping the shots as well as they could, keeping enough blood in my body, helping us out of there, guiding us to the hospital. If anything, I am grateful, and I love and kiss everyone and everything involved. I regret Rosalind had to go through this. I'm sorry for her suffering. But I don't hate the boys and I'm not angry with them and I don't hold it against Newark. In a way, once it happened I was glad it did, which doesn't mean I wouldn't prefer that it didn't. I suffered a few months from a stiff jaw and swollen neck, but there's no permanent damage except for the bullet that lodged in my neck and was never removed and, as I say, I forget it's there unless I'm telling the story to someone and press his or her amazed finger to the center of my neck, a little to the left of the windpipe.

When I describe my "state" after I was shot I say I was totally alert and responding in a manner to save both of our lives. I'm certain I argued a little but after the bullets started coming I had the usual rush of adrenaline and reverted to the fight-or-flight pattern, however it's described medically or physiologically. I didn't go into shock, in spite of the loss of blood and the trauma, though when we got to the hospital a certain "forgetfulness" set in, maybe when I was released of responsibility and was under care and protection.

I do remember the doctors waiting for me at the entrance, that they cut my shirt off, laid me down, stopped the bleeding, and examined the wound. I remember there was a long consultation, a discussion, and I was a part of it. The question was whether to remove the bullet or not, given how close it was to the artery since there was always the danger of the instrument slipping. I don't know whether we took a vote or what, but the choice was against operating. Apparently, there had been some problems in Vietnam. My dear friend, Alex Greenberg, a head surgeon and poet, told me he would not have hesitated to remove the bullet, but all ER doctors are not like him. A surgeon *was* called and he agreed with the others.

In the emergency room I was attached to a half-dozen machines and instruments and my face—which I saw in a mirror—was covered with blood and my neck—black, yellow, purple—was swollen grotesquely. I asked Rosalind about my poems, in an old leather briefcase, which she set down beside me. For the next two hours, while I was undergoing tests, I was busy orchestrating the immediate future. I directed Rosalind to telephone the conference leader—it was the middle of the night—to explain what happened, and to reschedule my appearance for Sunday, but the shit-head said he couldn't change the schedule until Rosalind, under my direction, battered him into submission. I told Rosalind that it was extremely important for me to attend a part of the conference and to read and talk. I didn't care, as such, for the conference itself, nor for the measly bucks they were probably giving me; what I cared about was being there, going back to my life, not letting the shooting defeat me. And Rosalind drove me there—Sunday afternoon, a day and a half after I'd been shot. I gave a talk on Gil Orlovitz—one of the lost poets—and read some of my own poems. I must have been a pretty sight, on whatever stage they were using, neck of three colors, rotten clothes, wild eyes. Rosalind, dear supporter, says I was "clear, spontaneous, coherent, witty, profound, and brilliant as usual." I don't remember who the other writers were. Friends, I know, but they were—some of them—resentful and embarrassed when I appeared. They had learned I was shot, I'm not sure when, and had a reading of my poems in absentia as a memorial service. Then I appeared, a blood-swollen ghost to interrupt the order of things. I wanted to apologize to them, but I had to quickly demythologize and *locate* the shooting, to put a skin around it just as my body eventually put a skin around the bullet, so I could go on with my life's work.

Orlovitz, a native of Philadelphia, died on the sidewalk in front of his apartment building on the upper west side. He was a poet, novelist, and playwright who published over a hundred poems—most of them sonnets—in major and minor periodicals, but never had a serious book publication. At his best, he was a powerful and original writer, but he is virtually unknown today. He is probably remembered by writers in their seventies and beyond, but younger than that only by severe scholars and devouring readers. He popped pills and drank unmercifully and died at fifty-four in 1973. He was incredibly well read, passionate, and generous. I lent him money, read his poems, and got him a couple of readings. I'll never forget him descending from the bus for his reading at Rutgers. He wore a stylish suit, a black tie, and an overcoat. He was modest and self-assured, a beautiful reader. He drank gin straight, with a bit of a chaser from time to time.

As for Rosalind, it was crazy not to do something for her in the hospital. They should have given her a sedative, talked to her, maybe offered her a bed, let her undress and take a shower, see if she could or could not drive home. I remember her washing the blood out of her coat and my jacket in a tiny sink. She describes how her hands were plunged in red water and the padding came out of the shoulder of my jacket where a bullet had lodged. She was more or less ignored and had the fear and pain—and boredom—of waiting, and going over and over again the events of the evening. She describes herself trying to sleep on a couch somewhere in the hospital, of a nurse giving her a blanket, of waking up to the cold morning with the sudden knowledge of what happened, of confronting the car, blood on the windshield, rearview mirror, door handle, seats, and windows, bullets embedded in the steering wheel and the dashboard, and a two-hour ride home, alone in the car, weeping, screaming, pounding her head, pounding the steering wheel. She said she screamed for two hours.

Me they treated well—almost like a guest rather than a patient. They seemed to have a collective guilt, as if I were mistreated on their watch. I *was* mistreated, but it was surprising to me that they assumed anything like responsibility. I had to reassure *them*, tell them how conscientious they were, even kind. They were ashamed of their city. It may be that they were acknowledging class. I was educated, a college professor; they were professionals. In a city that had exploded fifteen or so years before over race, poverty, red-lining, corruption, brutality, injustice, I got the treatment that doctors give to each other or to the privileged. Moreover, the hospital never charged me and I don't feel it was an accident. I don't mean my Blue Cross (from Iowa) covered the whole thing. There was no paperwork, no processing, no bills, no ER charges, no statement that said at the bottom "this is not a bill," no surgeon's fees, no giant profit on bandaids and tapwater. It was as if the hospital itself was ashamed.

When I was being wheeled into the intensive care unit, I joked with the doctors, reciting the names of famous people in history who had been shot—presidents, kings, and the like. For some reason, I couldn't remember the name of Emma Goldman's lover, whom she sent off to Pittsburgh to shoot Henry Frick. He arrived at Frick's office in the early evening while he was still at his desk and shot him with a little revolver that barely wounded the bastard. Frick stayed at his desk till the accustomed time and Berkman—his name was Berkman—was thrown in jail for a couple of decades, then deported to *Russland*, home of the pink and the brave. Berkman was a good anarchist, but a poor marksman. Red Emma didn't want anything to do with him when he finally came home; I think he disappointed her.

Later, when I got to my room and finally lay down on the coarse sheets, I alternated between pure joy and grief. Joy at being alive; at having escaped the way I did; at having such amazing luck—and grief that there was such malice, such willful indifference to life in the world. I kept saying to the nurses, to Rosalind, to my callers, "I can't believe one person would do that to another." And I wept over it uncontrollably.

I thought of two things. I know that because I have kept track. One was the shooting of Bruno Schultz by the German officer he encountered on the street in front of his house, after he had brilliantly and devotedly painted the officer's nursery for his children. The other was the malicious destruction of a small animal, a frog, by a friend of mine when we were both about twelve. He had stuffed a bullfrog into a No. 2 Mason jar, screwed the lid on, and threw him from the third floor onto the sidewalk in front of our apartment house. A bullfrog is not a Jewish slave, let alone a gifted and famous one, but the state of mind—of heart—may have been the same in those two murderers. I thought about the frog for years. I rushed downstairs and he was still alive with large pieces of glass embedded in his body. I had to kill him before I went back upstairs to beat the shit out of my friend. As for the murder of Schultz, that beautiful writer, it has become for me, as I know it has for others, a symbol of capricious and perverse human behavior. And it is the method of killing, a casual shot to the head, almost as an afterthought, or a preprandial bit of exercise, that horrifies me. I understand that in Belarus, during the war, German pilots shot Jews in the same way when they came back from their bombings and dogfights. As a sort of celebratory act.

I have taken up the trade of poet in part because of the difficulty in understanding—and the need to "explain"—just that willful, capricious, perverse behavior. It's as if there's no other way. Auden says that "wild Ireland" drove Yeats into poetry. Easy—if beautifully—said. I was driven into it by nearsightedness and unforgivable innocence. What I learned I learned with a vengeance even if it came late. And quickly enough I got used to my learning. When the two boys stood at the two sides of our car, whether engaged in an initiation rite or a robbery or just to see what it felt like to kill someone, I wasn't at all surprised, even if later I was grief-stricken.

There was one other book that came to my mind as I lay there—Thomas Mann's *Dr. Faustus*. And it was only when I reread it that I realized how direct the connection was. The pact with the devil itself occurs during a small afternoon nap of the "hero," Adrian Leverkühn. The narrator, one Serenus Zeitblom, a high school Latin teacher, is nominally writing a biography of Leverkühn, a boyhood chum and a musical prodigy who studied theology and then went back to music, but it may as well have been a critical history—a kind of allegory—of Germany in the first half of the twentieth century. Leverkühn became a great, little-known, deeply experimental composer, a cult figure and a recluse. His last composition was a symphonic cantata titled—naturally—*The Lamentation of Dr. Faustus;* brutal, pure, formal, expressive, "the most frightful lament ever set up on this earth." Leverkühn made the pact with the Destroyer, but so did Germany and even Zeitblom, with his flabby middle-class piety and his righteous scholarship, though he was *both* witness and spokesman, even if seen through Mann's irony and scorn. The year was 1944 when *The Lamentation* was released, just before the landing at Normandy. It is an ode to sorrow, the reverse, the opposite, the negative to Beethoven's "Ode to Joy"; in a way it is the revocation, and there is a chorus of grief to match Beethoven's chorus. The whole book—very German in this—is based on opposites, the daemonic, the dark, the uncanny, versus the humane, the enlightened, the civilized; the irrationalism of the "folk" versus reason, dignity, culture, science; the Nazi state versus the democratic. It's not a simple matter. It's not as if Zeitblom represents one side and Leverkühn the other. There is a hopeless mixture, and there is the limitation of language and of knowledge.

The most moving scene in the novel is the one where the divinely beautiful little Echo, Leverkühn's five-year-old nephew, first enchants the household in Leverkühn's country retreat with his goodness and innocence and then is suddenly struck down by cerebrospinal meningitis and suffers days of unmitigated agony. The child, whose name was Nepomuck, shortened to Nepo, called himself Echo, quaintly skipping the first consonant, and spoke of himself in the third person. Overcome with convulsions, vomiting, and skull-splitting headaches, his neck rigid, his eye muscles paralyzed, he pleaded with the powers. "Echo will be good, Echo will be good." I first read the novel—I remember—in Scotland, so the year would be 1953. Echo, and his cry, I never could forget. It compares to *Lear*, and there is the additional fact that my own sister, my only sibling, twelve months older than I, was struck down by the same disease when she was nine years old. I sometimes imagine her hydrocephalic shrieks, her heartrending moans, dear Sylvia.

It took me two, three months to recover from the wound. The

physical pain was greater than I thought it would be. I couldn't lift my chin up so I didn't shave. My neck was so swollen that I couldn't turn it. I slept ten hours a night—five, six more hours than I normally do. I was exhausted all the time. But emotionally I recovered quickly, which surprised me. Growing up in a brutal time, in a brutal city, I was always alert to vicious, unexpected, and insane behavior. I learned early not to be astonished at the undeserved and outrageous. I was a warrior, alas, and my one task was to preserve dignity and honor the human, though I didn't know such words yet. It was a sad way to be nudged out of one world into another and to achieve thereby not only a small kinship with the brutalized but an understanding of brutality itself.

It's ironic about the two worlds, isn't it? Sometimes the brutalized is brutal, the oppressed is oppressor. It's an agony to think of it, though sometimes it's a comedy. We can be both at once, we can even split the difference. Maybe only Diogenes was not oppressive. But who knows what his wife would say? And wasn't his dour, puritanical, and featherless message itself oppressive? Ah, lamb! Ah, your slit throat and the blood flowing on your white chest! Where are you here? Are you sheep or shepherd? Apocalypse would have it that the slaughtered lamb, albeit with seven horns and seven eyes, was the one who took up the book, and the one who sat on the throne. He was slaughtered, and yes he was a judge. Or was he a butcher, this lamb?

> . . . all those who worship the beast
> and his image and receive a mark on his forehead
> even those humans will drink
> the wine of the wrath of God, which is poured
> undiluted into the cup of anger
> of their God, and they will be tormented
> in fire and in sulphur before the holy angels

and *before the lamb*. The smoke of their torment
will rise forevermore, and there's no rest
day and night for any who worship the beast
and his image or wear the mark of his name.
Such is the endurance of the saints, who keep
the commandments of God and faith in Yeshua.

It's not that I imagine a world *without* butchers and it's not that I
ever forget the horrors of the century we have just gone through.
My friend Jerry Ostriker, an astronomer and spokesman for the
universe, says that it is entirely indifferent to this minute speck of
dust we call earth. In the dining room of his house in Princeton he
has a "map" of the universe that we can study as we sit there eat-
ing. I tell him that, after all, we have invented the universe, and the
dust is supremely important. We both make light of our dilemma.
A little gallows humor in both of us. The height of stubbornness,
and loyalty.

I hope the two boys are all right. If they survived the life in New-
ark, if they aren't dead yet, they would be in their thirties. They
could be in prison, or they could have made a breakthrough. Maybe
one of them went to college, is in computers, selling cars, studying
law. I want to apologize for turning them into symbols, or vehicles.
They weren't pernicious, though what they did was unjust and stu-
pid. And I want to remember how small was my brief "suffering"
compared to thousands of others', what cruelty, absurdity, insanity,
maliciousness they were forced to experience, how the lamb itself
was twisted and pulled in a thousand ways, how it wept for itself at
last, just as it wept for others—and continues to do so.

CHARITY

WHEN I WAS TEACHING at the Iowa Writers' Workshop, and living in Iowa City, I got an invitation to give a reading at a college in the nearby state of Illinois. It was an afternoon reading and it was close enough to drive, which was a relief after all the miserable plane trips I had recently taken. It was the fall of 1988. I know that because it was the time of a presidential election and Dan Quayle was running for vice president. I remember this because the town newspaper telephoned me the day before my reading to interview me and their last question was, "Do you have any advice to give to young writers?" to which I replied, "Don't vote for Quayle." The president of the college was going to introduce me at my reading and withdrew, I was told, because of what I had said, a punishment to me or, more likely, a protection for him. The choice of the English department would certainly be screened the next year.

I drove over, gave my reading, and most likely did make a few comments on the election—how could I not?—and obediently marched, or drove, off to the annual English department dinner at the chair's house, probably in my honor. The food was delicious, covered dishes of various sorts, homemade breads, pies, and there was an endless flow of good cheap wine. But after an hour or so I had had enough food and gossip and I retired, or hid, in an empty bedroom. I was joined shortly by one of the faculty, a lovely ironic woman in her early forties, who identified herself as a short-story writer and an ally. We sneaked out some French doors into the light rain, and walked up and down the slightly damp lawn before we drove off to her apartment. We intended to stay there, among her books, records, tapes, and prints, at least till things quieted down (we said to each other) at the chair's house. They called her two or three times "to bring the poet back," but we weren't cooperative. We were already kissing.

I was staying that night on a pullout bed in the living room of one of the English faculty. Susan, her name was Susan, brought me there a little late, and my host and hostess were red-eyed from the cheapo wine and exhausted from the long day. Susan announced that she was staying with me that night, more or less without consulting me, to the embarrassment, and probably horror, of the couple that was providing for my comfort, and we lay awake all night, talking and embracing, *sans consummatum*. But we did decide that we would meet a week and a half later, on a Saturday, midway between her city and mine, and spend the weekend getting to know each other better. I drove away in my Honda, a check in my pocket, Rudy Vallee, or the Schnozz, on my lips.

It was a bright morning in late November when I started off on my adventure. My route would be east on 80, then south on 74, a two- or two-and-a-half-hour drive. It was one of those mornings when I could go live with the cows, as Walt said, or for that matter with the trees and clouds, or with the good moon itself, which was fairly full as I recall and still visible; and I played my drum set, the steering wheel, the gearshift, the death seat, the windows, the dashboard, with all my might, two or three great songs. I was a little less than an hour out when I saw a strange couple—a man and a woman—hitchhiking and I stopped my car and put it in reverse. I think I wanted to see them as much as pick them up. They were in their late forties or early fifties, dressed in loud plaids and dragging several enormous plastic suitcases, the kind that are shapeless till you fill them with clothes and zip the wraparound zipper. They were waving their arms, shouting—at the world and at each other—and all but circled my car, all but opened the trunk and doors, before I came to a complete stop. He got in the back seat, she in front, and after we exchanged names and destinations, they assumed their postures, he leaning forward as if to miss nothing, she with her arms crossed and a look of dignity and contentment on her face.

They had left Northampton, Massachusetts, two or three weeks earlier, after quitting their jobs at a convenience store, driven their old Chevy west to find Denver, broke down in Denver, sold their car for fifty bucks, and were on their way back to Pioneer Valley and Northhampton. Someone had picked them up the day before in a large Cadillac, and took off, at a rest stop, with their suitcases containing all their clothes and some gifts for friends and relatives. They got their hideous "new" clothes and suitcases from Catholic Charities or Goodwill and they were anxious just to get home. I realized, after a few minutes, that they were not very bright, somewhere near the bottom of the ladder. I understood why the pig in the Cadillac had abandoned them but I hated him anyway, maybe doubly.

I asked if they had had breakfast and they—really "she," she was the spokesperson—confessed that their money was gone, that they had spent it all on clothes and suitcases and a little shelter and food. After driving a while I pulled into one of those giant truck stops, replete with gift shops, restaurants, video rooms, and truckers' windowless closets with showers, and looked at my watch to see how much time I had left, and a little nervously and maybe already resentfully, I guided them into the dining area. They ate a hearty breakfast, an unbelievable one, juice, ham, eggs, pancakes, toast, potatoes, coffee, pie. Then seconds. I excused myself and started to make phone calls. I called Catholic Charities, but they weren't interested in helping. Neither were the local police or the staties. I explained things to the manager and he said that he would take care of them and get them on their way. A strange and magnificent manager. I explained to my hitchhikers that we had to part now because I was taking a different route than they were, and reached into my pocket to give them some cash. I pulled out a wad from my left-hand pant's pocket and peeled off two twenties—I think it was that. They were grateful beyond belief, and would have gladly kissed my hands if that were the custom in our caste-ridden democracy. They were leaning back enjoying another cup of coffee and smiling like Buddhas when I walked out to my Honda.

I was on the last leg of my voyage out, alone and unhappy. I was full of pity, including plenty of self-pity, dread, regret, and anger, most of all anger. I was angry that I had picked up the hitchhikers; I was angry that they were so dumb and still had the vision of Denver; I was angry with the pig in the Cadillac who drove off with their suitcases and bags, he thought it was a great joke, I'm sure; I was angry with Catholic Charities and the police; I was angry with the 7-11 or Wawa that gave them four to five dollars an hour and no benefits; I was angry with Massachusetts and Washington—and God; most of all I was angry with myself, for picking them up in the first place, for being benevolent. Why did I give them forty? Why didn't I keep forty and give them the rest? Why didn't I give them everything?

Comfortable and comforting, charity. Not even approved by the IRS. What does Saint Paul say? The greatest of these is charity. Greater than faith and hope. But charity is love. It is not the giving, as such. It is the selflessness that accompanies giving, at least for Paul. "And though I bestow all my goods to feed the poor, and though I give my body to be burned, and haveth not charity, it profiteth me nothing," he says in the famous letter. And it is repeated one way or another throughout the New Testament. In Judaism charity is the very underpinning. There is no Judaism without charity, from the corner of the field to the *kuppah* to organized giving to redistribution, among the honest Left. To what medieval category did my ride, my phone calls, my forty bucks, and my free breakfast belong? Feeding the hungry? Ransoming captives? Why was I so upset, what touched me so?

I arrived at the designated motel three-quarters of an hour late, but Susan was waiting, marking papers, reading a book, studying me when I walked in. I explained to her what had happened, maybe leaving out the darker strains. She kissed me, in gratitude for the hitchhikers, and we registered at the polished desk. The lobby was like a small living room, fringed lamps, doilies, dark wood, rugs, portraits. It looked wholesome, something from Missouri or Illinois. It *was* Illinois. The desk clerk wore a white lace hat on the back of her head, a maid from the eighteenth century. We walked up to the second floor, found our room, and settled in. I'm sure we checked the noise level, the view, the air conditioner, the TV, the bathroom, and the bed. We acted as much out of shyness as curiosity. We were practically strangers, though we had spent the one night holding and fondling each other. We were both nearsighted, and that must have added to the shyness, for though we had been face to face, I didn't have a clear memory of what she looked like, and the same must have been true for her, though my photo was here and there, on a book or two. Picture two lovers putting their thick eyeglasses on nearby bedstands with one hand while they begin the search. A twentieth-century arche-typal cartoon.

I think it was shyness that drove us for a good while. We were almost reluctant to enter the next stage. Not that we weren't attracted to each other. The rules are hard on lovers. There sits the large bed in the middle of the room and, depending on the price, either a comfortable or a rickety chair or two. We could have sat on the edge of the bed and watched daytime television, holding hands, or we could have drunk the horrible coffee and poisonous powder while we talked about books—I would have smoothed her hair, she would have touched my knee. We finally got undressed and climbed into bed. I was still thinking about the hitchhikers and shaking a little. It was an odd mixture of dread and desire. She reassured me, this lovely woman, and as we settled into peace, or exhaustion, whatever it was, after our first outburst, I suddenly started to sob uncontrol-lably, and moaned and tried to stifle the moans.

I don't know if Susan understood it was the hitchhikers and the release that suddenly came and the absolute clarity at that point, the terror and the joy, separated and realized, or if she felt it was love that overtook me, but she responded with great tenderness, and a few tears herself, for tears are catching. We stayed in bed till it got dark, we sang at our showers, and we ventured out into the sprawl to find a restaurant of our liking, no matter how far afield we'd have to go. We had outwitted the theologians and the encyclopedists who constantly make their distinctions between *agape* (for which *caritas,* charity, is the Latin translation) and *eros,* sexual love, by combining them. The Spanish and Italian mystics had done this before us, and the Hebrew and the Persian, but we had stumbled onto it by our-selves, in an unlikely little village in the state of Illinois.

I remain still troubled though. Mystified. Maybe the question is not what to do about poverty, but about wealth. The Quran's emphasis on redressing injustice in social and economic life is an illustration. Individuals are urged, in the Quran, to spend their wealth and substance not only on family and relatives but on orphans, the poor, the traveling homeless, the needy, and the freeing of the enslaved. As in Judaism, the Muslim has a responsibility to develop a social conscience, as we would say, to share individual and communal resources with the less privileged. What does it mean when Jesus lashes out at the rich? Wasn't his audience mostly prepared for the famous metaphor, camel and all? Here I am, with stocks and bonds to my name, IRAs, two retirement policies, social security, asking these questions. Does money dull the soul? How do honey and locusts taste? What should the desperate son have done— left his dead father to the flies? Why are the poor blessed? Do they have a certain knowledge just by being poor? Are the rich denied this? The moderately rich? What are the very rich denied? Ah, Jesus! Did he mean it literally? Was it that the Kingdom was truly at hand? The ethics were impossible to follow, were the world to continue, but he never offered compromise or accommodation, nor, for God's sake, that ten percent, or fifty.

We sat on the bed in our underwear, palm of foot to palm of foot. We told stories, we ate oranges, we talked in tongues, we sang; and we caressed.

I told her stories of Pittsburgh, and the gold spigots in the bathrooms on Fifth Avenue. She told me how she dreaded supper, always cabbage, whatever fat or bone was served with it, growing up in Ohio.

I sang Jimmy Durante for her. "Try a Little Tenderness." She sang Janis Joplin. "Mercedes Benz." I did a Spanish-American War song and a World War I Canadian army song. She did Jeannette

MacDonald. Whoever's reading this, I wish I could sing "There's a Quaker Down in Quakertown" for you. I wish you could have heard my father and me harmonize.

I don't know when we got into first husbands and first wives, but it is the ritual of every affair, that bitterness, boredom, sarcasm, regret, respect, forgetfulness. I had only one to own up to. She had two or three. She either married men much older or much younger than herself, and she had a grown son from her first marriage, years ago, to one of her teachers. We talked at length about pyramids and angels, for she loved spirit and mystery and I didn't have much against it, and when we got to the holy books I remember we had one of those endless discussions about poor Jesus, and did he evolve out of the prophets, and what was old and what was new, and this led naturally to Paul, then Augustine, and since I had read endlessly in, and on, her religion and she had mostly only believed, I did most of the talking. I turned schoolman till I suddenly realized my foolishness and went apologetically back into the cave.

Anyway, it was getting dark and we were both getting sad. Though for me it wasn't just a question of darkness. Saturday night was my main time of grief—probably because as a boy I had to spend it alone with my mother. Susan had a Saturday-night grief too, but she never told me the roots, the details.

We sighed for the last time and went out to eat. We realized, both at the same time, that we weren't saying goodbye but had the night and the next morning together. We were giddy with happiness. I wondered, and she did too, where the hitchhikers were. I'll bet they're in New York State now and on the way to Massachusetts, she said, and I said Ohio, though neither of us knew the route to Northampton. We talked of the horrors man tenders to man. She talked of the flames consuming Joan of Arc and the noise they made as they steadily grew. I talked of the shtetls and how the Jews of one town were locked in a barn and burned to death by their Polish neighbors. She talked to me of Simone Weil's love of Christ and her hatred of the church. I talked of Weil's love of justice and how she said, at the end, that there would be no love without justice, they are identical. My own theme. When we kissed goodbye the next day it was cold, though the ground was still hot from the fires.

I looked for the hitchhikers all the way back to Iowa City. I thought for a minute they had taken the wrong road and I would have the chance to make it up to them, and I planned where I would put them in my house. I wondered if they brought T-shirts home with them. What was it like when they turned the light on in their trailer outside Amherst? Did they go back to work at the convenience store? Would they get robbed, or overload the coffee machine? Was I being tested, were they just souls planted there for my sake to see whether I would stop or go on, to see what shame, suffering, indignation, curiosity, would do? What if I hadn't stopped? What if I had neither pity nor outrage? The Talmud says a traveler out of money is one of the chosen; a child takes precedence; the secret giver is greater than Moses; it is forbidden to shame the poor. The war on poverty, what happened? Was the sacrifice, which was no sacrifice, too great? Should we just throw dimes in the street, like Haile Selassie, like John D. Rockefeller? Isn't it a marvelous way to redistribute wealth? Isn't it a nice communion—swallowing dimes? The body and the blood of Haile Selassie, of Merrill-Lynch? In a culture of greed, indifference, and ignorance; no knowledge or memory.

THE RING

IN MY PARENTS' CULTURE, at their particular time, it was the
custom for the husband, the breadwinner, to buy his wife a sec-
ond engagement ring twenty or twenty-five years after the first,
when they were a bit richer, if a bit broader and a bit more weary.
This would take the place of the old ring, the smaller diamond,
and would be a public statement not only of their improved eco-
nomic state but also of their commitment to the second half, the
long haul, in the face of children, maybe grandchildren—maybe in-
laws—something for the world to notice and appreciate.

Quite often the first ring was misplaced or the diamond itself was
gone, behind a stove, inside a washer or an obscure compartment in
a refrigerator, testimony to the wife's zeal and the pathos of her loss
under the pressure of endless labor for her husband and children. I
think my mother's was lost in a restaurant somewhere, maybe The
House by the Side of the Road, serving the best chicken in four
counties, and all you could eat, to boot. The stone came loose from
its mooring. It was like a loose tooth and my mother played with it
as she would with a tooth till she was suddenly left with a shock-
ing bare setting, where the blood had dried and the tongue would
do no good.

My mother had to do the conventional thing, lose the first ring.
I think there should have been, in that culture, a ritual reenactment

of the myth of loss, coupled with dances, tears, prayers, songs—
certainly about sacrifice and renewal, certainly about magic stones
and loose rings, certainly sexual. With shaking fingers the groom,
wearing a size 48 short, bends down to replace the ring, while tears
of victory fill the ancient bride's eyes. And her maids lead her to an
air-conditioned bower, replete with boxes of Whitman candies and
odorless roses and thin cigarettes. The three tenors are singing.

My father's idea was to circulate a little, talk to some friends
at Goldstein's or Morry's, and find something "wholesale," even
go down to Philadelphia, where he had some connections in the
diamond district around Washington Square or to Forty-seventh
Street in New York where a little Yiddish went a long way and
where he could bargain. Whereas my mother's idea was to go to one
of the two first-rate department stores in Pittsburgh, Joseph Horne's
or Kaufmann's, and sit down like a fine lady while a salesman or
two opened little cases of large beautiful rings and displayed them
for her on a velvet surface. My father went crazy when he heard her
idea. He punched one fist into the other, twisted his poor body, and
was practically speechless. It was a betrayal of the worst sort. The
very place he was the most cunning, the most wise, he was going
to be rendered impotent. There weren't words enough to explain
his desperation, there weren't enough facial movements. I don't
even think it was a question of the money; he was appalled, out-
raged, that she could be so stupid. And yet, from her point of view,
wasn't it enough that they had gone through empty stock rooms
and up slow-moving freight elevators to buy the sterling (Grand
Baroque), or that they had to walk through cutters and fitters in
ninety-degree weather for the fur coat, or travel to Jamestown,
New York, and a boring weekend with her cold sister-in-law's
nephews and nieces to get the furniture (sofas, beds, dining-room

set). Nor did she totally trust wholesale. She even secretly believed that she had overpaid for the fur coat and the silver. She called the department stores up on the phone and spoke in strange accents, so she wouldn't be recognized, to inquire about price, and made long lists and calculations clearing her throat all the while.

Goldstein's was a Jewish restaurant and delicatessen on Fifth Avenue uptown in the heart of the wholesale section in what is still called the Hill, once the center of Jewish—later African American—life in Pittsburgh. It was long and narrow, with a counter in front, booths and tables in back, and stairs going up behind the cash register to the upstairs rooms. Gambling and numbers went on and exchange of goods and information, but downstairs it also had the best pea soup and roast beef sandwiches I ever tasted. I think there were two brothers, both tall, pockmarked, with potbellies. The dry goods, clothing, and furniture wholesalers came there for lunch and early dinner, and the locals and passersby came in for coffee or a sandwich or a special. My father bought the ring at Goldstein's— he won out—after two years of war. I don't think my mother ever trusted the ring, a giant bluish stone, nor did it even give her the pleasure it would have if she had plucked it off the velvet.

As a widow, my mother took on the responsibility of bargaining. She bought clothes at unbelievably low prices at the sales in Jordan Marsh in Miami, and prided herself on her accomplishments. When she died in 1993 (age ninety-three) she had racks of dresses, pantsuits, sweaters, and blouses, turning color from the dirt and light, emblems, in most cases, of bygone styles. I went with her to a downtown Miami department store a year or so before she died. We were going to eat supper and look for bargains but she could barely move because of her arthritis. It was a nostalgic and dream-ridden trip; it was as if we were in Pittsburgh in 1940 or, say, the early '80s, when she could still move freely. We both knew it wouldn't work; she was silent and teary in the cab on the way back, and as usual, I tried to reassure her.

That ring, that bitter ring, was a symbol of the faded ideal and the ordinary reality my mother and father shared. It weighed them down a little, though seen in a certain light it certainly was brilliant and heavy. They were peasants, weren't they, or as peasant as disinherited Jews can be in the land in between, owning nothing in this America of theirs except what could be weighed and quantified. They were born in Europe, he in a shtetl near Kiev, with wolves as neighbors, she in Bialystok, daughter of a so-so scholar, and they came to America with their two families in 1905, she age five, he eight, to settle on a crowded hill, in the smoke and dirt, a ring now between them. They were both obedient and law-abiding though she had a little bit of wildness in her. They were Sunday Jews, non-observant, indifferent to the mind, scoffers at culture. I was the first person to bring a book into the house. And I was ashamed of the ring.

My mother wore it for maybe fifteen years after my father's death, in 1969. Then, fearful that she would be robbed, she took it off her finger and started hiding it in different places—in a silver cigarette case, in the drawer behind her cancelled checks, in the pocket of an old fur coat, in a blue discarded pocketbook with a tarnished snap, and finally in the small laundry bag in the hall closet where she kept underwear and stockings she washed once a week or so by hand in the kitchen sink. To make matters worse, that bag had a gaping hole in the bottom where certainly any ring worth its salt would eventually find its way. She had removed the ring because *they* (Haitians, Cubans) would cut her finger off to get it. I told her when *they* come to rob the old Italian and Jewish women they always look first in the freezer and then the laundry bag and I begged her to let me rent a safe-deposit box at her local bank. A bank several miles away was offering free use of the vault if you opened a checking account there, so we changed her bank, which caused its own problems, including the problem of getting her over there so we could clip Israeli bonds, which we now kept in that vault, during my yearly or semiyearly visit, without spending the whole day.

She didn't like putting the ring in the vault, and I don't blame her. At least when it was in the ripped laundry bag she could look at it from time to time, try it on again, hold it up to the light, feel its heft. "If only Rachael (referring to my daughter) would call me sometimes, I'd give the ring to her." But Rachael and she were estranged, nor would she (Rachael) be caught dead wearing such an ostentatious diamond. "It's between the two of you," I said desperately, not wanting to go to that place, where only horror reigned and my opinion counted for nothing, whatever it was anyhow.

In 1985 she decided to sell the ring, having read some ads in the paper or talked to some of the women in the lobby. The dealer, the jeweler, whatever he was, came to her apartment with his little glass and his book. Though I was in the woods somewhere north or on the rolling plains of eastern Iowa, I knew he screwed the glass against his eye, did a little measuring—probably with a small white plastic ruler, in inches and millimeters, and referred often to his thick book. She insisted on being present, probably at the card table in the living room, since she didn't trust him. What kind of pea game he could play I don't know, since she knew her ring and there was no time or opportunity to exchange stones, yet she watched him—I know this—with eyes of ancient hatred and cleared her throat many times. After much deliberation, indicated by a tapping yellow pencil and endless consultation in his book and the writing down of a page of figures—she told me all this on the phone—he offered her fifteen hundred dollars, or twelve, I can't remember which. If there wasn't a crack in the stone, if it didn't go all the way through, like a great fissure, he could have given her maybe two or three thousand, but he would not be able to sell it wholesale and he would not, out of ethical consideration, sell it to one of his customers. She turned him down, she was aggrieved. I think my father had paid a thousand, twelve hundred for it, but that was in the 1940s. "He's a *ganef*," she said. "I knew it when he came in." And we put it in the vault for keeps that day, wrapped in noisy tissue paper.

My mother died, oh, eight, nine, years after the visit by the *ganef*. Every time we opened the safe-deposit box and went into the little room she would examine the ring, hold it in her hands, stare into space—of which there wasn't much there—and rewrap it in the (pink) tissue paper. There was also a very beautiful gold watch on an intricately wrought chain that had belonged to my grandmother Libby, and a few other trinkets, besides the canceled CD booklets and the bond coupons. My mother never wore that watch. After she died I gave it to Rachael, who loved it. I emptied the box—it was the spring of 1993—and put everything in a cheap blue plastic bag, the name of the bank imprinted on it, a zipper all along one side. When I got back to Iowa I transferred the plastic bag to the glove compartment of my red Honda. I had to lock the doors now, which annoyed me. I intended to take the ring to a jeweler to be appraised. I had no attachment to it. Nor could I imagine any beloved of mine lusting after that ring. It summed up all that was banal, glitzy, conspicuous, and absurd about my mother's and father's life, their furniture, their cars, the lobby of their apartment building, the stupidity of the unused boat dock, the one thing that was peaceful and reached into the past, and made an eternal sound. It—the ring—made me fifteen years old again. It turned me into an unforgiving child. It made me a monster.

Ginsberg was the name of the jeweler—in Iowa City. He was an upscale jeweler who sponsored art openings in his back rooms—a little different from Goldstein's. He gave my package—the ring and a few other items—to his gemologist and told me to come back in a week. I've lost the paper on which each item was described and evaluated. It was a far cry from the *ganef* with the glass screwed into his eye. When I came back on the appointed day, Mark Ginsberg called out immediately from his perch in the back of his store, "That's a nice ring, Jerry, what do you want for it?" I thought, "Goldstein's, twelve hundred, *ganef*, fifteen hundred, fissures." "Ah, four thousand," I said. He handed me the gemologist's report; the ring was worth fifty thousand dollars—maybe sixty—and he offered me thirty thousand on the spot.

I tried to understand what happened and in less than a minute— well, a second—it came to me. Some upper-story man had quietly retrieved the ring one night—or morning—from a night table or a bathroom sink, and quickly made his getaway, maybe with some cash to boot. He sold it to one of the Goldsteins maybe for five hundred, an easy fortune, and the Goldsteins later sold it to my father at a nice 120 percent profit. Nobody, neither Goldstein, the thief, my father, knew what it was truly worth then. Ten thousand dollars? Least of all my mother. All those years she carried this weighty stone around, not realizing. God, would they have cut her finger off. Would she walk around in terror and paranoia. I'm glad she was relieved of this responsibility. "What about the crack?" I asked Mark. "There is no crack," he said. "It's a perfect stone, three carats in size and the cut and clarity, the brilliance, is quite unusual." How dumb the *ganef* was. Did he not know diamonds, or was he just greedy beyond belief? It was then I removed everything from the blue plastic bag.

I sold the ring Christmas of 2000 for a substantial sum to my local jeweler here in Lambertville. He found a customer in three days. Nor did I bother myself much with who bought it, or why, or what was the mystical connection and continuation, or would the ring reappear, or would the new owner catch a glimpse of my mother when she was fifty, or the poor original owner, bereft and not knowing whom to haunt, or the *ganef* with his screwed-up eye, or one or another Goldstein dealing in his upstairs room, or the original thief himself, furious at his loss. I think Poe would like the story, Maupassant more. It would make a good movie-of-the-week. My mother would have adored watching it on her fourteen-inch TV, sitting on the edge of her bed, one eye gone, one eye staring in wonder.

SALESMAN

MY ORDINARY RESPONSE to telemarketing is like everyone else's. Depending on how occupied I am and how much I am enraged at that moment by the national pastime of false witnessing, I can be bored, angry, or vengeful. I always know because there's a little delay on the line since my deluder is making several calls at once; and I know because of the hesitancy in saying my name and, simple as it is, mispronouncing it. My beloved says, "Why don't you get a real job?" whereas I either hang up, or lecture them about decency, or scream at them for calling me by my first name, as if they were intimate with me, like a dentist's secretary or a canvasser for the Police Benevolent Association. But this morning I was either lonely or touched by an unusual kindness because I listened to the spiel and stayed on the phone a good ten minutes, as if I were seriously interested in the product and the possibility. Her name was Adrienne and she was from Egg Harbor, New Jersey, and she hated George W. because he stole the election and was owned by the corporations, and she understood why I not only didn't want her to call me "Gerald" but to repeat the name at the end of each and every sentence. She did switch to "Mr. Stern," but she couldn't get out of the litany habit. Though I, in my new mood, forgave her.

Adrienne was selling Thermoguard replacement windows and doors. Her pitch wasn't strong and she quickly accepted the fact

that I didn't "need" windows and doors, but her ploy—if it was a
ploy—was that I should please order anything, at least express some
interest, since she would get credit, a bonus. I responded to the
personal appeal, I was, for a second, a good sucker, and I pitied her,
probably an overworked single mother with her kids at day care
or her resentful mother's house. I suddenly remembered that I did
need a kitchen door since the one I had installed maybe four years
ago, giving off to my lovely deck, had been split apart at the bot-
tom, probably by the rain, certainly because the door was made of
the cheapest material. Adrienne was overjoyed and told me I'd get
a hundred-and-fifty—maybe it was two-hundred-and-fifty—dollar
rebate on the door. That was the bait. And the offer was only good
for seven more days. Her supervisor, Stan, would call me in five
minutes sharp, to corroborate the foot in the door, and Dave, the
salesman, would be knocking on my front door at 1:00 P.M.—two
hours thence. Then we said goodbye. Stan mainly wanted to know
if I was the sole owner—he didn't want a recalcitrant spouse to deal
with. Dave arrived at twelve.

I knew I wasn't going to buy a door from Thermoguard but I
wanted Adrienne to get her bonus. I must admit I wasn't too guilty
about the salesman—Dave—and anyhow I rationalized that I *might*
buy a door and—anyhow—I would get information. I even thought
for a minute my mind was open and we would see. I always face
things when they're right on top of me and I suddenly realized that
I first had to go back to the lumberyard where I bought the door and
argue with them. But there was no time to do that now.

When I saw Dave on my front porch, I was shocked. He was
not a typical tin-man or window salesman, wearing a cheap suit
and tie and carrying a dispatch case full of samples. Nor did he
have an ingratiating, slimy, or arrogant manner. He had on a blue

V-neck sweater over a loose T-shirt, a short, rather flimsy jacket, jeans, sneakers, and no hat. He was in his seventies with a deeply lined face, long carefully combed white hair—the only hint of vanity—small feet, and eyes that showed cunning, fear, and exhaustion. He seemed humbled by life, but there was a reserve. Back-up wisdom. He went through the mechanics with no false enthusiasm and accepted my rules of the game quickly. I didn't want any windows; I wouldn't listen to any promotions; I wasn't interested in zero finance for six months. We walked to the back door, we looked at the construction, and the rot, he showed me pictures of replacements. It would be a steel door, the frame would be replaced, and, as I understood it, the steel would be covered with plastic and painted in the white of my choice and it would be guaranteed for either ten or sixty years, I can't remember which. I tried to guess what it would cost. I thought it would be a thousand but it was over two thousand, which, due to the recession (2002), was a bargain because the usual price was forty-two hundred dollars. I told Dave I would call him if I wanted the door replaced. He lamely suggested, after some prodding from Stan, whom he called on my phone since his cell phone wasn't working, that he would be happy to write up a contract, get all the paperwork done for convenience' sake, another standard ploy, but his heart wasn't in it and he acquiesced quickly when I rejected that idea. Of course if I signed up now the price would be guaranteed.

The thing about his face, in addition to the wavy hair and the sad eyes, was the broken nose. It had a sideways thrust and was obviously the result of some crushing blows. The way he walked, the resigned and graceful manner, convinced me that he had spent some time in the ring. I had seen those movements before. If he had, he would have been a lightweight. We spent only a half-hour together but I felt close to him. It was not just him, it was the type I was seeing. He was from my boyhood and my youth, and several of my high school friends had ended up selling storm windows and cars and ketchup. One of my college friends, Hymie Millstone, had wanted desperately to go to medical school. He had a perfect *A* average as an undergraduate but his father, a milkman, had no political connections so Hymie was denied entrance. There was a real if unofficial quota of 10 percent Jews and he was low man. He taught at the medical school itself for a while but ended up selling cigars, quite bitter about his lot and particularly angry with the other Jew who was admitted instead of him, since he *did* have pull, though *he* ended up in pharmacy school when he couldn't make the grade. Hymie probably was a cynical salesman, probably ruthless, and contemptuous of his customers.

I never did find out whether Dave had a family, where he went to school, where his parents came from. For a long time I didn't know whether he was Jewish or Italian and only when he handed me his card and I realized that his name was David Cohen did I know I had a landsman in the house. He responded to my Yiddish but in a modest and dignified way, and didn't try to capitalize on it. He told me he had worked for Thermoguard for twenty-three years, but I didn't believe him. In his second conversation with Stan he tried to get out of calling on another customer about forty-five minutes away from me, but Stan apparently had no one else to send. My heart almost broke when Dave said to me, "You have a nice house here," a standard statement but, in his case, coming out of— not envy—but a kind of matter-of-fact humility. I had to give him detailed instructions on how to get to his next call—he didn't have a map of New Jersey—and I walked him out to his car to say good-bye. His dark-blue something or other was sitting smack in front of my next-door neighbor's driveway, but I didn't say anything. Nor could I see through the windows of the car because of the blinding sunlight, but he explained that that was his wife sitting in the passenger's seat and I advised him at once where to go for lunch on his way up the river, my heart breaking at the domestic scene, Dave forever out of my life, the lost knowledge appalling.

I know I saw my father in Dave, or perhaps my own self in another life. It's an interesting question, how long salesmanship has been a separate occupation in the world of trade and commerce. I want to say that early traders, early merchants, knew whereof they carried, on camel-back or ship-back, and were themselves the "salesman," and in the bazaar, the marketplace, or the flea market they knew their goods well, be they shoes or rugs or pottery, all of which were family-produced. But that may be too romantic an idea. Maybe the Phoenicians, the Arabs, the Mongols, had special emissaries whose job it was to "sell" products. My father and his friends liked to say that a good salesman could sell anything, it was a truism among them, and most of them loved the very act of selling. For him, my father, it was men's and boy's clothing, later women's, though he started off selling cigars. I can see him in his early twenties; he had a Model T and loaded his cigar boxes in the backseat. Probably a display case of sorts. Young, handsome, vigorous, ambitious, optimistic. He was strongly attached to his product and when he switched to men's clothing he loved feeling the goods and rubbing his fingers over the lapel in order to judge the quality. The customer was never a "mark"—he was always given a decent buy. Even at the end when he was in the going-out-of-business business, buying bankrupt or solvent stock, reopening the store with big signs in the window, often employing the old owner who as often as not was retiring, replenishing the stock (*hélas*) with new merchandise, the principal source of income for one of the partners who was a manufacturer with a plant in North Carolina, he was always fair, fighting the partners in the name of honesty and good business practices.

I have an 8 x 10 photograph of the inside of one of the stores. My mother and father are toward the front, and a corps of salesmen, seven or so, are standing in their allotted ranks behind them. The room is large and the tables are piled with merchandise: shirts, sweaters, and the like. Suits and coats are neatly hanging in the rear. On the tables and walls, all over, are hand-painted signs, "Everything must go," "Sold to the bare walls," "Sport jackets, $8.95." They are all standing more or less at attention, formally dressed, not smiling—with the exception of my mother who has a wide grin and her right eye, the one she didn't see out of, squinting in front of the fearsome camera. I was in the selfsame store when Pat and I came back from our three-year stay in Europe with only enough money in our pockets to get to Detroit where I worked for three weeks or so selling scarves, socks, ties, sweaters, and underwear to the Christmas shoppers so we could go back to Pittsburgh and get jobs. I hated every minute of it. The year was 1955.

It must have been at that time that I helped my father move from one location to another. The way it worked was they got a license, from the city, to hold a sale for a given number of weeks or months and, if they overstayed their time, they were fined. They had to get the stock out of their downtown store, it turned out, by 8:00 A.M. on a given day. My father, in his late fifties then, was exhausted from the long hours he was putting in day after day, running up and down stairs—too impatient to wait for the slow elevator—supervising salespeople and bookkeepers, making decisions on stock, changing prices, preparing advertisements, altering the window, intervening with difficult customers. At 9:00 P.M. the night before, he and my mother left and I took over the job of preparing for and supervising the move. I hired three or four men off the street and we spent the night taking stock and loading a special truck we had rented. We swept up and locked the door at about 7:55 A.M. We ate breakfast, then drove out to the store in Dearborn, a thoroughly Presbyterian community then, not a Jew or African American in sight. It was a busy Saturday morning and the store manager, a greaseball brought in from Pittsburgh, had his salesmen erect a false wall of cardboard boxes so no one could see us carrying racks of suits and boxes of sweaters and shirts to the freight elevator, so we could store them on the second floor, out of sight. Naturally the wall collapsed and several of my troupe staggered into the store, full of customers at ten in the morning, suits, sweaters, and all. The greaseball was furious. As I recall, he called my father and told him to "get your fucking son out of here." The part I love best was when the wall fell directly in front of the greaseball selling a black serge suit to a minister, laying it on thick about the quality of the goods and what a saving the minister would make. The Presbyterian and I had a good laugh—he understood it all instantly—but greaseball was furious.

It was on an earlier trip, before the autumn of 1953—I know because that's when we went to Scotland—that I had a meeting over lunch with my father and his two partners in a private dining room of Karl's Chop House in Detroit. My father was the front man, the one who met the customers and ran the store; one of them was strictly the money man, providing capital; and one of them—as I said—was the manufacturer who made his profit in the retail outlet. One of the stores was a "gold mine," as these men with strange pick-axes used to say, and they planned to stock three or four floors of the

five-story building, eventually adding furniture and dry goods to
the men's and women's clothes, turning it into a small department
store. My father could no longer handle such a large undertaking,
so we were there for them to make me a substantial enough offer
for me to agree to assume the role. They knew I had the energy, the
skill in management, and most of all, that I could be trusted with
the money. My wife and I were living on fifty, sixty dollars a week,
if that, and if I accepted the job—a very large salary plus a quarter
interest—I'd be rich in a few years. But, against all the pressure in
that room, I turned it down. Everyone but my father was amazed.
Jake Wolk, the manufacturer, turned to me with a large slab of roast
beef resting on his gold teeth and asked me how much they were
paying me in Scotland, when I told them that was my destination
in the fall. I was much too embarrassed to tell him the truth, that
I would be teaching in a senior secondary high school in Glasgow
for ten pounds a week, which, at that time, was twenty-eight dol-
lars. They even told me I never had to sell; they even told me they
would find me a "nice house," God save us. Nor could I tell them I
was turning the offer down to save my life, that I was grateful but I
was on a different journey, and I couldn't explain.

On the wall of the little foyer you use to enter and exit from my
local bank, there's a list of services and products for sale so exten-
sive that it almost hides the cash machine next to it. There is family
bingo, the Lambertville story on video, various (insidious) work-at-
home programs, airport transportation ads, guitars for sale, hauling
and clean-up services, desperately needed items for dogs, a pancake
breakfast at the Legion (all you can eat), a chiropractic center, an
art gallery, and church notices. On the cash machine is a sign that
boldly—and falsely—announces that "we're here for one good rea-

son, to serve you." It doesn't say we're here to make money from your money. On the outer door, backward since I was inside, was the announcement that this financial center will be closed on President's Day, a compromise date between George and Abe that is convenient for sales but honors nobody. It's next to an American flag, which was pasted on the door to show unconditional, uncreative, and infinite loyalty in the fight against evil.

But who made me the judge and why am I so scornful and intolerant and why was I in such a rage for so many years? My own sense of the matter is that I was as much concerned with what seemed to me a logical position as I was with justice itself. My sense of justice—when I was sixteen, say—was expressed through an angry or impatient logic and clear-cut arguments, as I saw it. I was at war with my teachers, most of them, the politicians, and my parents. We fought over civil rights, imperialism, corporate greed, the First Amendment, religious issues, sentimentality, bad logic. I was ruthless and furious. One time I pulled a finely laundered tablecloth from under the plates, salad, cold fish, meat, potatoes, gravy, wine. I was horrified at my own anger and didn't know how to apologize. My father bent his head in embarrassment and grief; my mother was red-faced and open-mouthed. I acted as if I were one of the prophets, a part of that long line; though nobody said words in my ear or placed anything on my tongue. Is it that a poet (a future one, at least) is especially sensitive to language and redeems himself that way? How else to attack stupidity and injustice? But I was as angry over false language as anything. Or I felt that through false language injustice somehow occurred. I may have been righteously expressing the banal or overzealous, but I didn't care in the least since I felt it so personally, so keenly. What I admired in the prophets was their plainness of speech, their unprofessorial cutting through the fat, their simplifications, their understanding of where (and what) the enemy was. I paid no attention to and didn't care about their admonishments and preachments as such.

I remember an occasion in 1958 or 1959, when I was a new instructor at Temple University in Philadelphia, the president of that college, a Doctor Gladfelder, called a meeting of the whole faculty to discuss the "Philosophy of Salaries" at Temple. There we were, row upon row of distinguished idiots, listening to the foolishness that came from that foolish mouth. The *philosophy* of salaries. Something to do with a choice between buildings and livable wages. At the time I was making forty-three hundred dollars a year, and delivered yellow pages or borrowed money from an interest-free company fund for just such as me, or luckily sometimes I taught a course so my wife and children could have food on the table in those miserable summer months. Gladfelder's speech went on and on, in the tone of an unctuous bill collector, after which he asked for questions or comments. We were in the large room of an ugly, cheaply built building, a cross between a classroom and a theater, and the rows of foolish professors neither questioned nor complained. I remember someone congratulated Gladfelder on something, maybe the new stadium, or his necktie. After the silence I stood up and said we wanted both decent salaries *and* beautiful buildings. Not like the one we were in. I said, in the voice I used when talking to a four-year-old, that a building should last a millennium, which I explained to him was a thousand years. What I was most angry about, and had the most contempt for, was his *language*, his use of the word "philosophy," his lying heart, and I was countering his "philosophy" with my "millennium." And using it *accurately*. I think my goose was start-

ing to cook then—though the fire was still low. And I walked back
to my office alone.

What I found, and find, unbelievable, unacceptable, is the lie of
false identity, just as appalling in its way as the outright deliberate
lie, say, of a president or the CEO of a giant corporation. I first came
across it when I returned to the U.S. after a long absence and saw,
and heard, on TV two bad actors hyping cars, beer, banks, laxatives,
soap, in a banal and meaningless conversation. It was embarrass-
ing, hideous, and what was more hideous were the pathetic view-
ers in their hundreds of thousands of seats, watching and listening
like half-drugged cows before the hammer fell. The actors could
be well-known basketball players or fake pharmacists in white with
unrimmed glasses to express wisdom and sincerity and benignity.
But they were fakes. And you understood they were fakes. That
was the charm. I know it might sound ridiculous, what I'm saying,
I can see a sixteen-year-old making the cuckoo sign. He might roll
his eyes or look at me in wonder and exasperation. In his—or her—
short life, begun in 1986, how he had been surrounded, injected,
subdued, directed by an overwhelming propaganda. And how wise
he or she was by this time, resisting the boring arguments of a few
loose-enders, mothers and such. I was conditioned by radio, I guess,
and preferred Phineas Barnum to Walter Disney. When I heard the
gruff or lilting voices of one of the daytime barkers, some Arthur
Godfrey or other, I loved the sheer sound of the voice, and though I
knew all the information was distorted, whether it was news, pub-
lic service, or product, I loved that it was all of the same delicious
tone and I listened to it all with the same pleasure. It was as if there
was a different pact then, or understanding. It wasn't as if I expected
honesty, just a little decency. Daytime radio today is different; it's a
kind of Chinese torture, my apologies.

I am talking about dupery and diddling. My God, our politicians, our preachers, our generals. Only last week I read the now-famous story that the Pentagon was planning an "information" agency that would deliberately include "disinformation" (the Office of Strategic Influence). The good hearts in the Defense Department were worried, though, that it might spoil their image—as truth-tellers. A General Worden, who was supposed to head the new agency, "envisioned a broad mission ranging from black campaigns that use this disinformation to white ones that rely on truthful news releases." Good old General Wordy. What does it mean, "Thou shalt not bear false witness?" Grabbing your genitals and beating your chest like a Neolith? Kissing the Bible? The office had to be abandoned after it received excessive negative attention. The secretary of defense, a brilliant liar, insisted that the Department of Defense would never lie. The president, who was in China diddling and being diddled, was upset. He said the secretary of defense would certainly do the right thing. His nose gets longer and longer.

My father loved Arthur Miller's *Death of a Salesman*, only he felt there should be some additions and modifications. I can't remember what now, but he was an expert on the subject and Miller wasn't. He was much taken by the scene in the hotel, maybe horrified or embarrassed by it. I don't remember there ever being a conversation between the two of us, even a teasing one, about his cheating on his buying trips. I went with him several times to New York and there was a strong undertone of sexuality in the glittering lobby of the Pennsylvania Hotel or the New Yorker or the Edison. I knew it when I was twelve, and I knew my father was puritanical and looked at the enterprise with distaste, at least in front of me. There was a friend of his who sold raincoats on the road and had an affair on one of his trips. He had a wife and a daughter named Louise, my age. He was treated with scorn, sort of banned, because of the affair. And the banning went on for years. It was as if he was to be punished forever. I was fourteen or fifteen and felt sorry for him. Louise and I made out in the fruit cellar. When we were old enough and had become more self-conscious or delicate we stayed clear of each other. I suspect we both had good memories a decade or two later.

Recently I saw a video of the Maysles brothers' *Salesman*, a study of Catholic Bible salesmen and their wiles and ways in the mid-1960s. It was a documentary of the salesmen prodding good believers into buying Catholic Bibles and encyclopedias out of guilt or sheer helplessness. They usually entered the little kitchens and living rooms on false pretenses, making claims they were connected to the local church or that the family's name had been recommended by the priest or by another customer. The salesmen gained the confidence of the potential buyers by being folksy and exchanging family tidbits, yet remaining aloof, dignified, and authoritarian as if they were a type of priest themselves. Indeed they were well-tonsured, wore black suits, and conducted themselves as if they were attending to a mystery instead of taking money out of a poor man's pocket. The Bibles they sold were large and leather-bound and came in gold or red. They were filled with pictures, last suppers, mother and child, and the like, and they sold—in the mid-1960s—for $49.95. I think that would be between two and three hundred dollars in today's money. They used a multifaceted assault, drawing from piety, blarney, notions of childhood education, superstition, ethnicity, mother's guilt, religious pride, shame, and class ambition, using every trick from flattery and fear on one end to threats, clichés, and direct abuse on the other. They all drove big American cars, Buicks and Mercurys, none of the Japanese or German imports that were beginning to take over the market, and they were totally conventional in everything they said or did, not only to the "marks" but to each other in their cheap motel rooms after.

They were predators, and even saw themselves as such. They were as angry, frustrated, and disappointed when a customer got away as a leopard would be after chasing her prey and even leaping at it and missing by a few inches. Such a leopard—or wolf—licks her poor paws, looks away, and pretends she is interested in, say, a stray leaf or blade of grass as she quietly closes her case and snaps it shut before making a quick exit. In the meantime the deer or lost baby buffalo averts her own eyes in guilt and hopeless—if stubborn—inadequacy. "Everything in this life is a sacrifice," one of the salesmen said, referring to the hard-earned money the customer would have to spend. "The Bible is the best seller in the world," another said, and "This will be an inspiration in the home," and "The longer you have it, the more you will enjoy it." Just after one of them said, "You have a lovely home here," he concluded his sale with, "the important thing is to have it (the Bible) blessed because if it's not blessed you won't get the benefit of it."

Yet I don't know what was more painful, the encounter between the salesman and the customer, sometimes two salesmen, one working off the other, or the salesmen by themselves in the horrible motel room, playing cards on the fold-out table. I'm sure that the Maysles brothers, whatever their initial impulse was, eventually felt almost as much pity as disgust for these men. They seemed sad and worn out. Sitting in their motel room with their coats and ties off—they may have had two rooms—they reminded me of the Hollywood version of gangsters in their shirt sleeves waiting around for the heist, waiting for the telephone call with instructions, bored out of their minds, playing poker, of course. Only the salesmen didn't have holsters, and didn't wear hats inside. Their code was simple, "You've got a job to do and you do it." "Ninety-nine percent perspiration, one percent inspiration." "Push, push, push, push." "Go out there and hit 'em."

The boss, a kind of foreman, was tough and unrelenting. He was both inspirational and threatening, though when the men were relaxed he treated them as equals. He was, by the way, beefy, a body like someone on the force, whereas all the others were thin, even skinny, eating poorly and smoking constantly. The centerpiece of the film was a meeting at a hotel in Chicago where individual salesmen stood up and testified how hard they worked, how focused they were, and how much money they pledged to earn the next year. A prayer meeting was the model, or an AA service. Brother of EST. There were some bigwigs present, including several smiling priests. The highlight was an inspirational talk by a Melborn I. Feldman, Ph.D., designer and theological consultant and vice president of Consolidated Book Publishers, "the world's greatest salesman of the world's best seller," one who "needs no introduction to no one." He told his audience that they should hold their heads high, that it was a privilege to be of service to others, that they held a position of esteem in the eyes of the world and they should be proud. That the Father's business was selling Bibles. The mystery was his name and his face, both Jewish, indicating a possible sinister underplot. But no one seemed to get it but me, so I guess Feldman is from one of the more obscure shtetls. How the bros got their subjects to cooperate, it's difficult to know. That's always the case with these documentaries.

In 1965 or '66 my parents were already living in Miami in a new apartment complex, three pools, Friday-night movies, a lobby filled with lights and mirrors, a restaurant, a card room, etc. My father, handsome, social, verbal, accommodating, was well liked by the men and beloved of the women; and my mother, always perfectly dressed, even glittering when she came down to the lobby, was respected as being intelligent, beautiful, and wise. They were a perfect couple, in their mid- to late sixties, enjoying life and turning more conservative as the Vietnam War, the protests, the wildness, and the great political and social collisions were happening. Pat and I were living in Edison, New Jersey, quite hideous, our children were in elementary school, and I was struggling, in my mid-forties, to get recognition for my poetry, to make enough money for food and shelter, and to understand what was happening in the world and how to respond. I still bought cars for under a hundred dollars. I was isolated, yet close to New York and quite happy.

It was at that time that I heard from my mother and father, in one of our weekly telephone conversations, that they were being chosen as "honorees" of the State of Israel and that there was going to be a gala dinner to honor them for their lifelong service to Israel and Judaism. By this time, I had learned the art of deciphering, and I understood that my father—superb salesman that he was, and beautiful couple that they were, my mother and father—was actually selling State of Israel bonds to the dozens of just-retired couples in the three "towers" where they all lived; and my mother and father were being paid this way for their service. Not that anyone was cynical or abusive—it was a kind of ritual among the newly blessed—Italians, Jews, whatever—perfectly corrupt at its source. When my mother died she had spent twenty-seven years in Florida, twenty-three of them as a widow. After her funeral I attended to all the things in her apartment, and on her coffee table, the wood bleached from the sun, was a large book containing photographs and testimonials—of the dinner—which her guests leafed through or studied a page at a time. I've thrown the book away, though my good angel did tell me to keep it, and I did save some of the photos. One was of the Israeli ambassador to the U.S. congratulating my mother and father, and there were dozens of others, friends and relatives from Pittsburgh and Miami, sitting at attention at their tables.

I wasn't there and there was no attempt to have me come. God knows how uncomfortable or enraged I would have been. Nor did I send a telegram, as some others did. It was one of the many things we never talked about. I was poor, radical, had ambiguous feelings toward Israel, and despised the comfortable and dishonest hum. In one of the photographs my father was wearing a beautiful blue tuxedo and his face was shining; my mother had on long white formal gloves that came above her elbow and a white matching gown. They were of the Conservative persuasion and went to services twice a year. They were absolutely conventional members of the Jewish middle class in Pittsburgh, with all its virtues and faults. Though my mother had a little wildness in her and often—in her younger days—stayed up all night reading my books.

When she was in her mid-eighties, that would be 1985, she called me one day to tell me she had been invited to join an organization called "Parents of Famous Children." I was of course suspicious and started to ask her questions, which made her angry and defensive. "Was it a national organization?" "Where was its headquarters?" "What kind of people belonged to it?" "Why are you so suspicious?" she asked, "What does it matter?" And gradually

I learned that the "organization" consisted of Miami widows and that the organizer was a rabbi in the *schul* she went to every Friday night, and that it probably consisted only of women—maybe a man or so—from that *schul*. It was just a rubber chicken dinner in a second-rate hotel somewhere, the rabbi officiating and handing out 4 x 6 framed "diplomas" on which were handwritten "Parents of Famous Children" with my mother's name, Ida Stern, inscribed in the bad slanty handwriting of the rabbi. My name was nowhere to be seen, though I was the "famous child." It was pure scam. The reb was a first-class con artist. If he took in gross a couple thousand, assuming he was charging a hundred a head, and the frames cost fifty cents a piece, which would be ten bucks, and the dinner ten bucks a head, maybe twelve with some wine, and the room was donated, he would be making about $1700—at least $1500—for the one-time affair (no more famous children after that). My mother proudly nailed her diploma to the wall. The person sitting next to her was Mel Brooks's mother.

Different lambs, different scams! How much they hurt, how evil they were, could be measured in—what? How the victim suffered? What if he didn't know? What if the con and the mark were both "innocent"? Say one was signing up for Jin Shin Jyutsu, the "ancient art of harmonizing life energy," or the Power Optimism Workshop, where you learn to replace negative patterns with positive practices, or "On the Verge" or "Coming Out Group for Women" or "Fat Chance" or "Coping with Sibling Rivalry" or even going to a postseason sale, or buying anything from underpants to credit cards. Stocks. Tanning. Resorts. Is it all swindle? Lying? False information? Partial information, fake fondling and kissing?

What about plain decent commerce? Buying a hundred-year-old rug, in yellow and crimson, as I did in Crete in 1976, and carrying it with me, tightly rolled, on a plane, a train, and a bus, to my old house on the Delaware River. Or buying a Bedouin wedding dress that must have weighed twenty pounds from an Arab in Jerusalem after we haggled and hollered for a good half-hour, after I slammed the beaded door and walked righteously off and returned back over a small bridge just as he was hurrying to catch me, and smoking a single cigarette together and going back to give him money while he carefully wrapped the dress, my sworn brother. Or buying a new car in Easton, Pennsylvania, from a fat farmboy with a crew cut, in short sleeves and tie, nailing him down to one hundred dollars profit as he kept going back and forth to an empty office, I knew that, to get nonexistent approval or disapproval. (It had to be red, with a roof rack, manual shift, and excellent sound system.) I love bargaining and I'm terrific at it. My friend and guide in Jerusalem said she never saw anyone get a Bedouin wedding dress for that price—whatever it was. It is not exploitative, what the Arab did, what I did. Is it an issue of degree then? Is it motive? When does it become a con? Consider a daytime religious maniac. Consider the Lorillard Tobacco Company claiming it was not misleading anyone when it labeled cigarettes "light." Consider the president of the United States on any subject.

Does anyone still love Diogenes? He who went everywhere looking for an honest man. He who told Alexander to get out of his light. What would *he* think of prayer breakfasts and the fight against evil? What would he do with our lies? How would he respond to a telephone solicitor? Where would he go with his lantern? Blessed art thou, Diogenes, for being born in the fourth century B.C.E. What if he was being sold some bells to help the Messiah be born in a little airless trailer in Brooklyn, or Iowa? Almost as small as his tub. What if he were offered a free trip to Hawaii—with certain miserable conditions attached? What would he do with a gun? What would he think of the two caterpillars, Pat Robertson and Jerry Falwell? I hear there was a sect of cynics in Galilee 350 years before Yeshua preached. I'm sure there's a connection.

A DAY WITHOUT THE JEWS

I'VE BEEN LOOKING at a small photo of my father, taken in the mid-1930s sometime, and thinking about what he went through in the new country, his good and bad luck, the difficulties he experienced as an immigrant, a kind of orphan, and a Jew. He is wearing an undershirt—the kind they wore then—and holding his pants up with suspenders. He has a broad smile on his handsome face and his head, like mine, is small and round, more reminiscent of Khazaria than Poland and old Spain, his body short, thick, and muscular, made for riding wild ponies on the steppes. He is on his older brother's farm, in Mars, Pennsylvania, north of Pittsburgh, and he seems happier there than anywhere else, as if the smells and sounds of the farm were what he was born for, not those of the city.

In the Ukraine, his family occupied a small piece of land—technically owned by an ethnic German since Jews weren't allowed to own land under the czars. His father, Jacob Duglepiet (or Dolgiapyat)—changed at Ellis Island to Stern—owned a small sawmill, some houses, and a fishery, and lived in the shtetl of Ruzhyn, near Kiev. He and his wife Anna had eight children, all of whom emigrated except for the oldest, Eliazar. My father was the youngest, eight when he came; he and his mother were the last ones to leave, in 1905, during the pogrom.

Certainly Eliazar and his family perished during the Second

World War, if not sooner. We still heard from them even in the late 1930s, but they couldn't have survived the German and the Ukrainian onslaught—though there were rumors of a son who was a senior officer in the military, and in the 1970s a second cousin who was working with Soviet refugees in Austria came across a Dolgiapyat. But I think of my father, born Aaron, named Harry, who didn't know exactly when his birthday was, who as a boy went from older sister to older sister, who was full of life and love and truly blessed to get out as easily and early as he did. Of all my family, he was the one I couldn't bear to think of in the Germans' hands. Because of his trust, his obedience, his conventionality, his total lack of cynicism, I would say his belief. How I thought at times I was *his* father, the sorrow I felt for him when he sat on the edge of the bed every morning putting on his pointy shoes with a kitchen knife, the pride he felt in his handwriting, excellent as it was, the fine respect he had for me and my books, even a kind of awe.

It wasn't easy with us. He had worked since he was twelve, and couldn't understand how, in my twenties already, I just wandered and read and worked on my gray Underwood, how I turned down four or five juicy scholarships just to do nothing, as the master Walt advised, how I constantly switched vocations (façades) in order to carry on my secret one—wasn't I going to be a rabbi, a lawyer, a social worker, an economics then a literature professor, a labor advocate, a rug buyer? I never made my father the enemy, though I had to struggle with my love for poetry lest I give up, even though it appeared to him hard, stubborn, destructive—even disloyal. And I had to be strict about the money—I couldn't take *anything* from him if he didn't comprehend and support what I was doing, and how could he when I myself was half living in uncreated darkness, as Bach said.

If he had stayed in Europe he would have been in his early forties when the *Wehrmacht* came storming in. He might have been in Kiev by that time, or Odessa; by 1940 there were 160,000 Jews in Kiev alone; but unless he got away—one way or another—he would have been rounded up or shot on the spot. I can't imagine him striking out on his own into the forests. My father in the camps is unthinkable to me. Him waiting for the work detail, him eating the stinking food, him terrified of whips and dogs, him on his hands and knees eating grass—my father—the humiliation, the fear, unspeakable. It shames me to think of it, he who didn't drink baby's blood, who was not perfidious, in spite of Roman teaching, and who didn't wallow in anybody's money. In his world the worst he came across was a sign or two in Miami saying "No Jews or Dogs Permitted," poor animals, or a drunken Polack or two, or a Gentile snob. If necessary he used his fists, and he did that once or twice, but he came from more of a closed community than, say, his son, who was harassed endlessly, and given his anger, his pride, and his sense of justice (the son), became almost fierce, particularly in the golden years of the late 1930s and early '40s. There was a woman who lovingly told my father when he went wild over her little dog, I was six or seven at the time, that the dog loved people—except for Jews. I was there, I heard it. It never occurred to her that my father was a Jew, or might have been one. She might even have believed it.

I don't know if Ruzhyn was near Babi Yar or not. There had to be enough ravines near home to line Jews up on the edge and machine gun them down. I don't know what was most appalling, the deceit of the German government, which led the naïve Jews to believe that it was going to be "merely" a deportation, or the perfidy of the Ukrainians and Ukrainian Auxiliary Police, or the thorough planning and methodical procedures of the many German army units involved, or the horror of the exhumation and the burning of already decayed bodies. How could Aaron have put his clothes in a pile and run naked through the clubs, maybe with a son or daughter at his side?

As far as his life in America, he and his mother made their way from Ellis Island to Pittsburgh, where his father had established a business: Stern's Stogies. Though *his* father died young and the family ceased being "rich," and he had to leave school, he grew up quickly and took up as a salesman, oh, at seventeen or so, for this life. He had a daughter and a son and needless to say a wife, and moved in his very early thirties to a suburban neighborhood, for he was in love with America and a sucker for every dreamlet. His daughter died suddenly at age nine, the country went into an endless Depression, his wife had a nervous breakdown, and love and hate fought with each other for fifteen desperate years. He found himself shocked and dismayed at the persistence of bigotry and hatred and partly because of this, and partly because of his daughter's death, he moved back into the city and into a Jewish world again. His son, a year younger than the daughter, thirteen months to be exact, was sketching incessantly by this time and the father used to show the son off, whom he loved dearly, by having him draw likenesses at the men's clothing store where he was manager and buyer, especially on Saturday nights.

The only other catastrophe he had in his life was when the business he later owned with a crooked partner went into limited bankruptcy in 1938 and he was betrayed by "friends" and found himself suddenly penniless when he was on the brink of a great killing. He wouldn't even take a suit (44 short) from the rack to look for a job because he didn't own it anymore. Hitler he knew about, the evil one, but in his mind's eye he conflated him too much with Haman and shook a rattle in his face. He understood bigotry but he was unprepared for the total depravity of the German government and its clever manipulation of centuries-old Jew-hatred and the harnessing of it to modern technology, organization, and thought-control. And was as shocked as anyone else by the revelations of the Allied armies. He was, like everyone else, embittered and saddened; and felt betrayed and outwitted by false friends and liars, and guilty that he hadn't paid more attention, and ashamed that so little was done by American Jews who, after all, gave so little—but what could he have done, he argued, and wasn't it too close for comfort in America itself, and anyhow he was growing old before he expected it, and his thoughts were suddenly on the second half of his life and what he wanted to do with it.

He didn't like to think about the lost Judea where he was born, a country within a country, or within over twenty countries, a land more than a country, that his son, more than he, remembered incessantly, blood-stained Europe that I came back to with my mouth open and my cultured tongue sticking out. In his thoughts, my father went back to his youth, to what a swimmer he once was, the Allegheny River his pool; and boxer, and ballplayer. How he once outfought his nephew Mo, ten years his junior, who himself had fought in a hundred fights, amateur and professional, and was the only one, ever, to knock out Fritzie Zivic in the first round, Zivic who was welterweight champion in 1940, the dirtiest fighter in history, Pittsburgh's own. Who—my father—watched his son drift away and encase himself in a strange shell but had no words to penetrate it and was fearful of that cultured tongue, who made a little money, retired to Florida, adored his grandchildren, beat everyone in shuffleboard, and died obediently on his way to the hospital in an ambulance, no one to close his eyes.

In the summer of 1955 my former wife and I were moving from youth hostel to youth hostel in the Mezzogiorno, mostly along the coast, and had reached a small village named Praiano overlooking the Mediterranean not far from Amalfi, close to Positano. The sea there probably has a particular name—I think it does—and I'll probably remember it after a page or two. What I do remember is that we were staying at one hostel, two, three thousand meters up, and we spent maybe four hours walking downhill through the trees and rocks till we reached the sea road. Pat remembers that we climbed down steps built into the mountain and that there were level spaces in between with little farms among the trees. She remembers the long walk, and a large sand-colored shepherd-like dog that followed us down from the first hostel and wouldn't go back no matter how much we yelled and pushed, and how I developed a footful of blisters from the walk and how we stayed in Praiano, at Papa Luigi's, for almost a week to nurse my blisters.

Luigi's wife, Carolina, answered the door when we knocked. The whole town was taking a nap at the time and her slamming the door and screaming "lupe, lupe," when she saw the dog, woke up Luigi who opened the door and invited us in, after calming Carolina down with a few barks. The dog was panting from the heat and his huge teeth were encased in juices. He looked at Luigi with approval and lapped up the water he gave him. How Luigi got to be on the hostel list I don't know—he had a modest Mediterranean house with a few rooms downstairs and maybe four bedrooms upstairs. There were six guests beside us, a French couple, two Welshmen, and a German woman and her teenage daughter. The task now was to return the wolf. We spent a good two hours in the large open bar down the road, Luigi, me, Pat, the dog, a telephone operator, and some bystanders, trying to return the dog to its owner up the hill. The telephone operator put on a kind of hat with a green shade and garters to hold the sleeves up. It was the only telephone in town. I don't want to rub it in, but he did crank the phone before shouting into it. (It was the Tyrrhenian Sea.) When the owner drove the nine kilometers through the hills to pick up his dog he seemed angry with Pat and me and practically accused us of stealing his dumb beast. So much for good deeds along the Amalfi Coast.

We spent a week there waiting for my feet to recover, swimming in the salt water and eating from Carolina's garden. Every evening was a kind of party. We sang songs in several languages, and talked about art and beauty and geography and politics in the broken, half-literate way you do in such linguistically mixed company. The Welshmen mostly drank and after a while gave up any attempt at real communication except for a pound or two on the back and toast after toast in the old language. With the French it was North Africa, but I can't be sure. The sixteen-year-old fräulein was bored out of her mind. Her mother was "educating" her, but this trip was confined exclusively to classical matters, so the Middle Ages, the Baroque, the Gothic, and the Renaissance were passed over.

When we got to the War, and one way or another we got there, the German, who was in her mid-forties, reminisced sadly over her husband's death in an air raid, and bemoaned the ruthless English and American bombings. She was from Hamburg and worked, it turned out, for the Lutherans in some capacity or other. Her husband had been in the German army and was home on leave when he was killed in 1944 in the brutal firebombing. When I pointed out to her, in a calm and patient voice—we spoke English mostly— that both sides were guilty of aerial bombardment and the Germans were early practitioners, not only in England but, even before the war started, in Spain, she denied this and expressed surprise at my unfounded notions. This, mind you, in 1955, ten years after the war had ended.

The subject of the Jews came up soon enough. She expressed regret for their treatment but there was no acknowledgment of the enormity and the brutality of the German action, no horror, no sorrow, no condemnation. Rather, she once again blamed the Jews for Germany's ruin, and talked about the "international conspiracy." When I was foolish enough to argue with her, to *reason* with her, she expressed scorn for American naïveté—innocence she called it—and said we Americans didn't understand the Jews and their ways. When I told her, in the nicest voice I have, that I do indeed understand, that I am myself a Jew, she froze a little but still kept to her position until I told her in bald plain German, "Ich bin ein Jude," and that seemed to convince her. I don't know what the Welshmen or the Frenchmen said, or if Papa Luigi was there or not. Carolina didn't speak English, let alone German. And I don't know what we said next, or how we said it, or when we drifted off to bed. Pat Stern is still horrified by the event, and remembers it keenly.

At two in the morning, I was out on the road looking down at the sea and up at the moon, peaceful enough and even sober, when the German woman came out to join me, certainly in her nightgown, with a shawl around her. After a minute she started to sob and ask my forgiveness. I remember with embarrassment that she tried to kiss my hands. How long we were there and what we said to each other I don't exactly remember—more than being angry with her, I was shocked by her change of heart and her new knowledge. I probably said she did me no wrong personally and it would be cheap grace for me to "forgive" her. That I myself wanted to ask

forgiveness of the dead Jews for being alive and swimming in the
gorgeous salt water of the Amalfi Coast. That I would have to live
among the Germans and recognize them as human before I could
forgive anybody. That she should read, and read about, the Chris-
tian leaders who opposed the Nazis, including some who died for
their beliefs. That she could make a start by visiting the camps in
Germany and learning what happened to the Jews there, and she
could take her daughter next time to Poland and Czechoslovakia to
further her education. That she, as a Christian, should compare the
anti-Jewish measures of the early church with the Nazi measures,
in which she would find an eerie replication: "Jews may live only
in Jewish quarters, it was forbidden to sell land to Jews, Jews could
not obtain academic degrees, Jews must wear a distinctive sign on
their clothing, Jews could not show themselves in the street during
holy (Nazi festival) days, it was forbidden to eat with Jews." And
that her own Luther, who in his early arguments with the Roman
Church became a kind of advocate of the Jews, ended up writing
a passionately anti-Jewish work called *On the Jews and Their Lies*,
where he repeats the usual medieval slander about poisoning wells
and making matzos from Christian blood, and calls for the burn-
ing of synagogues, the destruction of Jewish houses, a ban on their
religion, confiscation of their cash and jewelry, hard physical labor,
and, finally, banishment from Christian lands—all of it useful to
Himmler.

Did I say all of that to her, or some of that? And did I realize
that this was a pivotal moment in my life, that I would never again
be so focused? That the whole war, and in particular the consum-
mately organized murder of Jews—as well as Gypsies, mentally ill,
and homosexual populations—was reencountered, even particular-
ized, at that moment? That I had to struggle with a postwar German

caricature, under an Italian moon, as if the two of us were deciding more than just our personal fates?

Well, forty-seven years later, I was riding a stationary bicycle in my gym, one of four (bicycles), when I noticed that the man next to me was reading Simon Wiesenthal's book *The Sunflower*, the astounding story of a dying German soldier, a member of the SS, asking Wiesenthal, a Jewish slave, for forgiveness. I was amazed by the coincidence. Wiesenthal was on a work detail in Poland, in his own hometown it happens, in front of the Technical High School where he was once a student, albeit hated and treated with contempt because he was a Jew. The high school had been turned into a hospital and the detail's job was to load trucks filled with rubbish from the building, bloodstained bandages, packing material. A nurse from the hospital, wearing her cap and uniform, ordered Wiesenthal to follow her inside. She took him to the former dean's office on the second floor, which Wiesenthal well remembered, where the dying soldier—completely encased in bandages, his head, even his eyes and face covered—was waiting to talk to a "Jew" before he died. It was altogether at random and by chance that Wiesenthal was beckoned. The nurse waited in the hall, behind the closed door, while the soldier made his "confession," since he wanted to die in peace. "He was not born a murderer, twenty-one was too young to die, he was brought up a Catholic, he joined the Hitler Youth," and so on. "His mother had a Jewish doctor, his father was a Social Democrat who hated the Nazis," and so on. In the Ukraine his troop was ordered to drive more than two hundred Jews, all ages, into a house, they doused the house with gasoline, threw grenades at it to set it on fire, and shot the Jews who tried to escape. Imprinted on his mind was a family, father, mother, child, their clothes on fire, leaping out a window, screaming. He drank brandy and sang songs that night.

Wiesenthal listened to him, a weird scene, allowed the German to hold his hand, didn't interrupt him, brushed a fly away, and at the end walked silently out of the room. He, Wiesenthal, was unsure if he had done the right thing by *not* verbally forgiving the dying man. He consulted with his friends—at the death camp—and good Jews that they were, even though they could be torn to pieces by specially trained dogs at the whim of a German guard, or whipped by one of the Russian or Ukrainian overseers if they were found loitering, or just shot to death for one reason or another, engaged in Judaic debate over the role of men and God in forgiveness.

The second half of the book consists of a series of short responses to the issue of forgiveness by theologians, writers, philosophers, and politicians, such as Robert Coles, the Dalai Lama, Matthew Fox, Mary Gordon, Abraham Heschel, Primo Levi, Herbert Marcuse, Cynthia Ozick, Albert Speer, Desmond Tutu, Arthur Waskow, fifty-three in all. There are no big surprises, but the details are fascinating. By and large the Christian, particularly the Catholic, spokespeople wrote of the need for endless forgiveness and the Jewish and secular spokespeople argued the difficulty, sometimes the impossibility, of forgiveness. Here are ten quotations from the book: "There are some evils forgiveness cannot wash away" (Cynthia Ozick); "It is a cardinal principle of Judeo-Christian ethics that forgiveness must always be granted to the sincerely repentant" (Edward H. Flannery); "I personally feel bound by tradition to summon up some compassion (*merhamet*, as Bosnians call it) for every sufferer" (Smail Balic); "Even if Wiesenthal believed that he was empowered to grant a pardon in the name of the murdered masses, such an act of mercy would have been a kind of betrayal and repudiation of the memory of millions of innocent victims who were unjustly murdered, among them, the members of his family" (Moshe Bejski); "Bring me a Jew, was the dying Nazi's request. Any Jew will do. Karl has learned nothing. His desire is to 'cleanse' his own soul at the expense of the Jew" (Alan L. Berger); "—how often many of us who profess the Christian ethic of forgiveness succumb to smugness, arrogance, pretentiousness, a cocky self-importance that is utterly incompatible with the kind of absolution and reconciliation implied in the act of forgiveness" (Robert Coles); "Why can't they forgive? We Christians do. Why can't they let it alone and get on with the living?" (Eugene J. Fisher); "Only the victims were in a position to forgive; and they are dead, put to death in the most inhuman ways conceivable" (Eva Fleischner); "How many ordinary German citizens—and clergy and bishops—knew something evil was going on and still lived in denial?" (Matthew Fox); "Had he never grasped the intent of the statements equating Jews with vermin? . . . if not the fine detail that Zyklon B, the gas by which those three (souls set ablaze) multiplied by millions were exterminated in their death chambers, was a roach poison?" (Rebecca Goldstein); "If the dying Nazi soldier wished to atone, he should have insisted that he be placed in the camps, so that he could die in the miserable circumstances of those in whose name he is asking forgiveness" (Mary Gordon); "Apparently, no living German was ever a Nazi" (Mark Goulden); "My whole instinct is to forgive. Perhaps that is because I am a Catholic priest" (Theodore M. Hesburgh); "In Judaism, where forgiveness requires both atonement and restitution, there are two sins that can never be forgiven: murder and destroying someone's reputation. In these two situations atonement is possible, but not forgiveness" (Susannah Heschel); "Forgiveness is of the heart. I would have forgiven, as much for my own peace as for Karl's" (José Hobday); "On the other hand we are all born in original sin" (Christopher Hollis); "The question of whether there is a limit to forgiveness has been emphatically answered by Christ in the negative" (Cardinal Franz Konig); "The act of 'having a Jew brought to him' seems to me at once childish and impudent" (Primo Levi); "The Jews who had been burned to death by this soldier had not authorized anyone to forgive on their behalf" (Deborah E. Lipstadt); "cheap grace" (Martin E. Marty); "Let him go to hell" (John T. Pawlikowski); "God can presumably forgive a murderer, but as far as people are concerned, *murder is unforgivable*" (Dennis Prager); "For a Buddhist, forgiveness is always possible and one should always forgive" (Matthieu Ricard); "That S.S. officer should take up his case with God. I personally think he should go to hell and rot there" (Sidney Shachnow); "It is God's grace that has touched me through you" (Albert Speer); "There can be no counterargument against forgiveness in such a case, or indeed against a reconciliation based on pity" (Manès Sperber); "The request was absurd" (André Stein); "Besides, those who committed these crimes are old now and in poor health" (ironic, Nechama Tec); "Indeed, he does not even want to know who the Jew is" (Nechama Tec); "It is clear that if we look to retributive justice, then we could just as well close up shop" (Desmond Tutu); "I cannot do it" (Arthur Waskow). Well, thirty-one quotes.

I came back to my German woman, after the long bout with Wiesenthal, somewhat edified but still mystified, as I will be for the rest of my life. She, shawl or no shawl, was not a murderer, didn't throw hand grenades, didn't shoot at falling burning bodies, probably wasn't a member of some brutal idiotic *Jungen-grup*, and probably held suspended some righteous self-serving notions in her head. And I, of course, would not be returning to a work detail in five minutes and marching back "home" in an hour to the tune of a Ukrainian or Belarusian whip. Yet to deny or excuse the German government's debased inhuman behavior is itself an act of complicity, as so many of the witnesses in Wiesenthal's book affirm. "While the evil was going on, to turn aside from it, to avoid noticing it, became complicity," Ozick says. "And in the same way, after three or four decades have passed and the evil has entered history, to turn aside from it—to forget—again becomes complicity. Allowing the evil to slip into the collective amnesia of its own generation, or of the next generation, is tantamount to condoning it." Matthew Fox says that "This story—the entire Nazi story—lays bare the *sins of complicity and the sins of omission and denial* that render our participation in evil so profound." He goes on to write about other sins of complicity and denial, including most especially those in the Western countries and, particularly, America.

This hits close to home. Unless I, as a privileged American, a male, a Caucasian—and a Jew—come to terms with these, intellectually, politically, personally, I have not paid my own debt. And I hope *that* doesn't sound too holy and self-righteous. Frau Shawl—I'm glad we met. I'm sorry that her husband died and her city, a hotbed of socialism between the wars, was destroyed. My father—and his mother—actually could have sailed from Hamburg in 1905. I have been there. Oh Germans, we loved you so much we adopted your language when we reached the Rhine and took it with us everywhere; so much that we modified and even abandoned our ancient religion. We were your best guests. I think of young Wiesenthal in his hometown, Lemberg, Poland, as a high school student at the Technion. He is on Sapiehy Street on his way to classes. It is maybe examination day and the "Young Radicals" have put a banner over the school entrance proclaiming that day as "A Day without the Jews," and they wear ribbons with the same inscription. They have fastened razor blades to the end of their sticks which they use as weapons against the Jewish students. This is all told in *The Sunflower.* "Since the campus of the Technical High School was ex-territorial, the police were not allowed to interfere except by express request of the Rector" (himself an anti-Semite). Ambulances waited on the side streets and sometimes a "patriot" was taken to jail, but he was released a hero. Since "A Day without the Jews" always occurred on examination day, the Jewish students, most of whom were poor, lost a term and that "inevitably meant an end to their studies." That was the building in which the SS officer made his confession. Well, Jews lived in Poland a thousand years. And they lived in Rumania—with *great* difficulty from time to time—for 1600 years. Frau Shawl and I would certainly not want to miss the sights on our grand tour, the gore notwithstanding.

In 1995, maybe 1996, I was traveling by bus from Easton, Pennsylvania, I think it was to Reading, Pennsylvania, to look at a house that was for sale and to visit some friends. There was no direct line and I went on at least two buses, maybe three, through major towns like Kutztown, Dryville, New Jerusalem, Seisholtzville, and the like. I had to wait at miserable bus stations or along questionable roads and boarded the final bus at six or seven in the evening, at sunset. It was one of those delightful ancient buses with roomy leather seats and a door that made a heavenly swooshing sound when it opened and closed, reminiscent of 1940s and '50s buses. There were two people on board, the driver and one passenger in . the front seat to his right. I, social and inquiring as I am, took the seat immediately behind the driver, so there were the three of us up front and no one in the rest of the bus.

The driver had a kind of bullet-head, close-cropped gray hair, and deep creases in his fat neck. He was heavy and his movements were slow and deliberate. He had on a short-sleeve shirt over a see-through T-shirt, a disgusting uniform, and, I think, a stick-em-on leather bow tie. The steering wheel was huge and he seemed to positively enjoy the immense constant turnings to left and right. It was a delight to sink into that old leather and to half close my eyes. The driver and the other passenger were having a conversation and if their voices weren't so loud, particularly bullet-head's, I would have dropped off immediately.

He was telling the other passenger—obscure in his corner—about an event that had happened a few weeks past at the Port Authority in New York. It seems that he was climbing up the back stairs, probably dirty cement with pipe banisters, probably even two at a time, when someone (he identified him as "colored") came rushing down holding a beautiful new-looking briefcase and offered to sell it to him, cheap. Obviously the briefcase was hot and bullet-head considered it, but he finally decided against it. He was relieved he made that decision because when he arrived in a few minutes at the locker room he discovered the briefcase belonged to a colleague of his, another bus driver, and it was stolen from him—picked up from a bench, snatched from a shelf or table. And he was happy he hadn't bought the briefcase, though he was tempted and the price, bullet-head said, was good enough, though "I could have 'Jewed' him down," said bullet-head.

I was a little shocked to hear the old phrase, no more than two feet in front of me, the bus purring, night coming on, the leather seat deep and comfortable, the sound of katydids, with the window a little open, penetrating the interior. "Don't say a word," I said to myself, "he won't get it, don't make a fool of yourself, be tolerant and understanding, they're just having the stupid talk that males do, as a way of vaguely bonding, breaking the silence, saying nothing, much better than shooting each other—out of boredom or what-not, he has no idea." So after a half-minute of silence I said, "What do you mean, 'Jew him down'? Why didn't you say, 'Christian him down,' you fucking asshole!" To which bullet-head replied, calm as could be, even sweet, steering the bus with pure love and devotion, "Oh, it's just a way of talking we Dutchmen have, it don't mean nothing." "Dutchmen," of course, meant German—these eastern Pennsylvania Germans called themselves Dutch, from Deutsche, from Pennsylvania Dutch. "My people always say that." "Your peo-ple," I said, "killed six million of mine and you still don't get it, you dumb Nazi."

I was shouting by this time. The other passenger, the one hunched in the corner across from me—I half-forgot about him—said (Oh, God!), "Gerald Stern, you're Gerald Stern, the poet!" Now I wanted to hunch in my corner. I had to admit who I was. I had to listen to his words of praise. I had to smile when he told me his favorite poems of mine and nod in gratitude when he recited some of my lines. But at least it released me from the Dutchman and from my insane attack on him. I was embarrassed of course, but relieved. But now I had a new problem: Hunched-in-the-Corner asked where I was going, wrote down my phone number, and tried to set up a meeting with me the next week in New York, where he went every Tuesday—or Thursday—to work, or go to museums, or maybe it was Tuesday *and* Thursday.

I was paying for my anger, for my Jewish pride. If that's the word for it. Yet I can't help thinking I did the right thing, Hunched-in-the-Corner or no Hunched-in-the-Corner. Where in the hell do Germans, or German Americans, or Swedes or Slovenians, or God save us, the Scotch-Irish or the French or English get off accusing Jews of just those special skills? Or, more important—for me—when are they going to give up scapegoating? "Jew him down." What a great word, "Jew." It's the only case I know, though there may be others, where the descriptive noun is by itself also an insult. Jew! You don't even need "dirty" Jew. Try Italian. Italian! Pole! Lithuanian! Indian! Englishman! Because of this, those non-Jews terrified of being taken as anti-Semites use the adjective "Jewish" as a euphemism. "Do you know Abe Feldman?" "Yeah, he's Jewish, you know. Terrific guy! Never killed Christ! Hates the taste of Christian blood! Doesn't have any money. Works in his garden. Builds his own furniture." Never "He's a Jew," God forbid. Of course, "Jew" as in "Jew him down" is not a noun—it's a verb. As in "Mexican him down," or "Chinese him down." And look at me making such a big deal about nothing. We Jews are so sensitive, and no harm was intended.

The upshot was that the next morning I was walking through town, maybe getting a bus back, maybe going to Philadelphia, when I ran into the Dutchman in fresh shirt and T-shirt, bow tie in his pocket, walking by me. He was very friendly, as if nothing had transpired between us, and asked whether I had found my friends in Reading and did I have a good time. I was shocked. Neither his words nor my assault on him seemed to have mattered—or even penetrate. I, in turn, was doubly nice. I even think I said, "Have a nice day." Squeezed-in-the-Corner, though, called me several times and I met him in New York City for lunch and a conversation a few weeks later, after countless calls. I guess he was a nice enough guy, though I have no need to enlarge my stable of friends, with the obvious obligations, missed dates, and hurt feelings. All I want in life now, besides a little happiness, is a table and chair, or anything that resembles it, the bench where I'm sitting, a large rock, senior citizen coffee at McDonald's.

BURNING MONEY

EASTON, PENNSYLVANIA, is one of my cities. Along with Philadelphia; New Brunswick; Pittsburgh; Iowa City; Miami Beach; Paris; Montpellier, France; Indiana, Pennsylvania; Lambertville, New Jersey; Ocean Grove, New Jersey; and New York. Over the years I bought—and sold—seven or eight houses in Easton. The city went downhill so fast that you could buy an eight-story art-deco limestone and brick building, with a bank on the ground floor, elevators, offices—the works—for $40,000 or $50,000; or a small eighteenth-century downtown brick for $5,000; or a rich man's ten-room, two acres for $30,000; or an old factory, everything intact and working, for $10,000 or $15,000. You could live in them, or hold on and pray.

Easton is at the confluence of the Lehigh and Delaware Rivers, a little over an hour west of New York City, a canal and a railroad town, the site of Indian treaties, the home of the first American flag (not Philadelphia), a great trading, transportation, and manufacturing center, the home of Lafayette College, one of the many great economic centers on the East Coast, the gateway, for two centuries, to the rest of America. Its population is less than fifty thousand, probably more like thirty-five thousand, or thirty thousand.

It is the classic model of decline that swept industrial America in the East and the Midwest after World War II. And the reasons

themselves are classic: old factories, outmoded systems, popula-
tion shift, easier modes of transportation permitting the buyer to
be at a distance from the producer, abandonment of the rivers as
a necessary ingredient in the process, high labor costs, greed, stu-
pidity, shortsightedness, suburbanization, racism, archaic house
and factory stock, banker caution, new cities, interstates, suicide,
shopping centers, dumb architecture, dumb city planning, dumb
government.

The height of its power was probably 1950, earlier maybe. By the
1960s, the Lebanese population downtown had already been exiled,
their beautiful small houses and gardens destroyed, and their culture
scattered. We bought our house, on the river in Raubsville, six miles
south of Easton, in 1968 and moved in in 1969. At the time, Easton
downtown was crowded with restaurants, stores, shops, markets,
department stores, and you could barely walk down the wide side-
walks. Truth is the blight had already established itself, the factories
were closing, and the neighborhoods were in the early stages of a
crisis. Route 22 had split the city apart in 1950, making it easy for
cars and trucks to *pass through* Easton, and by 1970, work was under-
way on Interstate 78, making it possible to bypass—and ignore—the
city altogether.

Easton had a large number of factories and workplaces that
employed anywhere from just a few to hundreds. Breweries, brick-
yards, textile mills, cordage companies, foundries, railroad repair
shops, box companies. It produced pig iron, railroad switches (frogs),
Dixie cups, bathing suits, flags, silk, pretzels, furs, film, curtains,
hats, dresses, shirts, pants, underwear, electric coils, machinery,
phonograph records, paint, and it was home to Crayola (Binney
and Smith) and Alpha Cement. The American Flag Manufacturing
Company—in Easton—was the principal manufacturer of Ameri-

can flags. In addition, Easton was the county seat (Northampton County), with all the services and amenities that this carried, by way of health care, welfare, job training, therapy, special bus service, and the like. Of course, all that meant, in addition to the businesses, the businesses that served the businesses, the lumberyards and hardwood stores, the joiners and unjoiners, and those that fed and clothed and entertained, and propped up and buried and educated and protected the workers and their bosses and those in between.

Things change hands. Spaces are converted. The more that dies the more conversion there is. The latest stage—I almost wanted to say "the last stage"—is art. Every decayed city in America turns in desperation to art and the artist. They're not *interested* in art; they're interested in filling the empty spaces. They have discovered the word "loft." They think those huge empty buildings have a value. They advertise, they post photographs and articles in the papers. Even the *New York Times* gets interested. My friend, Karl Stirner, himself a magnificent sculptor, bought a 40,000-square-foot downtown building in 1982 for $40,000—excellent condition. It was built in 1903 and was, most of its life, a food distribution center, canned goods and such—gigantic spaces, four stories, an elevator. He uses about a fourth for his studios, his living spaces, and storage for his enormous art collection, Mexican, Renaissance, Oceanic, African, Classical, American. On Sitgreaves Street, a few rough steps from the square, in a building that Lou Reda once used for filmmaking, two painters have moved in to spaces that would have been unthinkable in Manhattan or Queens. And in various places—on the main streets, in side streets, in abandoned churches and store rooms, other artists have sanded floors, rebuilt ceilings, and put up sheetrock to establish living and working spaces. I know seven, eight of them.

There are also dealers, dancers, musicians, printmakers, of various kinds. Two people I know bought the Salvation Army store, formerly a shoe store, and created a central garden in the center of a block-long storeroom. My son and I planned the same thing in the center of a two-story gigantic ex-bathing suit factory I came within two inches of buying and moving in to. On Ferry Street, across the alley from the beautiful old post office, King's Cleaners, which for years shrunk my clothes, is right now, August 2008, being massively upended to make room for someone who does exotic doorknobs—all 10,000 feet—a church somewhere under there, a shape or shadow, one ruined window visible. Even Lafayette College, the art department, has moved some studios downtown, a distance from the educated hill. Only a few years ago there were three or four galleries in town and on Friday nights there were openings, replete with cheese, wine, skimpy dresses, and some things on the wall. Serious talk. Sex.

Speaking of which (sex), it should be mentioned that in the late 1920s and '30s, Easton supported sixty-four brothels and gambling establishments, and barkers at New York City's Madison Square Garden prizefights on Friday night would cry, "Going to Easton! Going to Easton!" to draw large numbers of customers to a late-night train headed for Pennsylvania. Water produces this. It was that way when I was in high school in Pittsburgh. We went to Steubenville, Ohio, carloads of us. The Ohio River, not the Delaware.

It all comes down to one corner facing the large square. For years a restaurant was there called the Sweet Shoppe, where they served decent, inexpensive Greek diner food, though the cherry pie and ice cream were excellent. The booths were small, the waitresses smoked, and there were little doors in the back that opened into makeshift closets for fairly high-stakes gambling. Now the

Sweet Shoppe has been magically changed to a rather high-class Portuguese-lite bar and restaurant, called Valenca, with faceless expensive decor that is totally nonlocal and could be in any face-lifting world in New York, Chicago, or Dallas, where you can dine on salmon ceviche. There is not one cheapo eating place left in Easton. It's gone to the dogs. The Swellhounds.

It all comes down to that corner—to those two restaurants and to what those two restaurants symbolize or suggest. I don't wish the new restaurant any harm, and I love salmon ceviche, but I just have to say that it's dead and boring and badly planned and too big and forbidding and inappropriate for the place; and that, stubborn nostalgic that I am, I actually have a photograph of the Sweet Shoppe, circa 1980, hanging on my wall.

There *is* something to say for the absolutely elegant, privileged, and expensive side by side with the dirty, old, and encumbered, that poor city's fate now for several decades. The future of the city is hashed over everywhere you go. There are official clubs for this purpose, private and civic, certainly T-shirts, and weekly meetings. Seven A.M. is the right time, the rosy cool optimistic hour, but where do they go now that the Sweet Shoppe is gone? Portuguese-lite doesn't open till 11:30. Here and there are some holdouts, little clusters of bitter old men or wise old women, who prefer to talk about the past, and are cynical about the future, or just indifferent. They talk about the great floods, especially the one in 1955 when the two rivers suddenly overflowed downtown and all but destroyed the free bridge, twisting and bending it in the great flow of water. They talk about Pomeroy's Department Store and the slow narrow escalator, one of the earliest, that eased your way upstairs. And they talk about the Boyd Theater, the fake Moroccan masterpiece, where they saw movies and stage shows, and had bouncing-ball sing-alongs, and its casual destruction in 1972 to make room for fifteen or twenty cars to park in the dirt. I was there, as I said elsewhere, and retrieved a length of beaten Spanish steel, which is now the rail for the staircase in my former house in Raubsville, recently raised fifteen or so feet above the ground after the last of the many "hundred year" floods that befell the river towns, that house of stone and mud that literally grew out of the earth underneath it.

I don't want to give the impression that my cynics are sentimental, that they weep over nothing, that they sit in an empty lot and drop dust on their heads like some Hebrew wiping away his tears in Babel-Land. Though I rather like that image. I particularly like it if they are in the wrong lot mourning the wrong building, rat that I am. And I like that the empty space—the empty lot—is most of all like a red gum in a beleaguered mouth, and I like even more that the dentist pulled the wrong tooth, and they are mourning the wrong hole.

Sentimentality may be perceived differently in different circumstances and at different times, but it is always a question of inappropriate feeling, or language, or action—so we teach. Though *extreme* behavior, that which goes beyond mere "excessive feeling," not only becomes appropriate, whatever the circumstances, but it even justifies itself, I would say with or without an object. It's going crazy over the tooth you never had. Like Hamlet.

Me, I can't bear the pain of being separated from anything. I take over everyone's past. I mourn the life I never lived. I want to stay in every city I ever touched or even heard of. I long to walk through the streets of Carthage and talk to the half-naked wives, to drink wine in sixteenth-century Cadiz, to tear a loaf at 11:00 A.M. in one of the cities of Central Africa—before the Portuguese. I can't bear that life was lived on Third Street in a Lebanese house without me.

That in 1925 they drank the sweetened coffee and recited a smart Semitic line out of Beirut or Phoenicia just before I was born. Not to mention 1910 in a classroom at Lafayette, discussing Racine—or Rabelais. Or the argument in 1901 I had with my wife at the corner of Fourteenth and Northampton, on the second floor rear, the wind blowing the curtains apart and saving our marriage. And since I'm a ghost here, I have to struggle to remember pain. How about the swollen brain where a badly paid cop hit me with a club because I was carrying a piece of cardboard back and forth in front of my factory? How about the doctor's office where he put my broken shoulder back in place after I tried to retrieve the huge bucket full of liquid ore, wrenching myself apart and burning my hands raw on the speeding rope?

The Easton Area Public Library was closed on Labor Day, but on Wednesday, September 3, 2008, I visited the Marx Room on the first floor, a large glass enclosure containing dozens of volumes on the city of Easton and nearby communities. There were albums of old photographs, with quaint titles like *A Time to Remember, Forks of the Delaware River, The Old Home Town,* and *It Seems Like Yesterday.* There were histories, minutes of old clubs, biographies, private papers, encyclopedias, guidebooks to art and architecture, lives of public officials, stories of the Dutch, Welsh, Mennonites, Germans, and African Americans, sketchbooks (poems, stories of coal, minerals, uprisings), journals, "Notes and Queries," memoirs, diaries, war stories, lost causes, famous women, Jews, bad novels, poems, tax lists, archives, records, folklore, court proceedings, anniversary books, newspaper extracts and articles, reminiscences, recollections, autobiographies, minutes of school boards. I liked the photographs, Centre Square in 1896, old department stores with clerks standing at attention, lunch counters, cityscapes.

There were pictures of Bixlers, America's oldest jewelers, the new Mayer's Clothing Store (1949), snow-covered, tree-lined streets, the old Herman Simon residence (later a YWCA, later the Third Street Alliance), the Boyd with its giant interior, diners, drugstores, hotels, churches, the Paxinosa Inn, a huge summer resort destroyed by fire in 1905, the *new* Paxinosa Inn, destroyed by fire in 1931, the Drake Building, replaced by a parking garage in 1972, the Glendon Iron Furnace, a stretch of the Lehigh Canal, an outdoor theater (on Island Park), Canal Boats, Schaibles Bakery trucks (1934), the Dixie Company, the Home for Friendless Children, Simon's Silk Mill, Veterans on Decoration Day (1940), cemeteries, movie palaces, hospitals, donkey carts, the inside of a cordage factory, Laubach's Department store (predecessor to Pomeroy's), Bushkill Amusement Park, roller rinks, dance pavilions, roller coasters, boaters, old taxis, grist mills, general stores, swimming pools, grocery stores, bookstores, Keller's Music House, school buildings, Spanish-American War soldiers, trolley cars, a soapbox derby car, a tug-of-war (Trinity Presbyterian Church picnic), bathing beauties on the Delaware (1932), gasoline stations, the American Horse Shoe Works, high school bands, ice cream stores, a railway car barn, roustabouts arranging tents, a drum and bugle corps (American Legion Parade), a fire company running team, barber shops, Jim's Doggie Stand, a baptism in the Delaware, George F. Hellick Coffee Company trucks, a merry-go-round at Island Park, the Edison Cement Co., sleigh rides, *Daily Express* carriers, the Hotel Huntingdon barroom, the gentlemen's dining room at Seip's restaurant, the Lehigh Valley railroad passenger station (1910), a butcher shop, the trolley to Raubsville on a hill over Delaware Drive, Orr's Department Store, Woolworth's, the president's house at Lafayette.

I thought I'd spend three or four hours in the Marx Room, but I gave up after an hour. I was tired of old things. I was bored by the faces, the fake smiles. I was irritated by the useless destruction, the slaughter. I was more irritated that in five thick books of photographs there wasn't one African American, not a laborer, not a ball player, not even a porter from one of the passenger railroad cars. None building the free bridge to Phillipsburg, though more than thirty men posed on the trestles. No references to the segregation in swimming pools, movie houses, churches. Not one black customer in the stores, or on the trolley cars. Plenty of pictures of parades, American Legion or otherwise, but, amazingly, no reference to the Great Depression and unemployment and strikes and policemen and billy clubs. The left's contempt for nostalgia was driven home, with a vengeance. Two centuries of disgusting boosterism on the Forks of the Delaware.

The great mystery, for me, was, is, my fascination with the city. Its hold on me. I wasn't born there, I didn't go to school there, or work there, or, except for a few months—less than a year altogether—live there. No girlfriends, no friends. No library at thirteen—no weight lifting at fifteen. No running. I did live in Raubsville, six miles down the river, and we shopped a little—and banked—in Easton, but that was in my forties and fifties and it's not like Pittsburgh or Philadelphia or New York—or even Iowa City. I think partly it had to do with a certain time, with my age when I fully realized the place and, in this connection, seeing it whole—in time—and contemplating it as a living entity. Also it was small enough to see it whole, to realize its boundaries as if it were a mock city, a board game—yet large enough, deep enough, to be more than fully graspable, to contain the unknown, the unexpected, the uncanny. And it had alleys. And, most of all, it had hills and a river, like my original city. It even had two rivers. And it had layers.

My first neighborhood was the Hill District, in Pittsburgh. Steep hills, row houses, exotic (Yiddish) speech, small stores, cobblestones, empty lots, churches and synagogues, certain places, trees, rules, monuments, a river below. On a smaller scale, Easton resembles Pittsburgh. When I first moved there, there was a crumbling abandoned Jewish center, a kind of Y, and two synagogues down the hill. There always are two—facing off. A new building was built on the site of the center, for battered women. The synagogues have seemed to disappear. One was turned, years ago, into an African American church, the Hebrew characters intact. The other was turned, at least for a while, into a warehouse. The manager, a lovely woman, told me—it was the early 1980s—that there was a "swimming pool" in the basement. I didn't have the heart, maybe even the interest, to tell her what a mikva was. It is now, 2008, called Nature's Nook, and sells exotic animals and pet food.

It was in a two- or three-block area—I get it now—where the old Jewish neighborhood was located. As in the Hill District in Pittsburgh—on a much larger scale—the center now of black culture, the Jewish institutions transformed—the Irene Kaufman Settlement House, for example. I gave a reading there (in the Hill) two years ago in a former Yeshiva, the Hebrew writing over the door. Where the Jews of Easton eventually went I don't know. I assume to the boroughs and to College Hill. I know little of the Jewish history since I didn't actually live there, since I never had the "Jewish experience" there. Mine was mock, imaginary, metaphysical. When I climb Ferry Street, past the ugly McDonald's, past the site of the burned-out railroad station, my thighs engorged from the steep climb, I might as well be back home on Squirrel Hill Avenue or

Fallowfield Avenue, or Jane Street, in the South Side, climbing up the endless steps, or in Greenfield or the Hill itself, holy places of a few decades ago, as good as any Mexican pyramid, or Peruvian temple, I'm so benighted, obsessed.

I drove through Easton, after leaving the library, to take another look, or one more look, at the different houses I had walked through or made a down payment on or even occupied for a week or so: an incredible Victorian near the corner of Fifth and Northampton, $15,000 in 1989; an even larger one next door that had been used as a storeroom by the Easton Upholstery Co., around the corner, now painted and fenced and re-windowed, $20,000, in 1990; the enormous early-nineteenth-century mansion on Third Street, turned into a multi-unit apartment building, $30,000 "as was" in 1993. I was going to knock through walls, occupy two or three units, 2,500 square feet or so, and rent the rest out; a four-story Federal on Spring Garden Street, in perfect condition, complete with an elevator and various sitting rooms and "music rooms" in far corners, at the ridiculously high price of $110,000; the huge bathing-suit factory, off an alley in back of where the Boyd Theater had once been, I don't know how many thousands of square feet, where we planned that garden in the middle, a central courtyard, the owner offered to give me at any price but puzzled why I would live there (whose roof fell in one day—snow or rain—now another hole in the beleaguered mouth); the house, of course, on Sitgreaves Street I bought in 1984 for $10,000, which my son and I and Martin Desht worked through that summer tearing apart and building up, a laborer's house or servants' for the mansion across the alley, maybe the oldest brick house, I'm told, that's left in downtown Easton, my former wife lives in now and does her pots; and the one Diane Freund and I bought on Pine Street for $19,000 and sold ten months later for $40,000; and the two great turn-of-the-twentieth-century houses, acres of grass and trees, on College Hill that I would have been a desperate recluse in; and the isolated building on top of the hill at Sixth and Ferry, three floors of beautiful and unusual rooms just waiting for me, I bought and held onto for a week after daily visits, I had the key to. 1995. $20,000. My poor son drove down from Boston countless times, with measuring rod in hand, like Ezekiel. For this he had sat at his desk for four and a half years till three, four in the morning at Harvard's Graduate School of Design, always patient, David, never laughing at his mad father.

Sometimes, when I was in Easton maybe sitting in my tiny back-yard on Sitgreaves, I would get an urge to look at one of my "prop-erties." It could have been ten at night. A policeman followed my car one time back to my house because I had stopped too long, or was driving too slow through town. He thought I was cruising for whores and warned me about AIDS when he stopped me. There may have been forty, forty-five years between us. I was moved, excited really, by the houses. Sometimes I climbed the stairs to the front porches and stared into the windows. I was overcome with melancholy.

I found, in general, I was more interested in transformation—in conversion—than in revivification. I wanted to tear down walls, raise ceilings, move bathrooms. I leaned toward gigantism. The last thing I wanted was to refurbish and bring back, paint the right Victorian colors, add an authentic lost leg to some forlorn rooster buried in metal on some half-hidden roof. I was, after all, not a weepy nostalgic with a Book of the Rules in my hand, I was a ridic-ulous subcontractor, without wings, imagining some new creative space among the bygones, just like the unacknowledged carvers and sprayers from Manhattan and Brooklyn, tools and buckets hanging about them, just like the sawbuck dreamers with leases in their hands. First and last month's rent in advance. Which after all made me one of the new "investors" I sneered at—though I had my own rights, on many levels, and I insisted—I insist—on them, and like a tin god I hold myself apart, and tin I prefer to silver, for tin is magic. What gold ever covered a sardine, what ruby even more precious than tin!

It was the bathing-suit factory, the great wooden building (really two buildings) at Fifth and Ferry and the mini-skyscraper at Fifth and Northampton I lusted for most. David actually started drawings for Ferry Street and Bathing Suit. I thought I might take the top floor of Northampton National Bank and create a ten- or fifteen-room apartment, even if I didn't have the books and poems to fill them with. Maybe a swimming pool up there, made of polished local cement. Maybe a soundproof music room, a handball court, an indoor garden. I just needed a tin bucket to reach down to the bank below for some of the mazuma. How do you spell it?

I only lived in my house on Sitgreaves in spells. I was mostly in Iowa City, central Pennsylvania, or New York. I owned a house in Iowa and rented an apartment—26 Vandam—in Soho, at an insanely low price. Sitgreaves I rented out from time to time, from year to year, but mostly for security, not for income. I was robbed there twice, when the house was empty. One of my tenants was a city planner, Tom Jones, who lived by mystery, innuendo, and conspiracy. He paid me practically nothing, but he always paid on time. Business was business. He had a party one night in the tiny backyard where he had constructed a kind of stove out of soft brick, and cooked sausages, wieners, hamburgers, and veggies on the grill. I came, as invited—I was staying someplace else in town—but there were only four or five men there, which spelt utter boredom to me.

I left and came back with my friend Guido, an Italian painter and preservationist from Genoa who worked for Karl Stirner and stayed in his building—and a beautiful young ballet dancer who had a dance studio on the first floor of the building. Guido spoke not one word of English. He talked to Karl in broken German and to me in a Genovese dialect that I partly understood. (I actually preferred the German, for Karl's—and Guido's—southern German was a lot like Yiddish.) Guido was mad for the dancer and she, a little demure and flirtatious, loved it. The men in the backyard completely changed when the dancer arrived. It was now dog eat dog, forget bonding. There was an immense, full, low-lying moon and I walked through the "close" (grocer's alley) to the front of the house to appreciate it. I was accompanied by one of the guests, Chris Comacho, angry, smiling, wound very tight, who was putting together a mansion on College Hill. When a thin young man walking by us in the alley stopped to ask us for money—his story was he had been recently released from jail and was sleeping on the river—Chris cursed and threatened him. I remember I gave him a twenty-dollar bill and that when we returned to the backyard all the men started to burn money—Washington, Lincoln, Hamilton—to show . . . what? their generosity? their indifference? their contempt? their wildness? Or was it only for the dancer? Though Guido didn't waste his gelt, his lira. Not him. They did it with a flourish, with a bow almost, one at a time holding their disgusting lucre up to the moon for a few seconds before they put it in the fire. At which point I gently guided the dancer through the close and up the open garage next door to her house on the next street over. It was the kind of garage that housed maybe twenty cars, and there was an ancient rusted Amoco gas pump in front. The Valentine's Day Massacre occurred in just such a garage. We were together for maybe three months.

She ate large steaks and talked about her muscles like a football player. When Jones went on to greener pastures, she became my tenant and, like Jonesy, she always paid the pittance on time. Her name was Christine.

Binney and Smith were the original owners of Crayola and the factory was on Bushkill Creek, in the city, but they later moved out to Forks Township and the firm, as I understand it, is now owned by Hallmark, though McDonald's could buy it up, or General Electric or Peiping Toys, and it wouldn't change.

In 1995 a corporation was formed, a kind of trust, that bought up a huge corner of Centre Square in the very heart of Easton, consisting of five buildings, in order to create what is called the Crayola Factory, a slight misnomer since it is not a factory where crayolas or anything else is produced but a kind of museum and a kind of Disneyland where crayolas—chalk, colored pencils, markers of all kinds—are celebrated, and hundreds of people pay good money to tour the "factory" and use crayons, clay, and related objects in a variety of ways in specially designed rooms, and look at movies, TV screens, photographs, and legends, tacked or posted against walls that detail the heroic story of the origin, rise, and expansion of Crayola, the many-colored dream, not to be cynical, great-grand-moms with scissors, daddies finger painting, babies eating clay, the canal museum on the third and fourth floors, volunteers explaining the locks, families posing for shots in front of the six-foot smiling crayon wearing oversized Mickey Mouse shoes and gloves.

What's to say about Crayola? Mr. Binney and Mr. Smith were from Peekskill, New York, and founded their firm in 1885. Originally they made red paint for barns and carbon black for car tires. Alice Binney, wife of Edwin (the founder), coined the word "cray-ola" in 1903. It comes from the French "craie" (chalk) and "ola" for oily or oleaginous. Hallmark Inc., of Kansas City, Missouri, bought Crayola in 1984. They are the "world's leader in social expression." In 1996 Mister Rogers molded the 100 billionth crayon. The building, erected in 1996, is actually not called the Crayola Factory, it is called Two Rivers Landing. The rivers are the Lehigh and the Delaware, my river, the Delaware.

The trust, the corporation, that threaded together the various businesses and organizations that were the foundation of Two Rivers Landing was—as I understand it—the Easton Economic Development Corporation, certainly a brainchild of urban renewal. It, they, consisted of the city of Easton, Binney and Smith, the Canal Museum (formerly on 611 South), the National Park Service, the State of Pennsylvania, and the Delaware Lehigh Visitor's Center. The architectural firm they chose to do the design was Schwartz Silver, a Boston firm where David—my son—was employed, and, an absolutely amazing coincidence, he and Bob Miklos, a fellow architect at Schwartz Silver, did the drawings and made many visits to Easton to see the job through. David was nine years old when we moved to the Easton area and lived there essentially till his mother and I left, one to New York, one to Iowa City. We sold the Raubsville house in the early 1980s, at which point David moved to Cambridge—and Boston. He and Bob Miklos stayed at a B & B on College Hill when they were in Easton and the three of us—when I was in town—ate Italian food and talked space, material, and contractors. I remember David had a hard time securing the nineteenth-century industrial windows he wanted from a firm in North Carolina; the contractor, an Eastonian, couldn't quite understand that the *preferred* windows were as cheap or cheaper; he thought he would save money by buying inferior and less appropriate windows, so for a century or two the total design will be less relevant, less interesting. But what the hell!

The buildings that were replaced were the Easton Press and Bindery, some warehouses, and Orr's Department Store. The eight-story building next door to Two Rivers is the Alpha Building, original home of Alpha Cement. There is a "Crayola Store" on the ground floor facing the square where they sell pencils, markers, calculators, toy tools, games, chalk, paper, putty, glue, aprons, piggy banks, coffee cups, T-shirts, plush dolls, shirts, slippers, sweatshirts, hats, sketchbooks, and mess-free paint. Also, lying on its side, the world's largest crayon—purple. There is a little McDonald's inside the main building where you can refresh yourself with high-fructose corn syrup. I like the Canal Museum best—toy boats, waterways, locks, aqueducts, steep slopes, inclined planes, coal chutes, lock-tenders' houses, and toll collectors. In miniature.

The Alpha Building's main entrance is on South Third. It houses City Hall now, in addition to the Crayola Store. The stretch of South Third from the Alpha Building to the railroad bridge, where Route 611 starts its descent south along the west side of the Delaware, is the most shameful stretch in the city of Easton. It's the outer boundary of the once densely occupied Lebanese community, houses, yards, alleys, stores, offices, a city within a city, ripped up and thrown away by the urban planners, for nothing, for a little shitty gold. Now there is a huge parking garage that has replaced the Drake Building, a turn-of-the-century eight-story iron front, the only one of its kind in the area. It also houses the Easton Police Department and the Transit Authority. Across Ferry Street is the Max Center—insurance, investments, trusts; a very ugly Perkins restaurant, now, in 2008, empty and abandoned; a multiplex movie house; half the time for sale and a very ugly motel as of this writing, a Quality Inn; and across Larry Holmes Drive (Holmes, the "Easton Assassin"), a rather dilapidated McDonald's, waiting to be bulldozed. Behind the theater (now the Marquis) and Perkins is a huge swath of cement where cars occasionally park. This is a major downtown area, the center of a one-time important ethnic community that formed the population understructure of the downtown. What is most horrible is that Perkins, a study in abominable food, ugly rugs, and wasted space, replaced the one or two small Middle Eastern restaurants with their exquisite tastes and smells—E. E. Cummings called it somewhere "unfeeling." The urban planners and architects, in their wisdom, decided to suburbanize these buildings by planting grass between the sidewalks and the entrances, one of the new stupidities of the 1950s and '60s.

There is a rather large Victorian on Sixth Street, up the hill on the way to the lawyers' offices surrounding the lonely county office complex. It sold for a dollar, sometime in the mid-1970s; that is, it was given away with the pledge that the new owners would restore it and paint it and plaque it. I think I would rather tear it down than that. Nor do I have any fond hope that the forges and silk mills will come back. Nor do I want to hear a lost cello sobbing away in an ancient paradise. Which wasn't so very ancient and wasn't so much of a paradise really at all. I hoped for a new idea. I still do. What they should have done was build the community college (Northampton County Community College) in the vacated downtown buildings instead of in the meadows outside of Bethlehem, Pennsylvania. They could have occupied the empty hotels, department stores, and office buildings, and even nearby factories. A "scattered" college, the way NYU is in New York. And, if necessary, they could have built a few new buildings. Imagine the Drake Building or the Northampton Bank Building full of offices and classrooms. Imagine Third Street after the disaster, with, say, a ten-story stone and glass building stretching from Larry Holmes Drive to Ferry Street, housing laboratories, classrooms, theaters, restaurants, stores, libraries, gyms, offices, art galleries, swimming pools. Or a series of buildings—and no grass.

This is, of course, beyond the imagination of planners, builders, politicians, architects, bankers, lawyers, and bagmen that create our seats of learning. They want large campuses, preferably covered in trees, red brick, and latterly, cement buildings with dedicated walkways between, immense parking lots, and an even immenser stadium. Maybe a statue. Maybe a fountain to commemorate a *new tradition*. And grass. Grass is what you need for knowledge. Grass is the stuff of wisdom. Imagine the gall of the Sorbonne.

Aside from the fact that Lafayette College on the educated hill, Lafayette College, the great center of learning that has grossly ignored that part of the city which is downwind from their serious noses, might not like it.

Or something else, if not a college. If it must be art, then let the college and the city go into partnership and buy up some factories, turn them into studios, and rent them for next to nothing or *give* them away—don't make money on hardworking artists. Patrons don't rent. Realtors do! You like art? Pay for it! Though now it seems to be restaurants, and there are several restaurant rows developing and customers come from a distance. Antiques never took off, nor Russian Jews. Flowers—what about flowers? Or hardware? Hardware Row. Thousands of screws.

On the north side of the square is a very large statue commemorating the Civil War. Hundreds of such statues in hundreds of squares. It's like a stacked wedding cake, crossed swords, a bugle boy on top, the names of the battles, the names of the (Union) notables, carved into the stone, a sailor with spy glasses, a soldier with a sword, another with a musket, another with a cannon stick.

Lincoln, Grant, Mead, Hancock, Porter, Farragut. Shiloh, Look-out Mountain, New Orleans, Antietam, Fredericksburg, Chancel-lorsville, Wilderness, Gettysburg. Liberty and Union / Now and Forever / One and Inseparable are in large caps. On the side facing Third Street North, about ten feet up, are a few famous lines from Horace embedded in the limestone: *Dulce et decorum est pro patria mori* (it is good and proper to die for one's country), immortalized in our time by Wilfred Owen's World War I poem "Dulce Et Decorum Est." The lines are fairly well known by anyone who takes 101 ("My friend, you would not tell with such high zest / To children ardent for some desperate glory, / The old Lie: Dulce et decorum est / Pro patria mori"). Maybe it's taught now in the seventh grade. In 1970 or so there was an antiwar rally in front of the monument, on the side where Horace is incised, and not one beard or short skirt there caught the irony. That is why we are going to war with China. Stupidity and death are inevitable.

The city is my mother—my reclining mother—or my Aunt Bess. She is my sixty-year-old mother and I am thirty-six, or maybe she is ninety-three, lying in bed and dying, and I am piecing together her life. I always expected things from her that she thought were unreasonable, and she the same from me, though what we expected from each other, those things had no logical connection with one another. I am never going to resolve it in this life and I don't know if she resolved any of it in her life. Maybe when I say the city is my mother I am thinking of something archetypal and not that real Ida whose life—as she saw it—was a ruin, who was lost and frightened, who was deeply depressed, who had moments, but only moments, of wildness and joy, who gave reluctantly, who was terrified of dogs, who was born in Bialystok, who lived the lie, whose secret was guarded by the merciless wolf that kept watch over her day and night. My Aunt Bess was a little different, we were more honest with each other, more frank, less anxious. But I wasn't her son and she wasn't my mother.

The city could never be my father, and never was. The idea is absurd. Not that the other one isn't. It's the beginning of an insane metaphor, nor could I prove it, even if my name were Euclid. Nonetheless it's true. Almost always, when I drive or walk past the Covenant of Peace on the steep hill in Easton that is South Sixth Street, I remember that the abandoned synagogue was first a warehouse before it was an exotic pet store and I remember the "swimming pool" in the basement. Ida met her lifelong friend Pauline in a mikva, the day before each of their weddings, when they both were twenty. For seventy years, they talked almost every day. Pauline's husband, Hymie, was a greenhorn and sold herring from a barrel, which he wrapped, all dripping with brine, in old newspapers. Later he owned a countrywide chain of supermarkets and a dozen shopping centers. Ida never recovered from the death of her daughter, Sylvia, who died when she was nine. But it was Ida's loss—no one was permitted to share it. Nor even to mention Sylvia's name.

For a moment or so, even for a day, the two cities—Easton and Pittsburgh—become fused, or maybe blurred. With each other. One cobblestone street, one river, one hill, becomes another. Or one memory. The P&LE railroad station on the Monongahela River was changed into a four-star restaurant. Or at least three stars. Whereas Easton's railroad station, the one above McDonald's, didn't have such luck. The restaurant—the former depot—burned down just as it was about to open. A gas leak, or a cigarette. Pittsburgh is a City of Asylum, a sanctuary for persecuted writers from around the world, and I am reading poems here, September 2008, to music—to jazz—at what is going to be a large gathering on the North Side.

I am staying at the Hampton Inn and Suites directly across from the Heinz Historical Museum, lodged in a huge seven-story former icehouse. Everything lays itself out for me, presents itself when it's needed, a little eerie but true—and so it is this weekend. On the first floor of the museum there is a 1937 stainless-steel Ford, a red-and-cream-colored trolley car circa 1946, a fire engine circa 1919, a Conestoga wagon from 1784, and a Bantam Jeep from 1940, prototype to the World War II Jeeps made by Ford and—earlier—Willys Overland in nearby Butler, Pennsylvania. There are glass exhibits, old Heinz ads, statues of Indians, an in-depth history of the mining disaster of 1907, photographs of immigrants packed by the hundreds into ships, a history of sports in Pittsburgh, including baseball, hockey, football, harness racing, and fox hunting, with such heroes as Arnold Palmer, Roberto Clemente, Billy Conn, Josh Gibson, Satchel Paige, Terry Bradshaw, Marshall Goldberg, Willie Stargel, Honus Wagner, and Tony Dorset. There seems to be a dispute about what caused the mine disaster. The workers—mostly Italians and Hungarians—complained for years about unsafe conditions, but the owners blamed it on the bad working habits of the immigrants. Almost seven hundred died, in two explosions. There was nothing (in the museum) about the Homestead massacre (called a strike) in which Frick and Carnegie set loose the Pinkertons, nothing I could find, but there was a Heinz family tree. Lots of ketchup. My favorite item—on the wall of the restaurant—was a large photograph of Fifth Avenue, the main downtown street in, I think, 1940 or '42. It is dense with street cars, streamlined automobiles, buses, stores, pedestrians—ten abreast—on both sidewalks—theaters, tearooms, banks, bowling alleys, Five & Dimes, cobblestone streets—everyone well dressed, hats, scarves, neckties, umbrellas, heels, overcoats. It's November, or March. The nostalgic cover of a box of chocolates.

When I came back from the army, I walked over the bridge from the railroad station to Second Avenue and on the way threw my barracks bag into the water. The Pennsylvania railroad station where I pulled heavy wagons and loaded boxcars eight hours a day in the sulphur is now an apartment building. In both cases, I came home at one in the morning, but in neither was there an old nurse nor a dog to welcome me back. The cork factory on the strip, Pittsburgh's *Les Halles*, has been put to a higher use, as the icehouse was. I am contented in all cases and happy with everything. It sounds like "not guilty on all charges." Corruption is our only hope, said Brecht. Too good not to be repeated a third time. I just noticed yesterday that, in Easton, the Children of Abraham's great upper windows were bricked in. Less space for God. The important question is that when there are clashing memories, who are the police? Or *who* the police are, or *what?* This memory hangs in a spirit of inquietude, like a dark cloud, like that sulphur we used to inhale.

We gather by the Delaware River, all thirty thousand of us, waiting for the cloud to lift. My uncles looked more like Mongolians than Ukrainians. The round head, the skin at the eyes, the small bodies. When they left one pasture for another, they broke their tents and swept the ground, like the Iroquois, so there shouldn't be any excessive attachments, no hard feelings. Certainly one bowlegged milk-drinker from Central Asia remembered a certain hill, a stone well in the wild. If he were blind his memory would survive in his fingers. One of the virtues of a seventeenth-century cello, or a seventeenth-century tune, is that it permits us—even encourages us—to remember, to exercise memory. A constant, a permanent, destruction prevents that from happening. We have never really tried wiping out the past altogether, although the Albanian and Romanian monsters in the 1960s and '70s thought about it. We should thus keep old radios and old cities for their therapeutic value. No sentimental journey there.

There was a room full of people at a certain college in Illinois attending a poetry reading and no one there, except two aliens from some absurd East Coast pocket, knew what a "stoop" was. So he who read his poem—me, in this case—failed somewhat to connect. To his immense surprise. "But they didn't have those things there"; or—collaterally—"that was before I was born." We are mourners all, following the wagon on foot, as W. C. W. in "Tract" insisted. Those of us who are true mourners weep over what is not even past, we are so knowledgeable. But none of us are professionals, for our tears would then come from a flask. It is what a mother might feel holding her newborn. He will soon—too soon—be old and sick, the newborn. It is the melancholy attached to the new. A stove, say. Do we eat the past, the way a sexton beetle does? Does it refresh and renew us? I remember the apartments in the East Village we occupied in the late 1960s. How we created a kind of life there, nor did we worry about the temporary for we were always a step ahead of the sheriff, we beetles. The worst, the very worst is to *live* in the past. The very best is to wear a very old—black—suit and to go forth whistling, learning a language, memorizing verbs. At eighty. Eighty-three.

The only kind of home I could have been happy in in Easton was a factory, but I loved my house in Raubsville, on the river. I never had a home I had any affection for in Pittsburgh, though I did love to imagine living in a settlement under a bridge somewhere, among the Sumerians. We lived that way in Pittsburgh, in settlements, and each settlement had its own language, and its own soup. The language of the Hill was Yiddish, and its soup was knedel. Warhol was a Sumerian. "Home" is a terrifying, suggestive, hurtful, festive, engaging, overheated, drafty word. Home is good. Even wasps have homes. Bears have homes. But *heimat* is not the same. Heidegger's *heimat*. Hitler's. A drawerful of lederhosen. *Mit* suspenders. I wrote "The Expulsion" (*see end of essay*) in 1982, which drew its sustenance from Masaccio's amazing painting in the church of the Carmine, in Firenze. Adam and Eve, their mouths open in pain and regret, their hands covering their genitals, are oddly transformed into my father and me sitting on the steps (the stoop) of a row house, maybe the one we lived in when I was born, maybe one of the dozens I walked by and peered into on my long searches. We have been expelled—in the poem—from a dear early place, him too, not just me, for he talks about (and he talked about) his own house as a boy, a giant garden full of peppers and radishes and cucumbers that his sister Jennie made into pickles. That house I saw once on a Sunday excursion. It was in the Hill—I forget the street—an African American district by the 1940s, Fifth Avenue High School, the Irene Kaufman Settlement House, the Crawford Grille, warehouses, whorehouses—boarded up, unboarded up, old, new. His father, my grandfather, owned a small stogie factory and had eight or nine children, so it was a large comfortable house, say, in 1910, but certainly not when we went there. We sat on the marble steps for a second or two, but he was anxious to get away. He was always running. Nor did he have much to say. We did one of two things on our Sunday outings. We either visited "model homes" in the new suburbs and walked through rooms and walked off feet and yards, or we went to Goldstein's Restaurant for a roast beef sandwich and conversations about clothing and war. When it was warmer we went occasionally to a Pirates game at Forbes Field. The poem is a poem of mourning, a lament for what disappeared, an elegy for my father, an evocation of the rupture. Weirdly it is I—not he—who misses the row house and the garden. What did he miss, I wonder? What did he long for? My guess is it was the farm in Ruzhyn north of Kiev, in the Pale of Jewish settlement. His whole life he longed for the country and loved his brother George's farm in Mars, Pennsylvania; but his wife, my mother, was terrified of anything that crawled or crept or sprang or itched or barked or bellowed. So he wore suits. And stayed in the city.

The mayfly weeps, for the time five minutes ago—in her youth—when she had only one place to excrete; now she has four and a half. And tubs to match. The lizard who lives forever watched Charlemagne, a brief thousand years ago, shovel it in with his fingers. Einstein Bagels has the photo of an ancient delivery truck and country boys in overalls standing in front of a bagel store advertising latte in the window. Pure bullshit. Where is the very least amount of estrangement—in playing handball? Eating a pizza? Making love? Where is the race that was never disenchanted, that had no yearning? Are these the lotus-eaters? Doesn't leather crack, doesn't the eye soon enough show wrinkles? Odysseus is certainly not the first nostalgic, though he has become the mythical one. Eyes had certainly wrung them dry over old trees, old caves, and dead marsh grass long before bronze was created, for human beings just cling, and not only human beings, but Odysseus, he wept the best, and the longest. Of all the women he met along the way, the one who was a *person* was the most moving, including his own Athena. That Nausicaa I have loved for sixty or more years, as much for her wisdom and courage as for her beauty, and have come, over the years, to admire her more and more. Certainly she married, and had children, and grandchildren. I've done the math more than a few times, and the way I figure she was seventeen or eighteen and Odysseus forty. Thirty-nine or forty. Ten years at Troy and ten years coming back. When Odysseus was seventy-five, Nausicaa would be fifty-four. That would make it thirty-five years or so since she last saw Odysseus and reminded him—from the shadows—that she was the one who saved his life and urged him not to forget her. His skin would be pure leather and his handful of hair snow-white, if he were still alive, if he still had hair; and she would still be tall and beautiful, her hair held together by a precious clasp, maybe silver, with a legend out of Homer, maybe a brilliant ruby. I can't help it. She has loved her husband these many years but has found a place—a shelf?—for Odysseus, and wise as she always has been, she doesn't call him fool. Waiting, as they often do, women don't always get their heart's desire, whatever the theory is about choices and decision-making. As for Odysseus, though he was mad for home, you wonder how—in what manner—he remembered that lovely girl in Phaeacia who was not afraid of the salt-caked swimmer Athena led her to. Certainly it was her rare courage he admired; certainly her strong presence. I suspect that kind of presence, that wisdom, combined as it was with her grace and loveliness, made a deep impression on him. It's implicit in the epic, it seems to me, that she was somehow his equal, in speech, in understanding, in forthrightness, and this is what he thought about in his distant small kingdom, as he collected from time to time the memories of his brief visit in her father's house, in her mother's, for there is no doubt about the power of women in that society.

This adds a complication to the past, for it was two pasts he was involved in, two worlds to recollect, one piled on top of the other, two nostalgias, one of them Ithaca. He would not set forth again, of course, he would never return. He probably stayed away from salt water the rest of his life. He was no ridiculous character, out of Tennyson, Ulysses by name, who would sail again, "to seek, to

strive, to find, and not yield," a type of the stubborn greedy Eng-
lishman. A thief of Empire. He may even have had consolation—
joy—as well as melancholy, something to allay his grief. Though
I wonder if an Odysseus allows too much grief to enter, he was
so wily, and practical. There were probably other heroes, of other
petty cultures, who hung on to a piece of wood in some raging sea
or other, but none of them had such a poet to sing of their journey,
such a narrator.

Cavafy's "Ithaka" (*see end of essay for text*) was written in 1911,
when he was forty-eight years old. Given his time, his culture,
his character—his subject—he writes it from the viewpoint of a
much older man—as we would see it—a man who can look back
upon a "lifetime" of adventure, joy, loss, and flirtation with the
perilous both in his sexual choices and his verse. And though he
writes about Odysseus I would say in a new way, he is at all times
writing about himself, and the confrontation with the world on
Odysseus's return to Ithaka becomes, in Cavafy's poem, a search
for knowledge, and understanding. In both cases Cavafy insists
that Odysseus (read Cavafy) will not meet horror on the way,
neither "wild Poseidon" nor the Laistrygonians, if his "thought
stays exalted," "if a rare emotion touches (his) spirit and body."
For Odysseus it's adventure, for Cavafy it's knowledge, although
it is both for the both of them, both adventure *and* knowledge,
for one contains or reveals the other. The poem is touching in its
concentration on Ithaca. "Ithaka gave you the beautiful journey,"
says Cavafy. "Without her you would not have set out on your
way." "And if you find her poor, Ithaka (at least) did not betray
you." The nostalgia here is more temporal than it is spatial. It is
the looking back at a lifetime of adventure, physical, intellectual—
spiritual—and though it is rocky Ithaka that is the *place*, that is only

an accident. Ithaka is merely the mother, that which "gave (him) the beautiful journey."

But it is Alexandria that is Cavafy's city, his Ithaca, a place he described in one poem, "Days of 1896," as "prudish and stupid," a small place that lacked freedom, and he lived there in the old Greek quarter in a second-floor apartment first with his mother, then with his brother Paul, and, during his last twenty-five years, alone. The building housed a church, a hospital, and, on the ground floor, a brothel. Alexandria was a burden to him but it was his place of memory, his native country, his home, and it became the *locus*, the mythical city, of his poetry. There is a dual attitude to Alexandria—it is, on the one hand, a place where "the mind moulders," where the years are wasted; and, on the other hand, it is the very center of the great Hellenistic world, stretching over time and space, for hundreds of miles, and for centuries. Odysseus's village of course was nothing like it, and his *nostos* was radically different from Cavafy's—in spite of the poem. The Odysseus that Homer created was larger than life, too tremendous to be contained in the Ithaka he returned to, not counting the suffering, and boredom, that would follow. He would have to encounter at the gate a gang of stupid petty thugs trying to bed down his wife and a Penelope who kept them at bay—a pack of hungry dogs—through the modest brilliance of her strokes and counterstrokes. Filling and emptying her glass of water. Odysseus had to be shocked and embarrassed when he took his first walk after his secret landing. Maybe he felt cheated. I sometimes feel just a little like that when I come back to my earlier city, or my later, may I not be judged too harshly.

Everything is grist for the mill, and everything *becomes* grist for the mill if you wait long enough. My God, people are paying good money now for sectional sofas and blond tables—what they used to make fun of. I'm interested in what the age is when the pain sets in. Odysseus was thirty or so when he began his journey back. Proust was older. One place is reachable but another isn't. I was under eight when I had my first attack. I was in the basement of 1822 Fallowfield Avenue (in Beechview) searching through an old bundle of newspapers when I saw a two- or three-year-old comic strip—*Tim Tyler's Luck*—and started to cry. It starred Fang, a black panther, and Spud, his friend and master. It may be I was just discovering stiff and brown newspaper and realizing the passage of time. The passage of time certainly *is* the most painful moving tender bitter thing we know. It is either matched by or coterminous with, or perhaps identical with, the end of this universe in the sense that the end of one's own existence foretells or is the model for all of existence. Yet thirty—or forty—may be a keener age for this than seventy or eighty. Though gender matters, and culture, and individual sensibility. I think I am less sensitive to it at eighty-three than I was at fifty-three—or sixty-three. Even as I tell myself that it doesn't make sense. I would not be awestruck, at this point, walking through a street in Ancient Rome in 43 B.C.E. or standing on a bridge in Pittsburgh in 1919 eating a banana. *Tout égal.* Nor would I be shocked speaking another language or being a woman. I am about to be moved by a computer that fits under the soft skin of my left armpit and that turns on when I blink twice rapidly. I am about to pity the saliva that comes from my horse's mouth when I insert the bit, for I am a coachman in Lvov and I speak six languages. *Tout égal.* I take my place with the twelve-year-olds and sit there patiently amidst their impatience. I am relieved of loss—I am almost ready to live for others.

THE EXPULSION

I'm working like a dog here, testing my memory,
my mouth is slightly open, my eyes are closed,
my hand is lying under the satin pillow.
My subject is loss, the painter is Masaccio,
the church is the Church of the Carmine, the narrow panel
is on the southwest wall, I make a mouth
like Adam, I make a mouth like Eve, I make
a sword like the angel's. Or Schubert; I hear him howling
too, there is a touch of the Orient
throughout the great C Major. I'm thinking again
of poor Jim Wright and the sheet of tissue paper
he sent me. Lament, lament, for the underlayer
of wallpaper, circa 1935.
Lament for the Cretans, how did they disappear?
Lament for Hannibal. I'm standing again
behind some wires, there are some guns, my hand
is drawing in the eyes, I'm making the stripes,
I'm lying alone with water falling down
the left side of my face. That was our painting.
We stood in line to see it, we loved the cry
that came from Eve's black mouth, we loved the grief
of her slanted eyes, we loved poor Adam's face
half buried in his hands, we loved the light
on the shoulder and thighs, we loved the shadows, we loved
the perfect sense of distance. Lament, lament,
for my sister. It took ten years for the flesh to go,
she would be twenty then, she would be sixty
in 1984. Lament for my father,
he died in Florida, he died from fear, apologizing
to everyone around him. I walked through three feet
of snow to buy a suit; it took a day
to get to the airport. Lament, lament. He had
thirty-eight suits, and a bronze coffin; he lay
with his upper body showing, a foot of carpet.
He came to America in 1905, huge wolves
snapped at the horse's legs, the snow was on the ground

until the end of April. The angel is red,
her finger is pointing, she floats above the gate,
her face is cruel, she isn't like the angels
of Blake, or Plato, she is an angry mother,
her wings are firm. Lament, lament, my father
and I are leaving Paradise, an angel
is shouting, my hand is on my mouth, my father
is on the edge of his bed, he uses a knife
for a shoe horn, he is in Pittsburgh, the sky is black,
the air is filthy, he bends half over to squeeze
his foot into his shoe, his eyes are closed,
he's moaning. I miss our paradise, the pool
of water, the flowers. Our lives are merging, our shoes
are not that different. The angel is rushing by,
her lips are curled, there is a coldness, even
a madness to her, Adam and Eve are roaring,
the whole thing takes a minute, a few seconds,
and we are left on somebody's doorstep, one of
my favorites, three or four marble steps and a simple
crumbling brick—it could be Baltimore,
it could be Pittsburgh, the North Side or the Hill.
Inside I know there is a hall to the left
and a living room to the right; no one has modernized
it yet, there are two plum trees in the back
and a narrow garden, cucumbers and tomatoes.
We talk about Russia, we talk abut the garden,
we talk about Truman, and Reagan. Our hands are rubbing
the dusty marble, we sit for an hour. "It is
a crazy life," I say, "after all the model
homes we looked at, I come back to the old
row house, I do it over and over." "My house"—
he means his father's—"had a giant garden
and we had peppers and radishes; my sister
Jenny made the pickles." We start to drift
at 5 o'clock in the evening, the cars from downtown
are starting to poison us. It is a paradise
of two, maybe, two at the most, the name

on the mailbox I can't remember, the garden
is full of glass, there is a jazzy door
on the next house over, and louvered windows. It is
a paradise, I'm sure of it. I kiss
him good-bye, I hold him, almost like the kiss
in 1969, in Philadelphia,
the last time I saw him, in the Russian manner,
his mouth against my mouth, his arms around me—
we could do that once before he died—
the huge planes barely lifting off the ground,
the families weeping beside us, the way they do,
the children waving good-bye, the lovers smiling,
the way they do, all our loss, everything
we know of loneliness there, their minds already
fixed on the pain, their hands already hanging,
under the shining windows, near the yellow tiles,
the secret rooms, the long and brutal corridor
down which we sometimes shuffle, and sometimes run.

(FROM *PARADISE POEMS*, RANDOM HOUSE, 1982)

ITHAKA

As you set out on the journey to Ithaka,
wish that the way be long,
full of adventures, full of knowledge.
Don't be afraid of Laistrygonians, the Cyclops,
angry Poseidon, you'll never find them on our way
if your thought stays exalted, if a rare
emotion touches your spirit and body.
You won't meet the Laistrygonians
and the Cyclops and wild Poseidon,
if you don't bear them along in your soul,
if your soul doesn't raise them before you.
Wish that the way be long.
May there be many summer mornings
when with such pleasure, such joy
you enter ports seen for the first time;

may you stop in Phoenician emporia
to buy fine merchandise,
mother-of-pearl and coral, amber and ebony,
and every kind of sensual perfume,
buy abundant sensual perfumes, as many as you can.
Travel to many Egyptian cities
to learn and learn from their scholars.

Always keep Ithaka in your mind.
Arriving there is your destination.
But don't hurry the journey at all.
Better if it lasts many years,
and you moor on the island when you are old,
rich with all you have gained along the way,
not expecting Ithaka to make you rich.

Ithaka gave you the beautiful journey.
Without her you would not have set out on your way.
She has no more to give you.

And if you find her poor, Ithaka did not betray you.
With all your wisdom, all your experience,
you understand by now what Ithakas mean.

(FROM *THE COLLECTED POEMS OF* C. P. *CAVAFY,*
TRANS. ALIKI BARNSTONE, NORTON, 2006)

A Guest at
the World's Table

I. Dog

IN THE EARLY 1930S WE MOVED from the old Jewish quarter in Pittsburgh, the Hill District, an absolute replica, with its cobblestone streets, tiny shops, and synagogues, of some Eastern European corner, to a goyishe suburb of neat ugly houses and a woods full of black locusts and half-grown maples in a ridiculous attempt at partial assimilation. We had a new car every other year, two peach trees, and a kitchenette, of which my mother was very proud. I was the only Jew in the local public school and I got beat up more or less daily, or at least insulted and ridiculed.

My father, the youngest of nine, was born in a shtetl maybe fifty miles north of Kiev, and since he came to America in 1905 at the age of eight, he had no accent and bought completely into the American myth of cleanliness and equality. He adored animals but since my mother, a traditionalist, was terrified of anything that crawled, flew, barked, or roared, we kept no animals; though for a short while she relented and we had a silly nervous little canary named Dicky.

My father and I were taking a walk one evening—I remember our street was called Fallowfield Avenue—when we came across a woman walking her dog, the poor thing proud, erect, its mouth open, its tail high, alert for anything. My father fell all over the beast, petting him (her), roughing him up, half-dancing with him, almost kissing him. The dog was overwhelmed with pleasure and returned the favors. It was a love match made in dog-heaven. The mistress, the owner, for her part was also pleased that someone would love her dog that much, and stopped to take out a cigarette, which she would soon redden with her delicate lips. My father anyhow was in his late thirties at the time, a fine suit, a moustache, certainly a beautiful fedora, as handsome as they came. "He loves people," she said, "unless they're Jews. He can't stand Jews."

My father probably said nothing. I listened, and absorbed. Father Coughlin was already wound up and Hitler, in some faraway land, was making good headway. We moved away three or four years later, partly because my sister had died, age nine, and partly to rejoin, to de-assimilate. But whatever the meanness and stupidity was of that vile lady, her dog, maybe a spitz-Eskimo, maybe an Airedale, favorite dogs of the time, had more sense and, in spite of her, kissed to death and loved forever one dear Jew, who walked away holding tightly the hand of his young son.

II. Saturday Night

Saturday night as a boy, when I think back on it, was not always a time of gloom and dread, strange words I know, but it had a little joy to it—something I don't normally confess to the shrink I happen to be talking to or the loving partner full of sympathy for my grief and melancholy that century ago, caught in the clutches of my mother's deep depression, wandering helpless into her bedroom where she lay moaning on her bed or into the small living room where she sat

and I remember that I had "perfect pitch," and how, with his help, I was going to move with musical speed into crowd-pleasing performances, in spite of my late start.

We may have moved already into the contract phase, some money may have changed hands, even it may have been hinted that a used violin could possibly be found among his extended family of hungry friends, when my father suddenly appeared, earlier than usual, his look curious and suspicious, the whole medieval revel punctured at once by his totally practical, logical, demanding mien. Forget contract, used violin, perfect pitch, cold spaghetti. We had to start all over, and oh did I have sympathy for the three graces and their vivid explanations, how they stumbled over each other, and oh did I have pity for that ruined musician and his miserable plight, he who had almost succeeded. "No son of mine will ever be a musician," is what my outraged father said. He who had contempt for long hair, shiny uncreased pants, and moth-eaten violin cases. Sometimes when I tell the story, I have him throwing Orpheus down the front steps, but I'm sure he just "encouraged" him a little. And it was Saturday night, and a long, a very long, walk to the streetcar, empty cobblestone streets to go down, hills to climb. I'm sure he had some other resources, a genius here and there with perfect pitch, and of course he had the orchestra pit of the Stanley Theatre, now Heinz Hall, home of the Pittsburgh Symphony Orchestra; or the Casino, the best burlesque house in a hundred miles, where I spent many an early afternoon doing my geometry and such—torn down now for a small parking lot, the ghost of some Rose or Flo weeping for the loss.

My father meant more than music though, didn't he? It was chaos, laziness, dirt, poverty, that terrified him. It was that Europe he came from, especially the wild southern part, home of the actors and drifters, the gypsies—Romanians and Hungarians all. Though there was certainly something of the philistine there. And the weird bourgeois cult of hard work and punctuality. All of which he learned without even studying.

I guess I betrayed him, living my life on the loose for so many years, eating beans, serving the other master. Maybe I always felt I owed a little to that violinist, I'm sure a Galizianer or a Romanian, both of whose grandfathers played at country weddings. Maybe it was my stubbornness all along; maybe my perfect pitch.

MOTHER'S DAY

I

I HAVEN'T, to any significant degree, written about my political—
my agitated—activities over the years; nor have I tried to understand
what it was that motivated my action. It is not enough to say that I
was outraged by injustice, stupidity, complacency, lying, indiffer-
ence, and deception. I had to redress wrongs. What I saw as wrongs.
I had to sit on the seesaw and bring it to a level. But my nature
was—is—part comedic, part idealistic, colored in irony, smeared
with mockery and sarcasm. Nor does it matter that so was Isaiah's;
and I rant somewhat, and those that love me get irritated and bored
by my ranting. The fact that I mix up my ranting with the singing
of popular songs from the times of our earlier wars doesn't help a
bit. Nor, if I let myself go, do I miss one slur, one cut, one nuance,
from a song eighty-five years old, and still resonating. What I hate
is inexactitude, sloppiness, just being vaguely there, if there at all,
but even more, obfuscation and rote. Different kinds of injustice.
"One day they will get it right at the Sorbonne," sings Stevens. A
line to match Marlowe's "Look master, here come two religious
caterpillars." It is, in the face of confusion, which happens to be
the principal power of the powerful, that I claim my acre—or my

ounce—of charity, sunlight, and truth, truth as a carpenter uses it, doubly acute if we consider the Jewish carpenter. I would say that confusion will be the Pentagon's great weapon of the future, but isn't it theirs already? A dear friend of mine is writing a book on the corporations. It's not, he says, that they will take, or are taking, over our country, they already have. But I want to know names, salaries, perks, influences, futures. I want to surround the home of the bringers of stink and stink them out. Except they have large dogs and own the force. On the screen they actually get it right, though it comes off as entertainment. And the prophets, if they are male, are turned into cross-dressers.

I was surrounded by 150 motorcyclists the other day, fat men and women on hogs, and the noise was horrible. I screamed back at them my own motor noises, but they didn't hear me and I embarrassed my love's sixteen-year-old son. Anyhow, I liked them, mostly Vietnam vets. The next day we were eating dinner in an Italian restaurant in Doylestown, county seat of Bucks County, Bucks County, Pennsylvania, and at the bottom of the menu, Zuppa, Insalata, Primi, Secondi, was a statement, in bold print, that astonished—and upset—me, since I am prone to those two things with a vengeance. It said "Pray for those who have died to protect our freedom, and pray for those who died on September 11 because of our freedom. Never forget." I was asked to pray; and I was asked to pray for dead soldiers—on Memorial Day and, in the same breath, pray for those who were killed on September 11 because the attackers hated freedom, or our version of it. What disturbed me more than the idiocy was the sermon on the menu, the rude intrusion and maybe more than that, the foolishness, the impossibility of any real response. So I attacked the waiter or whoever the hell the person was who asked us whether we wanted to pay for our water or drink slime.

But it's always the same—the one visible is a bit player, he didn't set the policy, he didn't write the sermon, he probably, himself, prefers slime. And so it was—to make a leap—in 1959 at the Whites Only section in Woolworth's, the waitresses didn't set the policy, how could you involve them? And up and down the scale of unimportance, particularly, *particularly*, the retired state cop with a bad heart who collected the tickets at the segregated swimming pool in Indiana, Pennsylvania, home of Jimmy Stewart. "I have a bad heart, Dr. Stern," he said, "I didn't make the policy," as my son and I and our friends, Robert Vowels Jr. and Robert Vowels, later the president of Spelman College, prepared to go for a little swim one Sunday morning. As I remember. And I was ruining our evening, our dinner at the Italian restaurant, and I knew it, stubborn and angry as I was, and selfish. I feel it now.

II

How did understanding come to me, if only for five minutes, when I was fourteen? It was Mother's Day, 1939, a Sunday, of course, and my mother and father were sleeping late. I sat at a rickety secretary, with my knees pushing up the small board—covered with some torn green felt—writing a poem in a little booklet I had devised. My second poem, as I recall; the first one was on Christopher Columbus and the one following would be written in a cabin near the top of Mt. Chicora, in New Hampshire. The subject was the lies surrounding Mother's Day. I may have read a newspaper article, or just sucked up some feeling. Nothing important. More or less banal. But I was *fourteen* and there was nothing radical or inquisitive about my culture. In fact, I was a Western Union messenger boy who wore a uniform, including puttees, and delivered flowers as well as messages, though, for some reason, I wasn't working that day. What was interesting was the poem itself. I remember only the first four lines, the first stanza, probably enough to indicate the trend:

> On Mother's Day and Father's Day
> It is the custom now
> To harbor deeds of reverence
> That rival the kowtow.

Spondees, and maybe even a distant cousin to sprung rhythm, though I had never heard of Hopkins—and wouldn't for five or six years to come.

I gave the gift to my mother, later that morning, carefully written and neatly wrapped in a homemade envelope. She started to cry; and my father's words were: "Couldn't you have gotten her a gift, kid?"

III

There's a part of me that's extremely intolerant to clerics of all kind, whatever the religion. Though I have no proof that priests, of any faith, are actually less principled, less prone to kindness, less interested in "carpenter's truth" and justice than those of other callings, say, farmers, dentists, sailors, real estate salesmen, novelists. It may be the uniform that gets to me, or the windiness. I am over-friendly and guarded at the same time. And fascinated, in the radical meaning of the word. Once a week, or so, I eat lunch at a restaurant here in Lambertville, New Jersey, called The Galleria. It's a small dining room, seven or eight tables, and, without exception, the same two Roman Catholic priests are close by, eating quietly and talking in low voices. They are priests and administrators of the huge church nearby, with the food kitchen at the far side, the inviting signs in Spanish and the gravestone, displayed prominently on the main street, with a Virgin and child, on the smooth front and a legend underneath her, put there by the local chapter of the Knights of Columbus, announcing that the stone is "In loving memory of those unborn children who died before they lived"—somewhat at odds with the official line. There is a large garden behind, with a grotto in which a demure Mary stands looking skyward. She is adorned with beads and a cross, and there is a votive candle burning at her feet and a large jar with dollar bills and some loose change in it. There are rhododendron trees, pines, and a miniature kneeling stone woman, Elizabeth, I think. There is also a statue nearby of St. John the Evangelist—name of the church—I guess St. John of Revelation. The art is horrible.

One of the priests looks to be in his late seventies or eighties. And he has a hard time maneuvering. His companion, who is in his sixties, takes care of his older brother. They are both Polish, and the story is that the younger, a more recent immigrant, stole money from the church funds and then spent it, not on women, or trips to the Caribbean—or Atlantic City—but on fancy handsewn vestments from Poland. A forgivable crime, in my eyes. The "fascination" may, probably does, have something to do with the presumed connection to spirit, to the light, which they, however distantly, share with the poets. As such, any institutional compromise is doubly hideous. My demand is that they live on the edge, as poets (sometimes) do. No political bullshit, no windiness, closed eyes, false invocations, dumb breath, ugly compromise, accommodation. Women's clothes sewn in Poland are all right. Bad art and ugly propagandistic tombstones are not.

IV

Apologia pro sua Ranta

You must go to extremes sometimes and rub your own face
    in the dirt.
Who doesn't hate mother and father and sister and brother is
    no follower
of mine, said Joshua.
You must illustrate this with your body and with your words.
You sometimes have to burn all the poems to write a new
    one.
A teacher is a teacher all the time.
Our only enemy is the Liar.
I overturn the table when I hear him lie.
And rip the tablecloth and spill the gravy.
This is poetry; what I teach.
Another day: forgiveness.
Sometimes God rains on the just and the unjust alike.
Such a God.
Sometimes your love forsakes you.

V

I wrote about the tablecloth more than a few times. I used to be a
little pleased by it, but now I'm horrified and disgusted. What I did
was pull a freshly starched and ironed cloth off the table, covered, as
it was, with meat, gravy, peas, and carrots. Some rage over parental
stupidity, self-congratulation, fake feeling. You'd think at my age
I could finally let it alone. But I had to see my parents shiver. And
suffer shame.

VI

I had to *rise* to such feeling. When I was personally affronted. Otherwise I was polite, even self-effacing. When I was head of a teachers' union for four or five years I was manipulated by my "team" into the appropriate anger and took stubborn and even ridiculous positions. I was a madman when provoked and couldn't be beaten. How is 57 percent in raises over three years? How is the first compulsory arbitration in the United States?

VII

My activism, such as it was, was separate from my writing; that is, the writing, whether political or not, was not *in support of* the activism, nor was it itself an expression of the activism as, say, an antiwar poem might be. I know I wrote a few bad political poems during the late 1960s, but I never published them. In Indiana, Pennsylvania, at Indiana University of Pennsylvania, my tenure was threatened; I was summoned before a star chamber, and I was almost fired for publicly confronting and embarrassing a well-known war supporter, but by this time in my "career" I, and my friends, were smart enough to call out the students who threatened to strike if I were fired. And in that same city, I organized and led a large march to commemorate the murder of the Mississippi Three on a certain Monday when there were such marches in state after state, but it had very little to do with writing, poetry or prose. It was as if I were an activist or organizer *manqué,* a *métier* I flirted with and indulged in, as it were, for nostalgic reasons, a kind of duty, even whimsy, guilt-laden and filled with poisonous Pittsburgh oxygen, world of wonder almost religious I entered with joy, ludicrous in the extreme now—that early Hunkie rage—amidst the new sunshine of imported beer, boat parties, general selfishness, and spiritual gloom.

VIII

The murder of the Mississippi Three (the Civil Rights workers, James Chaney, Andrew Goodman, and Michael Schwerner) took place in 1964 in and near Philadelphia, Mississippi, and the marches were a few months later. My friend Mary Vowels went the Friday afternoon before to the minister (read priest) of the Red Brick Presbyterian Church, the church of note in Indiana, Pennsylvania, to try to get a march started, since we felt it was best to work through the churches. Mary—and her family—were the only African Americans in the congregation. The minister offered sympathy, confusion, and delay, and Mary ended up knocking on our door in tears and anger. In a matter of hours, using whatever resources I had, I got something going. I first contacted the minister and shamed him into "saying a little prayer" on the steps of the county courthouse the following Monday. Then I set up a phone bank, and several volunteers from the head of the student union, a friend of mine. They called every church in the county to inform them that the minister from Red Brick was leading a march for justice—they might have said Christian justice—and to announce it Sunday morning. I called the president of the college who couldn't be there, but gave his reluctant blessing. Then I called the deans and department chairs to tell them how enthusiastic he (the president) was. After that I called the state police for "protection" and informed the newspapers and radio stations. The march—down Philadelphia Street—lasted two hours. I think there were thousands of people there, including the

entire African American community, who were, by the way, ger-
rymandered out of the borough so they couldn't enjoy the privileges
of living in that boring city. After the speeches and prayers at the
courthouse, a contralto sang "We Shall Overcome" and the banner
headlines in the newspapers that day read "We Shall Overcome: A
New Song for Indiana." It was the largest march in Pennsylvania.

IX

I read in Wikipedia that Ratzinger, the German pope, in his first
encyclical, *Deus Caritas Est* ("God Is Love"), defined truth as iden-
tical with love. He explores the relationship of truth with toler-
ance, conscience, freedom, and religion. He believes in reason
(Aristotle, Aquinas) and feels the mind itself has the capacity to
answer the fundamental questions. Whitehead, whom I've tried
to read for over a decade, writes, "There are no whole truths; all
truths are half-truths." I have been obsessed with it for weeks now.
Did the bastards who tortured and murdered Chaney, Schwerner,
and Goodman believe they were acting in the name of truth or
did they secretly believe the opposite? Philosophy 101. My dic-
tionary of philosophy refers constantly to what it calls *reality* and
makes a distinction between scientific and philosophical truths.
The philosophical question, it says, is not what is true but rather
what is truth? Certainly only a half-truth. If *truth* is something
philosophers and theologians fight over, *true,* as I say, is a word
carpenters use. When a window isn't true, for example, it's *racked.*
Its sides then are at an angle, and we end up with a parallelogram
rather than a rectangle.

I think of that kind of true when I'm writing. Although it is
I who not only creates the window but even the frames and the

racked sides. Even the sun and sky. Words like *plumb, faithful, accurate, actual, verifiable* do get you away from poetry, where breath is the measure rather than the compass and the square. Though breath does have a subject. Even if the subject is literal, fragmented or—to some—irrelevant and boring. In Hebrew it is called רוּח "ruach"; it means the breath, the spirit, the mind, the brain, of God. It also means "wind." The closest we get to it in English is *inspiration*. I think of the Masons who used both the compass and the square in their symbolism, and remember that above them stands an eye. Does the eye measure, or does it receive a vision—that is, is it a scientific or a visionary eye?

What is mysterious is the Lie. Except in children and in childish situations. What is abhorrent is the Liar. Sometimes I think of the Liar for an hour on end. Billy Budd. The lie presupposes a kind of *sanity*, a kind of social health in which the lie is possible. It presupposes—it supposes—that the society in question is not delusional, not insane, for in an insane society the Liar would be telling the truth. I am writing this in 2008. Does the Bush and Cheney government truly believe it did not lie and is not lying? Lying not only about Iraq but constantly, consistently, as a matter of course and of policy about everything, and anything, that enters its field of vision. I am suggesting (with horror) that the government in 2008 is sane; and therefore despicable.

But the truth is that poetry uses its own kind of "truth," and it's not carpenter's and it's not philosopher's. Even if I long for a saw and want very little to do with philosophy. For rapture is elsewhere. Certainly it's in the language, certainly the music, certainly the subject. Most of all we can't know it in advance, so there is no way to prepare for it. Certainly great poetry advances truth, but that's something else. Truth is elusive yet plain, truth is shocking, truth is too gorgeous to stand. (I feel like Paul writing his letter about love; with due apologies.)

If Dante learned his ground rules from Aquinas, he learned his poetry elsewhere. And elsehow. And his "truth" is elsewhat. What German taught D. H. Lawrence how to write, how to feel? I know it's crazy to even talk about truth when it comes to poetry, but I rather like the absurdity of it. The closest we get to it is in the letters of Nietzsche, a little *Zarathustra*, some of the Presocratics.

Somewhere I read today—or last week—that "exactness is not truth," a quote from Matisse, and it made me hesitate about carpenter's truth. Certainly it's not a lie, it's "just one kind of truth." Poetic—artistic—truth can be reached by reversal, avoidance, paradox, subterfuge, and irony—maybe even *by* lying. And poets get it right by indirection. They point to the sun. Auden said Adam pointed to the sun when Eve was born out of his side, from a rib. Was it to make it bearable? Was it to tell the truth? Was it a work of art, a poem? Isn't narrative *parallel*? Isn't it metaphor, that is, an unfinished and unreached (unreachable) conclusion? Is it time to explain myself? Let us sit down! How do poets and prophets get connected? I saw a rainbow in the filthy water under a bench in Tompkins Square Park one day and wrote about it at the very end of my long poem "Hot Dog." I was Noah then—or I was thinking of the book of Noah, since a huge spring rain had just ended. In my poem it was "a muted oily rainbow" in which "I splashed my shoe and spread / the colors out, some greens and some reds . . ." I said "Never again," referring to the universal flood but also, of course, to the Jewish response to the Holocaust. My dove, the one that never came back, is, in my poem, converted to "two or three birdlets / getting ready again for the next eternity." They never came back.

X

Temple University, in the section of Philadelphia known as North Philadelphia, is—and has been for sixty years or so—the heart of an African American slum. It was built in an upper-middle-class neighborhood of large houses and tree-lined streets that changed, as almost all such neighborhoods did, in the deterioration of America's industrial cities in the middle of the twentieth century. When I started teaching there, in 1956, the English Department was located in a converted house on the southern edge of the campus. It was the *very* southern edge, for the house next door—outside of the "campus"—was in extremely bad repair and contained literally dozens of people—all ages, as did the houses down the block, and the next and the next as well. The administration (of Temple University) in its wisdom chose to build a six-foot-tall brick wall across the street, defining, as they said, the edge of the "campus" but effectively creating a barrier to keep the local residents off the Temple grounds. It was racist, and stupid. And you wondered, did they in the least believe, in any way, their ridiculous defense of this act? A few of us, after a while twenty or thirty—instructors, graduate students, some undergraduates—began entering the campus by climbing over the wall. Sheer theater, but a rag sheet—*The Daily News*—took pictures, the word began to spread, and they finally tore down the wall. Maybe they had some property on the other side condemned—I don't know. But it was exhilarating to take a subway down, walk to the wall, and hoist yourself over, all the while wearing a suit, a necktie, and carrying a briefcase full of folded "themes." I could still do it at thirty; thirty-two. The year was maybe 1957, or 1958. By now the monsters are long dead and

Temple has made peace with its neighbors; and anyhow, I am just as interested in the fact that I could climb that wall.

XI

I think about the prophets more and more as time grows shorter and find them ever more peculiar and mysterious. Abraham J. Heschel, the great Jewish thinker who marched with King, asks the question, "What manner of man was the prophet?" and calls attention to his explosiveness, his sensitivity to evil, the importance he placed on trivialities, his loneliness, his misery, his shrillness. He was, Heschel said, "one octave too high." "We and the prophet," he said, "have no language in common." His sense of injustice, his moral indignation at what we consider normal behavior—normal violence, say, or corruption or just complacency—is overwhelming. "Who could bear living in a state of disgust day and night?" Heschel asks. "They [the prophets] make much ado about paltry things, lavishing excessive language upon trifling subjects." "Indeed the sorts of crimes that fill the prophets of Israel with dismay do not go beyond that which we regard as *normal*," Heschel says. "Cheating in business, exploitation of the poor . . . to the prophets, a disaster." "A death-blow to existence." "A catastrophe, a threat to the world." "God is raging in the prophets' words."

This last is the critical clue. Whether or not Yahweh exists—or existed—whether or not he talked to, or through, the prophets, whether or not they were delusional, it was their constant belief that their god *was* communicating with them, that he made specific demands upon them, and that this combined with their words (their poetry) and their rage and compassion to make their witnessing possible. Quite simply, we don't have that kind of prophet today.

Although we do have "false prophets," an interesting and atrocious lot. We tend not to believe in the miraculous or the unnatural. We have social activists and political poets, sometimes they are one and the same, and we have journalists, politicos, saints, and comedians, of one kind and another, but we don't, generally, believe God talks to, or through, them, either literally or figuratively, even if they explode and are luminous and speak one octave too high. No one suspects it of Shelley or Adrienne Rich or Blake or Ginsberg or even Milton, on the one hand; or Martin Luther King or William Jennings Bryan or Ezra Pound or Lenny Bruce, on the other.

Yet it is the prophets, Amos and Jeremiah and Hosea and the Isaiahs, who serve as model and inspiration. It's like Yeats's ladder, though, and Shelley's famous essays; some do prophet-like work, and though they are truly "unacknowledged" show prophet-like anger and judgment—and love. In a small way. Others shout more, are better known, are "acknowledged." Some run for office, some write "articles," some cause great changes and make this life bearable, even sometimes beautiful. Some just write letters or make phone calls. One or two rise to greatness. Above all, dignity is never an issue, never. It is easy enough to say that God does speak—in one way or the other, metaphorically, so to speak—different than God a person, male or female, bearded or powdered. Some fool said God was punishing us for gay marriage by taking jobs overseas. We know he was doing this in Katrina because of the vice in New Orleans. America is full of caterpillars and angels are flying around. People of all persuasions and both sexes have gifts of prophecy that include visits from divine beings. The country is overwhelmed by the mystical turned literal. As far as Martin Luther King is concerned, he never said he "talked to God," though of course he prayed for guidance (if anyone had a divine connection, he did). He said he had a dream. If God could talk to us, he certainly would have talked to King. Maybe also to Malcolm X, Dick Gregory, Daniel Berrigan, Dorothy Day, Heschel himself. He might have talked to Red Emma but, God, she would have barked back. Rukeyser too. I could make a case for the muse and the living pen, but I'll let it go.

At Abbie Hoffman's funeral, he who said, "Steal This Book," he who wore judges' robes at his conspiracy trial, he who tried to levitate the Pentagon and threw fistfuls of fake money in among the traders at the New York Stock Exchange, his rabbi said that Hoffman's long history of protest was in the Jewish prophetic tradition, which is to "comfort the afflicted and afflict the comfortable." The prophetic *tradition*. Good enough for this life.

XII

Sometime in the mid- to late 1970s there was a knock on our front door in Raubsville, Pennsylvania—we never had a bell—and two of our neighbors, a husband and wife who lived down the road in a large trailer, were standing there, smiling and uncomfortable. Life begins with a knock on the door. They informed us that there was a move underfoot to convert our back road into a park and to buy up all our houses, eminent domain or Latin claptrap. We had a drink together and talked. We lived on an old bypassed state road (once Route 611) that ran south of Easton, Pennsylvania, and north of Riegelsville, literally on a mile-long island bounded on the west by the Pennsylvania Canal and the east by the Delaware River. Our land went from the canal to the river, both sides of old 611. There were three older structures on the road, the hotel (where between 1820 and 1900 the canal workers once stopped to eat and sleep), our house, in the middle, and an abandoned stone building complete with an exposed walk-in fireplace and high weeds over a dirt cellar floor, plus maybe ten other buildings, trailers, shacks, and basements. Somewhere, in Harrisburg, the state capital, or Easton, the county seat, at some ugly table or other, the idea was hatched; and the planners were busy at work making multicolored drawings in their office at the Allentown-Bethlehem airport. We organized a group with the acronym LOLA: Leave Our Land Alone. We were working people and small-business proprietors, electricians, cab drivers, factory workers, an auto body shop owner, and the like. They understood oppression and mistrusted fancy language. About fifty people showed up at our first meeting, at the restaurant in the hotel. I was elected president.

The whole thing took about two months. We printed up leaflets and sent out notices. Advertised. Rang bells, made calls. Ate potato salad. The hotel and my house, a large 1790 stone, were the only two buildings that were going to remain. I'm not sure if they planned a zoo there or not but the hill we owned above the river was turned into a ramp and canoes were going to be stored in our living room, where the piano and the mohair sofa were. We demanded a meeting with the commissioners, and it took place in the courtroom of the county building. There were two hundred or more people crowded in and the commissioners and artists (planners) were up front. They tried to hoodwink, delay, and confuse us but we were ready. The commissioners kept blaming the "artists," but those poor fools, B.A.s from some ex-normal school, were rather tongue-tied. We decided to take a vote there and then on the commissioners' upcoming election, and it was rather one-sided. We refused to leave until they formally abandoned the scheme—in front of us. Which they did. Our speeches were superb. I put my corn-cob pipe out, by way of theater, on one of their renderings.

We lived there five more years or so and not once—till I left for Iowa, did we ever get a bill for electric work, or plumbing, nor did our taxes ever increase. I had the privilege of living in a loving community for thirteen years.

XIII

It is astounding that the prophet Hosea, in the very first word God spoke to him, as recorded in the book of Hosea, is ordered to take a whore (a wife of whoredom) as his wife. It doesn't matter whether the marriage is meant to be literal or is a figure for God's relationship to Israel. It is astounding; brutal; direct; shocking. God, and Hosea, were not shy about fucking as a subject, here and throughout the fourteen chapters. The *Interpreter's Dictionary of the Bible* uses the word "harlot." What's wrong with "Lady of the Night"?

XIV

Blake had dinner with both Ezekiel and Isaiah. Believe it or not, at the same time. So he says. Chicken and sweet potatoes.

XV

Something's missing and it's a shame. What is lost? What great place did they tap into for two hundred years? Would I want to go there? Do I grow weary of the word "justice"? Wasn't it a relief to enter my aesthetic period?

XVI

What a joy it is to know you climbed the wrong mountain—or the right, for that matter, and not the wrong, or just to know there were two mountains. I haven't looked it up yet in Wikipedia, but I think I know enough. Zebulon Pike, for whom Pike's Peak, in Colorado, was named, was a second lieutenant in the United States Army. I think he was in the war of 1812, and my guess is that he climbed the mountain after that war, that he was on an expedition for the government, an exploration, that he could measure and describe things, that he used instruments. The story is that he climbed the wrong mountain—the next one over—but they named the big one after him nonetheless. When I was eleven or twelve I had a book that described the adventure. I guess it was a novel. It was called *Lost with Lieutenant Pike,* and it was the only book I actually owned. I wrote a poem about it, called "Lost with Lieutenant Pike," that appears in *Rejoicings,* published in 1973. The poem is about maturing slowly and outliving your string of errors. Here are the first few lines. No, here is the whole poem:

> How was I to know—in 1938—that anyone but
> Zebulon Pike could be the master of my imagination
>
> or that the one book belonging to my dead sister—*Alice in
> Wonderland*—did not have to lie for twenty years, hidden
> on a closet shelf
>
> or that I was allowed to throw out my stupid molds, my
> set, that never once, with all my pouring, managed to make
> one soldier without a leg missing or without an incredible
> wound in the side of his neck.
>
> Slowly I became a man, and as I did I looked back with

shame, which was the lawful payment for my ignorance and
meekness.

Whatever I have to do now to outlive my string of errors I
will do,
and I will live as divided as I have to, and as loose and as
senseless.

In another life it will be all masted vessels and sugar houses
and tea-pouring and little men running down their lanes;
this time around there will be no government for anyone.

I have to live on the lid of Hell, poor friend;
I have to leave the woods and the Shul and the chicken
standing on its wings and the white silk scarf
and the visit from Mars and the long journey to
Harrisburg, Pa.

It is something to stand on a hill in the middle of November,
9,000 miles from Jerusalem, with the ice forming
inside your nostrils, and to feel your own wisdom.

I am not suggesting a good allegory here, I am only naming two
mountains. Nor did I climb the wrong mountain in this life, though
I have climbed many a wrong crag and made my way back wildly.
In Ireland, a few years ago, while Anne Marie was taking an after-
noon nap, I ventured out the back and made my way down to the
sea, a hundred yards or so distant. There seemed to be a path but
after a while I was fighting weeds, burdocks and nettles, wearing
only shorts, as I recall, and a T-shirt. I fought to free myself of the
pricks but also to find the path, any path. It was very hot for Ireland,
they were suffering from a heat wave, and there was no breeze. I
never reached the water, I kept getting into the thicket deeper and
deeper and finally decided to go back to our cottage, but again I
was caught and couldn't find a way. I tripped over stones, fell into
holes, and was scratched and bitten. I eventually got to a barbed-

wire fence quite a bit out of the way, but with a mown yard on the other side and a road of some sort beyond the house. I was, by this time, sweating, scratched, and bleeding. I also heard a dog bark and was almost terrified of being attacked if I climbed over the fence. I also had to maneuver the barbed-wire. I slowly set my foot on the lowest strand and, though I was swaying, and the dog was barking, I managed to climb over the three wires, run across the lawn and out to the road. I was a quarter-mile or so away from our cottage. When I finally got there, Anne Marie was just getting up. I was elated—in an ecstatic state, singing and shouting. Anne Marie wiped the blood off and insisted I calm down. I was crazy, stupid, awkward, out-of-it, a type of hero, oh, poor Carlyle, if only for a minute, a nanosecond.

I know my mountains, and I knew—eventually—what I was doing. I chose to go there; it wasn't an accident. It's not that the mountain looked greener. It just also looked green.

XVII

Philadelphia is the hub for US Air so I tend to use that carrier more than the others. When I call up from time to time to get information from an agent, I find myself confronted by a voice—by a person—speaking in an English I struggle to understand, and when I ask the person, intruder that I am, where she, or he, is from, the answer is always "Manila, sir." At least it is in 2008, and always, after the struggle is over and the information is given, I end the conversation by apologizing for the Spanish-American War, to which the reply is, invariably, "Thank you, sir," though there is no certainty, or very little certainty, that the agent knows what I am referring to. I don't give any lectures on American imperialism, I don't mention Admiral Dewey, yellow journalism, the European jackals, or the atrocious betrayal of the courageous Filipino army and the illegal and immoral occupation by U.S. troops. Though I sometimes recommend to the agent that he, or she, read Mark Twain on the subject, especially his 1901 article titled "To the Person Sitting in Darkness," where, in biting satire, he details that betrayal and discusses—with outrage—how America's honor has been debauched and her reputation ruined before the world. Twain (I don't tell the agent) even takes on the American flag—he suggests that the white stripes be painted black and the stars replaced by the skull and crossbones. At one point in the essay, he makes reference to a letter that an American soldier in the Philippines wrote to his mother in Decorah, Iowa, after a battle (with the Filipino soldiers whose country we had come to liberate). The American soldier writes: "We never left one alive. If one was wounded, we would run our bayonets through him." To Mom! I must confess that I longed to tell the US Air agent to read my poem, "Just Say Goodbye to Mother," which is on page 40 of my 2005 book, *Everything Is Burning*. It's an antiwar poem and even mentions the Philippines and makes reference to Twain (Clemens) by name:

JUST SAY GOODBYE TO MOTHER

What about Damon Runyon, his cloth booties,
the pineapple upside down cake his mother
burned while caramelizing, the shower in the basement
that after all the wrenches and wrenching was only
a trickle, and after 1898 he
had to live without his mother—oh
the white boys in the Philippines—and carry
his gear on his back and you may not believe it
the sweet and milky songs they sang and what

Samuel Clemens said about *that* war
or how I banged on the door at the post office
and someone met me with his finger wagging
again and again from 1941 to
1945, my own mother howling.

The title of the poem is the first line of the most popular song of the Spanish-American War, "Just say goodbye to mother / and tell her there's no other." The tune is gorgeous.

Twain fights false patriotism, flag-waving, Christian kindness, corporation ruthlessness, "the Blessings of Civilization," exploitation, plain dishonesty, bullying, hypocrisy, stupidity, and Caucasian superiority. Above all, he fights the liar. And the lie. He would have had a field day with Vietnam and Iraq. He would have adored the liars: Wilson, Bush Sr., Bush Jr., and Reagan, particularly. Smart, realistic, even cynical as he was, he could never have possibly imagined W.

XVIII

I feel a little joy at recording some of these things, but only a little. The recorders ages hence, if they keep records, won't have that much to record, though a few more events keep bobbing up, some from my days at a badly managed, criminally wasteful, ethnically ravaged high school, some from the army, some from the hateful caste-ridden days in filthy Pittsburgh, and some from my ten years of drifting before I settled down to a real job at the other end of the state, in Ben's fine city.★ My regret, and my revision, certainly

---

★ The letter I got the other day, which refers to that period, is at the end of the chapter.

don't belong here; anyhow I probably have recorded that enough by now. At a certain point, beyond the nostalgic moment, beyond the "agenbite of inwit" (Joyce's term, in *Finnegans Wake*, for regret and remorse), the writer (the poet, the thinker, the living-soul), like Yeats's Caesar, sits in his tent moving his pen from left to right ("With no more sound than a mouse makes"), a gauche and sinister Caesar he, as if he were moving pieces on a board, as if he were *only* moving pieces, as if he were *finally* moving them, with his heart and his mind no longer separated, the two of them one at last. He sits in a plastic chair near a great woodpile leaning against a shed, not far from a noisy window air-conditioner named "Friedrich," his Puerto Rican panama on a round table next to his Heidegger treatise on poetry, language, and thought, and his cup of cold coffee. He is shaded by two gorgeous trees in full leaf and he is identifying bird sounds.

Dear Gerry, Sterny Babe, Mr. Stern—all of the above:

Sorry for my delay in getting back to you. I called the phone number Hunter College transferred from your email—609-000-0000. I left an apologetic message, whereupon a kindly gentleman called back to tell me I had the wrong number. He sensed my eagerness to reach you, so I hope this email address is correct. I still read your poetry in *The New Yorker*, especially the ones set in coffee shops near Columbia, but it is our past that haunts and inspires me. Whenever I hear one of Bach's *Brandenburg Concertos* or Beethoven's Ninth Symphony, your cozy living room in Mayall Hall comes swimming back—images of that primitive turntable plugged into your radio. Sam Goody was practically giving them away with a $30 purchase of LPs. And then there was your booming Dylan Thomas, quieter Eliot, and Joyce's *Ulysses* . . .

and in our senior English class, Othello's final words, "I have done the state some service and they know it," with chalk marks on your jacket and a touch of Paul Robeson in your voice.

Once, during your first year at Lake Grove (was it 1952?), you were a substitute in our American History class. We were discussing the election of 1896 when you leapt up on the desk and *became* William Jennings Bryan, raising your arms and shouting his cross of gold speech, or at least your version of it which prepared me for anti-war rallies in Madison, Wisconsin, and also for teaching Clifford Odet's "Waiting for Lefty."

We fondly recall the raucous evening you came for dinner and would love to repeat it and catch up. Our phone number is 212-000-0000. Among other news, we recently became grandparents for the first time.

Hope to hear from you soon.

Love, Norman

LITERARY ESSAYS

SOME SECRETS

I HAVE ALWAYS ADMIRED the relationship between younger artists and older ones, and when I read about the schools and the dear lofts and the desperate sofas where the one held the other's hand or pressed a cold washrag to his head, I have a certain envy that I was never one of them, neither the young taker nor, later, the giver. It's even a source of embarrassment to me—at interviews, for example— when I am questioned about my *origins* and find myself stammering or over-elaborating, trying desperately to account for myself, longing to be a branch of some tree, a leaf somewhere with clear veins and a regular shape. It may be that I am just being taken in by the silly morphologists, who after all make a living from branches, and other poets have also walked around without masters, holding their own disembodied heads against their chests like weird creatures out of Hieronymus Bosch, but when I remember *The Lives* I remember, case after case, two faces bowed over a text, two hearts watching a river together, or a dirty sunset. Of course, now that I've come through it all unscathed, or with very few scars showing, I am a little proud of my terrible isolation and even delight a little in its mystery, as if it were the result of a master plan, and certainly my poetry has resulted from it, but it would have been nice, I realize now, to have had a little help, to have had a sense of some nourishment somewhere, however tenuous or even symbolic it was.

I make it sound as if I suddenly emerged like an unknown blos-som in some incredible Alp, or burst full-grown out of the head or thigh of some Eskimo god, biting my own way through the great caul. After all, I did have school and books and friends and family and place and an identifiable decade. Probably my "separateness," if I can call it that, had a great deal to do with my own biology and my own history, with a certain shyness and a certain secrecy, cou-pled with a kind of arrogance, although that isn't exactly the right word, that made me unwilling to submit at the same time that I was too distant, too modest even, to do so. I think this is accurate, though it sounds terribly like mutterings from a couch. And I guess it's no accident that I use the word "submit" to describe my con-nection with the nonexistent master. Certainly that wouldn't be the word that Hart Crane would use as he thought of his dear Walt or his dearer Arthur, and if it was submission that Robert Lowell was engaged in on Allen Tate's front lawn, or Allen Ginsberg on W. C. W.'s side porch, or Rimbaud behind the smoking revolver, there were no apologies and no agonies. It may be that for me the issue is simply that I did not have one great influence, one master, but a number, even an endless number, and that's what's causing my confusion, and certainly, like everyone else, I did have a great number of influences, but I don't think that's the case.

Rather I think it's the case that I'm not accountable as the result of my apparent influences, except in the most obvious ways. The Left, for example, has been an influence on me, as it's been an influence on dozens of other writers, from Williams to Auden to Rukeyser to God knows whom. Each has used it in his or her poetry, or been used by it, in a particular way. But to identify my connection with the Left, mostly tenuous, even sometimes a little sentimental and nostalgic, does not identify in any significant way my poetry. It identifies my sentiment, it shows a little the nature of my loyalty, it says something about my history—and these are important things—but it is not a critical element in my writing. Likewise, Judaism has been an influence on me. But there too my connection has been a little tenuous and sometimes nostalgic—that is, the connection with my writing. Although, in that case, the historical idea of the Jew as an eternally stubborn, hopeful, and dreaming creature has been an influence, as have been some of the mystical texts, albeit I use those texts as a kind of midwife and secret metaphor for my own inclinations, and use the Jewish texts, as opposed to, say, Buddhist ones, as much out of loyalty as out of belief.

If I were to explore other apparent, even "obvious," influences on me, I think I might arrive at the same conclusion. Perhaps I am saying that I want to discount ideological or formal influences and find the "true" ones in my own personal, accidental history: the city I happened to live in, or being the victim of anti-Semitic slurs and physical abuse during my early childhood—until we moved into a Jewish neighborhood when I was ten, or living during the Great Depression but not suffering directly from it, at least financially, or being left-handed in the days of organized hatred of the sinister, or living for years in the same house with an Orthodox grandmother and a black maid, or wandering alone for hours through a large city woods across the street from my house. But I don't think these fully account either.

Maybe my sister's death, when she was nine and I was eight, is the one exception. This was important for me not only insofar as it generated a direct response from me, but also because it affected my parents so strongly and thus changed their behavior toward me, causing them, among other things, to overprotect and overnourish me—the one child left—and at the same time, in a subtle way, to reject me and even "accuse" me, crazy as it sounds, because I was the survivor in that visit of death. This experience is encapsulated for me in the sad Saturday nights I spent with my mother while my father was working late. She took me to bed with her and held me while she wept, crying "Sylvia, Sylvia, Sylvia" over and over again while I tried to console her. It may have happened only once or twice, but I remember it as a ritual occurrence. Clearly, I was being both loved and rejected. Clearly, I was helpless and uncomfortable and living in two places at once, with two debts to bear, my mother's and my own. If anything came close to being a direct influence over me it was this, and it caused me the most pain and confusion, although I still don't fully understand its connection with my writing.

I know little—really I know nothing—about the psychology of masterhood. I don't know if one is more, or less, inclined to seek out a master if one has a weak, or a strong, father. Maybe it has nothing to do with the father but rather with the mother, or with an older brother—or sister. Maybe, like baldness, it has to do with the maternal grandfather. So many things conspired in my case to provide a world without authority, if I may put it that way. For one thing, neither parent ever "interfered" with my education, and I had no older brother, and no teacher in my early years, or later for that matter, ever took an interest. I think I discovered college itself by sheer accident—I mean even the buildings. I happened to be passing by the University of Pittsburgh one day in the early fall and I wandered in and found myself registering for classes. It was during the war, so I had no trouble getting in. We had no advisers in those days. And a few years later, when I began writing, I had no one to turn to, although by that time I knew it was a good idea to have someone. I gave some poems, I remember, to an English professor

I was taking a course in the essay from, and after holding them for about two months, he advised me to read Kafka. I still don't know why. The poems were unmarked, possibly unread. There were no poets coming by giving readings then, there were only a few magazines in the libraries, there were no workshops, no small presses. We lived in darkness. Moreover, I wasn't an English major and I had no friends who wrote. I don't think I knew what a bohemian was. I did carry a little notebook around with me in which I wrote my poems, mostly sonnets in a kind of Edwardian style. I also carried a little book by Louis Untermeyer in my coat pocket. I wore white shirts, ties, wing-tip shoes, double-breasted suits. I was on the football team, then the debate team. I played nine-ball. I didn't know one was or could be an actual poet.

It wasn't until I was in the army, in 1946, and went to New Orleans and Washington and Baltimore, and started wandering through the bookstores and libraries, that I began to realize that writing was an occupation, and it wasn't until then that there began to stir in me the sweet idea of one day becoming a writer. But there still wasn't anyone I looked up to or even got signals from, except, maybe a little, Thomas Wolfe, whose novels I began to read. But there were no poets for me, not yet. The idea of going to a school and studying under a poet never occurred to me. I didn't know yet who the poets were, and later, when I did, I had no idea where they worked—or that they did work—and I didn't know you could study poetry, say, at Princeton or Iowa or Columbia, or that one even visited and talked to living poets. There wasn't one other soul in the world I could talk to about the books I read or show a poem or story to. But I was very happy and was not bitter and was not in longing. I lived and studied without direction, and if anything was going to be a permanent influence on me it was that.

By 1948, even as early as 1947, I was moving from shelf to shelf, devouring the major poets, putting together the odd history, listening carefully to the music. I read with no real logic, Spenser one week, Swinburne another, and like a threadbare angel, a poor naïf, I was moved all by myself as I encountered the great speeches, the breathtaking lines, the vaguely familiar passages in poet after poet, one marvelous writer after another. And of course, I was reading other books to fill the gaps: novels, history, philosophy, psychology. I made lists of the important books I had to read. I would be sleepless, sometimes humiliated, sometimes desperate, at the discovery of another great book I had not read or had just heard of. My former wife, whom I met in the fall of 1947, tells me that the iron stacks of the Carnegie Library are permanently embedded in her mind, that she remembers me reading nine, ten hours a day, that the first books she remembers under my arm were Herrick and Yeats and Joyce. I was in the 52/20 Club, a World War II G.I. benefit, twenty dollars a week for fifty-two weeks, a very tidy sum for those days. My dear president, the little scholar from Missouri, gave me twenty dollars a week to read old books and transform my life.

In the winter of 1948 I was reading the magazine *Poetry* and reading the thin volumes in the new-acquisitions shelf at the Pitt library. Sometimes, I quickly discovered, they were very thin. And I was piecing together the story of modern poetry—learning the language—and collecting my own library. I think Yeats and Pound were the two modern poets I cared for most then, though I began to know all the famous poems that were in the anthologies and all the names and dates and histories. I met Jack Gilbert and Richard Hazley that spring, or rather reencountered them since we all had been on the debate team together, and had indeed been the international champions, and they discovered, to their astonishment, that

I was reading poetry and writing, and I discovered, to my delight, that they were too, although I recall that Gilbert's plan then was to become a novelist.

We had to be the only people writing and reading poetry in Pittsburgh at the time. At least we never found any others. The peculiar thing about that period was that we didn't spend much time exchanging poems with each other but rather talked about the poets we were reading. It was as if poetry was a holy art, a religion, and we were not yet ordained. I know I was writing a great number of new poems, even if my friends weren't, but the idea was not the workshop idea—at least not then. We shared great poems, great lines, with each other, we talked about the mission of poetry, we developed our scorn. Pound was the poet we most admired. And after him the early Eliot, and MacLeish and Cummings, and Hart Crane. I was, as I recall, reading the late poems of Yeats and all of Auden and Marlowe. We didn't talk much about Frost and Stevens and Williams. Not then. I think our theme was "the poet in a hostile world." I don't mean to make fun of it. It's a real enough subject and as important today as ever. It has been the very mythus of poets, at least in Europe and America, since the beginning of the nineteenth century, in a way since Ovid, and it was the natural myth for three poets under siege in their real lives in inhospitable and merciless Pittsburgh. For us, poetry had to be serious and lyrical and personal and approach the sublime. The beautiful or moving line was the measure for us, even perhaps more than the whole poem. Thus some lines from Milton or a short speech from *Faustus* or a phrase from Yeats.

Of the generation just preceding ours, we would become most interested in Dylan Thomas and then Theodore Roethke and Robert Lowell, but not for a while. We were hardly interested in realists like Karl Shapiro or John Ciardi. Academicism was already in the air, but the cloud was slow in coming to Pittsburgh. I remember—with horror—how I greeted Richard Wilbur's first book of poems. I literally tore it up on the steps of the Carnegie Library—for which crime I humbly ask mercy from the trustees, and sympathy from Dick himself. We had all gone our separate ways by the early and mid-1950s, but in our periodic reunions we never failed to curse out the new academics, with their wit and elegance and politeness and forms, for their cowardice and bad faith, most of all for their disloyalty. To the Dream. Maybe, in some strange way, we were saved by our distance and our ignorance and our innocence. We didn't learn either the new style of writing or the new style of living. We had no insurance, no cars, no jobs. No wit. Maybe Andrew Carnegie's evil angel, which kept us blind and filthy and confused, should, after all, be thanked.

I spent most of the 1950s in Europe or New York City, living on next to nothing—a stretch of G.I. Bill, an odd job here and there. I was rather vaguely working on a Ph.D. at Columbia University, but had no identity with the other students and seldom went to classes. I quit forever one warm beautiful spring night. I had written a long poem in 1950 called *Ishmael's Dream:* my first epic. I remember writing ten gorgeous lines a day, on schedule. At the time I was living in Paris, a few blocks from Notre Dame. I prepared for the writing by reading from *The Bridge* and *Paradise Lost* and Isaiah out of a huge rotten Bible I had stolen from the American Center on the Boulevard Raspail. The subject, which I never consciously thought about, was the regeneration and transformation of the world, and myself as religio-politico-linguistic hero, a common enough theme for a first generation American Jew only son. Later, I showed the poem to Auden, who was living on Cornelia Street in the Village.

He made a positive comment about the ending, the last ten lines, and that was that. It was my only attempt to make a connection. Of course, he was the last person I should have sent such a poem to, but I was a little dumb. I eventually did come to use Auden in my poetry, years later, in an unforeseen way, and I took a course from him in the sonnet—at the New School.

By the mid-1950s I was writing some good poems and publishing them. The underlying theme was still transformation and the hero's call, but I was now more coherent. I occasionally used rhyme and the stanza, but I had nothing to do with the polite domestic verse of the day. The poet I was most involved with then was Wallace Stevens. I had reduced the number of useful "older" poets to two, Lowell and Roethke. After a while I turned more toward Roethke because of Lowell's subject matter and his turgidity, as I saw it then. It was early Roethke—the mystery, the strangeness, the loss, the love of small animals and plants, the sense of justice. I would return to Lowell again when *Life Studies* appeared. I was interested in Williams not so much for his language but for the way he combined health and madness, domesticity and wildness.

When I began teaching at Temple University in Philadelphia in the fall of 1956, I had a definite style. I read every poet and journal I could bear, and I was totally unknown. I was in no community of poets, either in person or by mail or by phone, so I figured things out for myself, as I always did. When everything started to blow, West Coast vs. East, beat vs. feet, I took an independent stand, finding in the poetic left an approximation of my own view, yet hating what appeared to me then to be its lack of imagination and its anti-intellectualism. I disliked the academics, yet I was working for a university. But I was slave labor, a subversive, a hater of their tide. Unfortunately, my separateness and self-absorption not only prevented me from transcending the two extremes but made me insensitive to what other younger poets were doing—Robert Creeley, say, or Robert Bly, or Denise Levertov—or made me judge them too quickly, and I was the loser for this.

In 1958 I began working on *The Pineys*, a long poem about the presidency. It was going to be my ticket. It was humorous, extravagant, mystical, buoyant, wordy, and very long. There were elements of the *Cantos* in it, and *Paterson* and *The Prelude* and *The Bridge* and *Song of Myself*. There was reconstituted prose and lists and lyrics. It was going to do everything. I was still an eternally old student and an eternally young instructor. I had a moustache and smoked cigars. I propped up the high chair with obscure dictionaries. I lived in a lovely timelessness. But one day, while rewriting the very last section, I realized the poem was a failure, that it was indulgent, that it was tedious, that it no longer interested me. It was 1964 or '65; I was going on forty, living in Indiana, Pennsylvania, and teaching at the state college there. I was devastated. I had been a practicing poet for almost two decades and I had nothing to show. I suddenly was nowhere; I had reached the bottom.

I remember walking around for months in that dull little city, teaching my classes by rote, not sleeping at night. Certainly I was going through a tremendous change—and a crisis. Certainly it was ironic that that crisis should be right on target, a real *crise de quarante*, on my own fortieth. As far as the poetry went, it had to do with realizing that I was taking an easier way than I should, or could, or must, that I was not wresting my own angel, that I had not arrived where I had to go. It also had to do with a realization that my protracted youth was over, that I wouldn't live forever, that death was not just a literary event but very real and very personal. It was a liberation, though I looked upon it at the time as a horror. I was able to let go and finally become myself and lose my shame and my pride. It meant literally starting over, but I didn't care because I was altogether interested only in the work and not in the rewards the work might bring. Not then. And suddenly I had very little envy of other poets and almost no sense that I was competing with them—even if they were ten years younger than I and winning all the prizes.

Maybe I'm not accounting for it enough. Was it because *The Pineys* was a failure that I fell apart? Why did I think it was a failure just then? A few years later, 1967, I had a chance to publish it, so in a few days I got rid of a lot of dead wood, did some rewriting, and sent it off. And it didn't look that bad. Wasn't it just the last stage of an endless series of rejections and abandonments that had plagued me since my early twenties? Why did I "come to" just then and start writing with authority and precision? Isn't that anyhow just what many other poets do, only they do it much earlier? Maybe if I had not got bogged down in such a long poem I could have made my move earlier—say, when I was thirty-five. But then, the very occupation with that poem was a way of delaying or deferring the change I was going to make. I'm suddenly remembering a visit to a doctor and his concern with my health—overweight and such. Did an ordinary event like that, producing a slight shift in my view, allow me to tap into material that was formerly warded off or ignored? Was it my lot to speak for the second half of life and not the first?

I think, when I look back now, that it was my own loss and my own failure that were my subject matter, as if I could only start building in the ruins. Or that loss and failure were a critical first issue in my finding a new subject matter, that they showed me the way. Or that my subject was the victory over loss and failure, or coming to grips with them. But I certainly started with loss and failure. Moreover, in a certain sense I always did start with these two and I was merely finally coming fully into my own, doing the thing more purely now that I had always done, more perfectly. It was as if I had been preparing for this all my life—certainly since my sister's death and my mother's sadness—and now I was ready. At any rate, after a little agony, the poems started to come easily and simply. The first group were written in the winter and spring of 1966, at the time of my forty-first birthday. Those poems are collected in *Rejoicings* (the name of the tractate on mourning in the Talmud), and there has been no letup in the writing from that day to this.

A couple of commentators have talked about the issue technically. Bly, for example, referred to my long lines. But I know that the issue is emotional and not technical and that it always is when a vital change is involved in art, although I recognize that the technical can stimulate, even make available, the emotional, that it can be a facilitator, that the challenge and demand of free verse in the 1960s, for example, helped James Wright make the changes he did in *The Branch Will Not Break*, that Whitman's change was aided by form, and Keats's also, in the odes. When I look at the statement I made for *Contemporary Authors* a few years ago, I see I emphasized my attraction to weeds and waste places and lovely pockets and staking out a place that no one else wanted because it was abandoned or overlooked. Aside from my attraction to these places because they are a relief from too much culture, I think I found in them a perfect location for my own emotions, although after a while I realized I had to be careful I didn't suffocate from too many weeds. At any rate, I could sink there as low as I wanted, I could be utterly alone, I could even be without hope and I found a kind of support. Such abandoned and neglected places have been used by many other modern writers, and by all the Romantics, and they have become a familiar metaphor for our lost world and a familiar arena for our holocausts and our ruined dreams, but they were for me very personal. I think I valued as much as anything else the secret aspect of such places and I have always loved the secret places that were just beyond the reach of our penetrating minds, the tiny black locust woods of my childhood, the obscure reading rooms of my young manhood, the hidden studies I go to now.

The longer I live, the happier I get, and the more I write, the more I arrive at my own place—I almost said my own assigned place—and I am ready to let Sylvia's hand go and I am finally ready to accept my abandonment, although I doubt if that's what it is, and simply call it a blessing. What I don't understand is why I waited till my fortieth year, although I'm sure I waited so long because I had no critical guide and I'm sure I had no guide not only for the accidental reasons I have mentioned, living apart from the mainstream and such, but because I couldn't find a way to incorporate someone in an acceptable manner, given my own impulses and obsessions, including my obsession against the very idea of having someone as a teacher or guide. I could have sought Kunitz, or Roethke, or Berryman, poets who were teaching and whom I admired, but already the pride and the secrecy had set in. It was truly as if I couldn't afford, and couldn't bear, any kind of accounting at the time, as if that would interfere with my destiny.

I can't imagine myself, say, at thirty, sending a sheaf of poems off to one of the middle-aged masters. Part of it was just habit, and part of it was just insecurity, but some of it, most of it probably, was a lack of connectedness. As smart and verbal as I was, I was totally impractical and artistically crazy. I was living in a stubborn, perverse, proud dream place. I went where I did go because I didn't have a guide and I became what I am for that reason, although I am not recommending it to anyone. If I did have someone, if I had belonged somewhere, the poetry would have been different—and would have come sooner—but it's the life mainly that makes the poetry and I don't think I really had a choice.

In the meantime, I've recently discovered that I must be on guard lest I am too impatient or too indifferent to the new poets looking for help, so I don't start mumbling in Hittite or arrogantly lecturing them on the self-made man, and so I don't lose the opportunity of making someone a little happier or a little less bewildered in the lovely and terrible struggle for beauty and understanding we call poetry.

THE SABBATH

Whenever I think of the Sabbath I think of lying on my back listening to Brahms and looking at the cracks in the ceiling. Or it could be Vivaldi, or Schumann. I am a recumbent angel. My shoes are off and though I wear pants I have the thinnest of T-shirts, or nothing, above the waist. It is seventy-five degrees, and October, and in the intervals between the movements the leaves can be heard, shuffling and coughing. Sabbath is the foretaste—in all the religions—so it gives you an idea of how I'll probably spend *my* eternity. I'm sure it wouldn't appeal to everyone. For all I know, I may be alone. I remember some Edwardian Utopia, full of a kind of English vindictiveness, where one did in the afterlife precisely what he did here, only presumably with a different kind of knowledge or what's the point, and therein lay the punishment, or reward. It was the same thing. So if you spent your Sundays looking at football on TV, you spent your immortality doing the same thing. And if you spent it in denial, likewise you spent your own forever, and if you spent it drinking and loving, well, our father's hill hath many valleys. It's a dull old idea, the kind of thing that comes up in a living room or a neighborhood bar, but it at least has a certain logic to it, even justice, which no depraved Calvinist would ever understand or respect. It is even a little Dantesque, for Dante liked to locate his sweet mortals in

251

ironic postures that were reminiscent of, or a logical extension of, their little lives here on earth.

It is interesting how bringing up the Sabbath immediately does bring up the afterlife. I said it was a foretaste. The Talmudists spent their Sabbath eating, drinking, and praising God. Mostly praising God. At least they were supposed to. And when it came to imagining Heaven, what else could they turn to but pleasing the senses a little and spending hour on hour in beautiful prayer, and study? And praising God was not only done musically, it was itself a form of music. If they had to do it with harps, what harm? Or even tubas. They were lucky, at least the men were, knowing that music so well. The poor women, though, whose Sabbath duty it was to light the candles and take care of the men and the children, were denied eternal instruments. Perhaps they could learn to play a little, if roughly; or they could bring unity and color—tone, as we say—to those gray-headed flocks, as they did down here.

I was reminded so much of just those *harpes* and just those *luthes* when I went to the Fiddler's Picnic outside Iowa City one Sunday. It was on the 4-H campgrounds, a very heavenly place, with farm buildings, a parking lot, a wooden stage for the fiddlers, some bleachers, and a marvelous green hill rising steeply up into the woods and meadows beyond. As you left your car and entered the grounds, the first thing that attracted your attention were the little bands of stray musicians behind buildings, alongside campers, or just out in the open, preparing themselves for the platform, or just contenting themselves with facing each other and making sweet sounds. There were kites, bicycles, and an occasional airplane. Kids were swinging from car doors and adults were lined up patiently outside the rest rooms. There was an Eyewitness News truck, Japanese tourists, half-grown dogs with open mouths and red ribbons chasing each other, and little families lying on the hillside with beer and dope and Pepperidge Farm cookies. There were ancient hippies in headbands and backpacks, there were skinny runners in satin shorts, there were Kabbalistic T-shirts.

In the distance was the corn and the blue sky. One young angel, a boy of about ten, came up to me as I stood beside the wire fence at the top of the great hill and asked me what the large leaves were hanging on the wires, were they grape leaves? His grandfather, he told me, made wine from Kool-Aid, and the Indians who lived near their farm loved to drink it. He was willing to tell me everything. His mother was there with his baby sister, he was in the fifth grade, he played the piano. I soothed him, I asked him his name, I touched his silken head. His glasses were thick and his eyes were magnified. He stared at me with wonder, and a kind of greed. Down below, hundreds of feet down, a religious group had just finished singing "I'm Washed in the Blood of the Lamb." Then they signaled for everyone to stand up and sing together "Amazing Grace." Everyone stood and sang. There was a bearded boy in fatigues and four girls, all in blue-jean skirts. They played guitars and fiddles. One played the harmonica. They sang, over the speakers, in low tough voices, swinging their hips. Did anyone even for a minute believe that either Heaven or the Great Sabbath would be different from this? Why should it be?

How you feel about the Sabbath depends on where you come from. If you were raised in western Pennsylvania, as I was, the Sabbath was forbidding, a day of mostly suffering, particularly if you not only had to undergo the public ordeal, the silent streets, the locked-up stores, the closed movies, but the private ordeal as well, the heavy Sunday of guilt and gloom, almost as the two Johns had planned it. It wasn't till I went to Catholic countries that I discovered Sunday as a day of pleasure. The emphasis was more pagan than Christian, but I didn't care. My own Sabbath came a day earlier, of course, since I was a Jew, and though I had to bear the sadness a little of their Sunday, I still had the pleasure of my own Friday night and Saturday, with its attention to feasting and celebration. There was an excitement, a headiness, to that Sabbath, and though various things were forbidden, or at least frowned on, that wasn't the *critical* aspect. On the other hand I wasn't *pure* anything. I was for a while bastard Orthodox and for a while liberal Conservative before I became nostalgic Agnostic at the age of thirteen years and one day. The Jews of Pittsburgh, I guess like the Jews of Schenectady and Cleveland and Houston and Detroit, developed a kind of adjustable Sabbath to accommodate the new gods a little, all except the surly ones, who lived by old time. You could see them in certain converted mansions, or sometimes in a restaurant, or sometimes standing outraged on the sidewalk glaring into our very hearts, our ruined souls, those of us who drove our Buicks and Chevys and Studebakers the two or three forbidden blocks to shul.

It is quite possible that in the earliest of times labor itself was taboo on certain days in order to propitiate the dreaming God—say, the moon—who was resting or thinking and would therefore have been offended by such activity. It was a day of abstinence, probably of penitence. To the early Babylonians it was a day of evil omen and mourning, called Shappatu, and on that day the shepherd of the great tribes, acting for the people, could not eat salted meat or cook or change his clothes or dress in white or offer a sacrifice or ride in a chariot or talk victoriously or make a wish. It was a time of terror and appeasement, of deep struggle. I can't understand how the notion of a day of blessing and rest came into being from this. If it did. It is an incredible idea, almost beyond imagination. How had human beings converted a fearful day into a day of great joy, how had they made the philosophical leap, and then *how* had they immediately converted *that* into a day of absurd prohibitions, as if they not only couldn't stand the freedom but the joy? As if there were no other way to do it. As if they were Babylonians.

On the deepest level, the state of "rest" is a state of complete harmony between mankind and nature, and man and man; and "work," be it lighting a match or lifting a blade of grass, is an inter-. ference. It intrudes. I think what happened was that the ideal condition, the dream condition, was located somehow illogically in the sphere of the real and the literal, and mankind, at least the Jewish variety thereof, was asked to do the impossible. To live perfectly. He should not have been whipped and stoned and lectured at and frowned on for his weaknesses. He should have been praised for what he did and pitied for what he could not do. Sabbath, among the Essenes and the Samaritans, and among the Mennonites and the United Pentecostals, became a day of obsessional overstrictness, but that was only because they had all but lost sight of the dream of perfection in their rigorous attention to failure and imperfection.

On the Sabbath we are free from the chains of nature and from the chains of time, for there is no nature, and there is no time, although it is only for one day a week. Is that not mad and beautiful, and impractical? Picture a whole community, picture a whole country, acting as if there were no money and no work and no sorrow, and no death. Picture the great delusion, if it is that. Picture living out an entire epic of eternity, and doing it serially, week by glorious week. It is as if, by claiming that day, one could claim for himself the fruits of that day. It is as if one could force the issue, through belief, through obedience, through prayer. Through will and imagination. The dance. The Talmud says that if all of Israel would observe the Sabbath fully only *once*, the Messiah would be here. Not that the Messiah would come as a reward for our good deeds, but that he would *be* here, as a consequence, as a natural result or fulfillment, of our Sabbatical lives. Some places it says twice.

The Sabbath can be seen not only as an anticipation of messianic time but as a nostalgic reminder of Edenic time, the time before the expulsion. There, probably, there was harmony also, at least we are told so, but the difference is that Edenic man hadn't opened his eyes yet, he didn't know of good and evil, he wasn't tied together—or separated—by bonds of love and loneliness, he was not yet cursed. And, therefore, if he knew peace and unity, it wasn't the resonant star-shattering unity of the man or woman who overcomes the limitation, who moves through existence and time and suffering into "restfulness"; it was the peace and unity of a rock or a tree or even a bird, something that sometimes the poet aspires to but, I think, in desperation, or hopelessness. In messianic time, and on the Sabbath, which is its precursor, man is free, that is he does what he wants, that is he has the consciousness to make loving decisions. What if it should happen that one day the world would be full of love, one Saturday? It would be called new-time. This is what the prophets imagined. The earth will be unpolluted again, and immensely fruitful. There will be no conflict and no pain and no destruction, a continuous Sabbath. *It* is the purpose of history, perhaps of existence. And it will happen, the prophets believed, from human efforts. But that which happens, is it a state of non-existence, or is it a state of existence? Is consciousness intensified or is it obliterated? Is total consciousness, or total absorption, a form of obliteration? I'm sure some bridge-makers from Colorado or Tibet have taken up the issue. I'm absolutely sure those rabbis' eyes are slanted, and that those great Chinese bow and kiss their scarves in the same way that we do.

Then what should we do on Saturday afternoon and Saturday morning? We may not sow or plow or reap or gather into sheaves or thrash or winnow or cleanse or grind or sift or knead or bake. We may not shear or bleach or heat or dye or spin or make a warp or make two thrum-threads or weave two threads or split two threads or tie or untie or sew two stitches or tear in order to sew two stitches. We may not hunt deer or slaughter or skin or salt or tan or scrape or cut. We may not write two letters or erase for the purpose of writing two letters or build or pull down or either extinguish fire or kindle fire or beat with a hammer or carry from one premise or domain into another. But not only can we not plow, for example, but we cannot dig or make canals, and not only can we not reap but we cannot pick fruit from a tree or tear off grass or mold that has grown on a box or a barrel, or cut a flower. For by so doing we interfere with the physical world, the state of peace between man and nature. We build and destroy. We reduce the perfection, or at least the balance. And we violate the commandment. We probably can't pare our nails, or swim lengths, or read the want ads. I know we can't swim, for we may be tempted to construct a bladder. And we cannot squeeze fruit juice, for that would be threshing. And we cannot slaughter, for that would be a derivative of dyeing. So say the texts.

We may eat, indeed we must eat, and we may drink and we may reason. And if a child is locked in a room we may batter the door down, of course, and rush someone to the hospital. And we may listen to music, may we not? And we may make music, although for some that was toeing the line, and it was perhaps better for a Shabbos Goy to do that for us, and although for the mad Essenes defecation itself was too much of an interference with the silence and harmony, lovemaking was—eventually—not only permitted but indeed encouraged—required—as a good Sabbath activity, for the Shekinah was present that day and the union was likely to be blessed. The logic, certainly from a modern viewpoint, is ambiguous, even confusing. Of all things, sexual activity *is* an interference, particularly with its threat of new life, but perhaps no more than eating and drinking, with its threat of continued life. But it is what the activity stands for that counts. However real it is to the individuals concerned, it must always be seen and felt as symbolic activity, as if life itself was a dream, or a work of art. Or at least the Sabbath was. That is the explanation! Saturday is a work of art, a dream. And what we do on that day is "as if." As if the Sabbath were eternal. As if we lived always on, and only on, the Sabbath. As if we could defy nature, in our tremendous love of it. As if we could pick and choose; as if we could be as arbitrary, and free, as we wanted to, selecting and combining whatever it is we had to, or wanted to. As in a work of art. And it would finally last forever.

That is why there was so much haggling. That is why we were permitted to carry a piano, or a bed, from one room to another, but we were not permitted to carry a handkerchief into the street. For that might be transferring property and therefore changing the social order. Or it might call to mind such a change. It was not at all a question of labor or effort, as such. It required more effort not to carry the handkerchief, not to light the match. We had to maintain the illusion, if it is that, of peace and permanence, and free ourselves from time. We were struggling with a work of art. A poem. The Sabbath is a poem.

My favorite movie is René Clair's *À Nous la Liberté*. Wherever I am, whatever I'm doing, I'll stop at once to go see it. And the scene

I love the most in that film is where the workers, having at last been released from the deadly struggle with material existence—in the form of a fully automated assembly line out of a technocrat's perfect vision—are free to do what they want, the burden of labor forever lifted from their shoulders, the curse undone. They choose to dance, and the company has erected for them, or they have erected for themselves, a kind of pavilion where all day long they hold each other and move around in a dream of love and dignity and peace. It is summer. The women have on lovely cotton dresses and the men are wearing dark shirts and ties. Some have on caps. They dance a quick two-step in the style of 1930. It is radios they are manufacturing, and someone or something must set the machine going and do the oiling and repairs and make certain decisions and store and release information, even if the production and the packaging and distribution are done by invisible and nonhuman hands. But that is not the concern of these people. They are finished with conflict and disharmony. With work.

The lovely anarchistic philosophy that underlies this film is the one that sees the possibility of human liberation through the wise use of technology. Machines will do the work. They will free us. Those same machines that once enslaved us. A romantic and discredited view, most of us now believe, in its oversimplification and naïveté, although the film itself was already partly ironic and critical, especially in its portrayal of the childlike and pastoral idyll. But the vision is sabbatic as well as technologic. It is poetic and religious and even mystical, as all anarchistic visions are. Not only that, but the technological Utopia itself is formed from and suffused with sabbatical thought and feeling, just as all sabbatic visions, even the most orthodox, now must take into consideration the thoughts of technology.

This is a strange time to be thinking about Shabbos. Half the world is at war or preparing for it or recovering from it. Moreover, a sizeable portion of the good people of the world are in political prisons of one kind or another, and a fourth are starving; and we are contemptuous not only of human life but of all life on the planet, if not the universe; and we are in a kind of trap, and coldness of heart has become the dominant mode, and the life we force ourselves to lead is degrading; and almost all governments are inept and corrupt and brutal; and we live by delusion, and there is very little dignity left and very little awe; and we may perhaps indeed be evil or indifferent creatures altogether, as the cruel incendiaries among us have for centuries suggested; and in my own country ugliness is apotheosized, and money is worshiped more than ever before; and we elect weasels to office; and we carefully destroy most of what is good from the past; and we murder and rape and thieve with ease; and we bore ourselves to death; and we either believe in dark and mindless things or pretend to believe in bright and holy things while we secretly hold them in contempt; and we allow both our public and private lives to be governed by systems and rules we neither understand nor believe in; and we hate the brain; and we are deeply pessimistic. Although there are some pockets of resistance: we produce art and we are somehow great in medicine and astronomy; and we dance and write poetry; and we still have some lovely cities; and though we are wavering, we still live for the future; and we are insisting on a presence, or pressure, we never did before; and for one drop of water the thirsty among us would gather and weep. But no matter what, I'm not going to give up my dream or my life because of this Nebuchadrezzar and that Nicanor, for I have my great-grandchildren to think about, and I am forever ruined anyhow by my teachers and masters. In fact, what better time could

there be to think about Shabbos? And why shouldn't we fly through
these fields, and over these bridges now?

Myself, I will write poems in spite of the rabbinical ban on writ-
ing "even one letter of the alphabet," for I will be writing in a dif-
ferent nature. And I will take it that praise and some blame, whether
oral or written, are acceptable; just as playing musical instruments
has to be acceptable, in spite of the loud noise; just as climbing a tree,
for the sake of a breathtaking view, might be acceptable, even if the
fruit, the apricots and the pears, are shaken loose by accident, and
it be construed as picking, as harvesting, which is a weekday rou-
tine. I remember anyhow that the ban against playing instruments
is not because of the noise, because certainly the instruments could
be muffled; and it's not because it's a diversion and a joy, which are
English and Swiss and Scottish crimes; but only because the player
might have to *repair* the instrument—it's the repairing that's prohib-
ited, so I will make sure that all my pens are flowing and my pencils
are sharpened. Or perhaps the nature of poetry itself will change
some Saturday, not that it will become insipid or sweet, not that
the pain will go away, for there is still death and memory; but per-
haps the pain in the life of the poet will stop being the main subject,
the endless romantic era will be over, and we will have our delight
back, or have a new delight. Perhaps the rabbis will even let us write
then. Although I also want to just sit and think, for that is my *great-
est* pleasure. I remember, even when I climbed my library steps to
do my endless rampaging, how I imagined that one day I would be
free of the compulsive need and I would sit in front of the fountain
down there, on one of the wooden benches, and let my mind drift.
At the moment—I was maybe twenty-two—I didn't worry much
about what I would think about on my small bench. I think I felt I
would live in a lovely animal timelessness, but now I see it is time

itself that gives me the pleasure, and the passing of time, and the living again—that which I call pleasure. It is contemplation, I am sure, but I call it "thinking," and there is nothing more delightful.

I will write poems, I will listen to poems, I will listen to music, I will talk and argue. And rage. I will sit. None of this is work. And I will worry a little about what my friends and neighbors are doing, trying to balance somehow my respect or tolerance for their own choices, no matter that they might seem to me boring or meaningless, with my need to make their actions and their dreams coalesce with mine, that dangerous violent passion. I have already, even this early in the week, achieved a little patience and a little interest in their lives. I am almost ready to become a decent citizen of this world, the first step toward becoming a decent citizen in the next. I think that's true. The last few days are a little cooler and the grass in front of my house is thick with leaves of all colors and sizes. I can't imagine a Saturday without them. A beautiful woman passes my front door pulling a tiny Chihuahua after her. It weighs a pound. She tells me it's called "dear little one" in Spanish. Upstairs the Chicago Symphony is playing Schubert's Ninth Symphony. In a little while I'll be listening for the hundredth time to Blind Boy Fuller wailing to the hills of North Carolina. Sonny Terry on the harp; Bull City Red on the washboard. I am thinking of my Uncle Simon and his last years in Miami Beach. I am remembering his clippings and his photographs; how he carried them with him to his furnished room; how proud he was of his last years as a labor organizer for the salesmen at Robert Hall; how delighted he was with the pictures of himself and Soapy Williams, governor of Michigan, and with the grandfatherly union officials in Atlantic City and New York and Chicago. He did that for nothing. He was five-foot-two and went to work when he was fourteen. He spent the long Depression years only sporadically employed. I remember his bitterness, his mean temper. I remember him reading Emerson's essays from a little bound set he had picked up somewhere. I remember his slow death. And turning the pages of his album with him, reading the articles and looking at the pictures, over and over.

I can see me some Friday soon walking out my front door to welcome in the queen. I have a broom in my hand since there are no myrtles growing here, or better yet two brooms, one for Exodus and one for Deuteronomy; or lest I am too silly or mocking, I can pick up two small maple branches outside my kitchen window. My rich stew is on the stove, my house is lit up, and the floor is swept. I am alone, but there is not one ounce of self-pity in my heart. I am thinking of that hill I saw, and that music, those harps and lutes, those violins and guitars. I am thinking of the faces of those farm-ers, fixed and transformed. I can't believe, whatever it is we do with our nervous lives, we were not better meant to sing for each other, and listen, and tune our fiddles and trombones. I can't believe we are not going to have that happiness.

GINSBERG AND I

How weary I used to get, and resentful and impatient, when people compared me to or mistook me for Allen Ginsberg, as they did. Particularly since it was such a crude comparison. Both of us East Coast Jews, quick-moving rabbis. Not that I didn't love him and wasn't a little amused by the comparison; it was the gross simplicity that troubled me.

Sometimes I patiently bespoke our differences. He had a darker complexion. I was beefier, he had a beard, I wasn't gay, I didn't have a programme, I wasn't trying to shock the bourgeoisie, our voices—pitch, tone, accent—were different. His singing voice was nothing, tinny, I thought, whereas I had a lovely second tenor. And our subject matter and our concerns were different. And we approached the political differently. And I was more metaphysical and mystical; he was more realistic.

More than anything, he clearly thought he had to choose between Stevens and Williams; and he chose Williams. Whereas I loved them both and didn't see it as a problem and I combined their strains and strands. But he felt that not only was Stevens's poetry too symbolist, musical, whimsical, evasive, cute—he told me this—but that it lacked true content and wasn't driven by subject matter as, he would say, Williams (and he himself) were.

I heard him once at a reading seven or eight of us gave at a reconstructed movie house in Rutherford, New Jersey, called the Williams Center—in honor of Williams's one hundredth birthday—complain to the person in charge that one of the readers—it was Dan Halpern—shouldn't be there because he (Dan) taught at Columbia, and Columbia was pro-Stevens (and I assume therefore anti-Williams) and Dan was therefore doubly guilty. It was both astonishing and ridiculous. The person in charge was a huge beautiful guy maybe a little overweight wearing a suit and tie and sweating heavily—it was close to a hundred degrees—but Allen persisted in the face of the poor man's sweetness and fear.

Of course, we *were* alike—Allen and I—in many ways. We saw through shit, we made unaccommodating judgments, we simplified. We liked the more severe prophets. But I never wrapped myself in an American flag, as he did, as an act of publicity; and I didn't scold and rant and I didn't make the news. Allen was world-famous years before I even emerged. Indeed, he was, I think, the most famous poet in the world. What there was was a physical similarity—I have to admit it—and we were the same age. We both were influenced by Whitman but he claimed Whitman, he was a direct descendant, a continuation—I was more resistant.

It was the mistaken identity that got to me. I'll tell a few anecdotes. Once, sometime in the 1980s, I went to a small coffeehouse in the Village—I'm sure it was a Saturday morning—to have a coffee and work on a poem. I noticed a young man whispering to the waitress and glancing over at me, so I knew something was happening. After a while he came over, rather fearfully, and asked me if he could show me a few poems. "Ah, they follow me everywhere," I thought; then, on an instinct, I asked him who he thought I was and he answered, "Allen Ginsberg." I was amused at first but after I told him who I truly was and he *withdrew* the poems, I was crestfallen. How (and *why*) to tell him who I was, how (and *why*) to tell him I was a "master," whatever that was, he whose poems I had absolutely no desire to see, he who didn't recognize me, he who *mistook* me, that wretched young *schnorrer*, that aspiring fool who showed no knowledge, no taste, no manners. That latter-day Beat—certainly a neo-Beat—full of ridiculous intensity, shorn of music, punctured with exclamation marks. Not to mention that I lost interest in working further on my own poems—not to mention the coffee was cold.

A year or so later—it was 1985—I was wearing a beard as the result of having been shot in the neck during a robbery attempt in Newark, New Jersey, and being unable to lift my chin to shave. The bullet, a .22 caliber, lodged in the soft flesh next to the carotid artery, and it was two months before the swelling and the stiffness went away. The surgeons decided not to remove the bullet because of its proximity to the artery. A few months after that I was walking up the gangplank in Miami, Florida, from some inhuman airplane, when a heavily dressed snowbird walking opposite me—we were both wearing winter rags in the tropics—shouted out Allen's name in great joy and, as we continued to walk, carrying our overcoats and bags, I told him who I was, the story of the mistaken identity in the coffee shop, and the shooting. To which he replied that it was he, Larry Lieberman from Illinois, that he knew who I was *almost* immediately, that he felt terrible, and so on. It was then my turn to apologize and I said something about not recognizing him behind the hat and the sheepskin coat.

We then shook hands and said goodbye—we were both going to see our ancient mothers, but I was also first going to give a reading in a local college. When I got to my host's house I applied the lather thick and painfully shaved off the beard. It was another case of mistaken identity, with me on the invisible side, if you will, and I was starting to get irritated. It was dispiriting that it was a one-way street; nobody told Allen he looked like *me*—at least I assumed so. He had the famous puss and I was a latecomer, so it would always be the same, if it was anything. Nor do I know of any like cases. Adrienne Rich, or Ed Hirsch, for example, don't have doppelgängers out there; and Phil Levine doesn't even look like his twin brother who, anyhow, is a painter. I'm the only one plagued like this.

The third part of the story is that in 1990, the centennial of Walt's death, we were giving a reading of his poems in St. John the Divine to what turned out to be an enormous audience that filled the huge space. There were eight of us, I think, Charlie Williams, Lucille Clifton, myself, Michael Harper, Allen, Galway, I think Sharon Olds. That's seven. We were sitting in one of the smaller rooms getting instructions on where to stand and in what order to speak when Michael arrived late, his huge raincoat dripping water, trying to close his umbrella. He was clearly struggling to adjust and when he saw me sitting there—though we know each other—he asked, "How are you, Allen?" I couldn't resist replying that I was Jerry Stern but "we all look alike." Which he, as an African American, certainly must have heard endlessly. Mean-spirited, and I'm sorry. For his part, Michael apologized profusely, and the next few times I saw him he was *extremely* friendly and attentive. And I have nothing but love for him. But there *was* something. True, Michael knew that Allen would be there, and maybe Allen was on his mind, and he was flustered from his late arrival and the rain. After a while I got used to the comparison and less irritated by it. When I hear it at readings I remark that he *does* look like me. I tell one of the stories and I let it go at that.

I am writing this in Walpole, New Hampshire, in the sum-

mer of 2000, not far from Brattleboro, Vermont, and the lovely
Laches Hotel and Sam's Army and Navy Store and even closer to
Bellows Falls and the old intact railroad station. Last night we had
dinner with friends; Anne Marie and I, and Jackie Gens, who was
Allen Ginsberg's assistant, were there. She said there *was* a physical
resemblance, especially in the eyes and the lips, as well as the way
we moved. There was some satisfaction in that. If we were alike,
we were alike. Come to think of it we were both bald, had round
foreheads, and wore eyeglasses. I love the fact that we both were, or
are, connected with New Jersey. Though he was born there and I
came later. He would probably have been amused, maybe unhappy,
for all I know, that I was the first poet laureate of that state. I don't
know why he was never New York's poet laureate, or America's.
He certainly was our unofficial laureate and we all knew it. Anne
Marie, who knows me better than anyone, agrees about the eyes.
They're both Russian, she says, which I translate as "tragic." But
we only look alike at certain angles, she says. I think she is think-
ing that her sweetheart does not have anything in common with
anyone else, famous poet or not.

We are staying at a bed and breakfast called The Inn at Valley
Green in the outskirts of Walpole and we're sitting in the garden
under a gigantic sugar maple. Anne Marie is rereading *Crime and
Punishment*. She read 150 pages today. There are seventeen rooms
in the inn, and a library in one of the downstairs rooms, maybe not
your typical bed and breakfast books: *The Passions of the Western
Mind*, *The Life of Bob Marley*, *The Book of Dogs*, Nabokov's *Glory*,
Zane Grey's *Tappan's Burro*, Wilkie Collins's *The Moonstone*, *Home
Pet Care*, *Treasury of Great Nature Writing*, *Berkeley's Essays*, Pearl
Buck, Robert Benchley, Thomas Mann, and between *A Guide to
Mushrooms* and *A Field Guide to North American Birds*, magically, *The*

Collected Poetry and Selected Prose of John Donne, 760 pages, the 1932 edition, edited by John Hayward.

I spend the afternoon reading and recollecting. I decide at this juncture that my favorite Donne poem is no longer "The Extasie," or "The Sunne Rising," or "Julia," or one of the Holy Sonnets (X, XI, XIV), but "A Hymne to God the Father," which begins "Wilt thou forgive that sinne where I beginne," and ends with the sad pun, "and having done that, Thou hast done / I fear no more." Naturally, I try to guess Ginsberg's favorites, though he may have left Donne a while ago. I wish I knew. He certainly was exposed to Margie Nicolson at Columbia, as I was.

This morning I walked through the fields. Wild carrot, cornflowers, fleabane, and a little trumpety white flower that looked like morning glory but, I'm told, was bindweed. In the orchard above, juicy, yellow plums and hard, sweet apples, a kind of winesap. Ginsberg would have loved it. This afternoon we're driving into Brattleboro on a little-traveled dirt road so we can see the ruins of Madame Sherri's stone chateau. It's in the woods, I understand, fairly inaccessible, a fireplace, a few walls and pilasters, some arches, some stone steps, some poison ivy. I read that there's a swimming pond by the dirt road, in front of the house, surrounded by a stone wall. I'm sure there are lily pads there now and a patient frog or two. Like poets, they tend to look alike.

In a newspaper article I read at the inn, I learned that Madame Sherri, Antoinette Sherri, a Paris-born theatrical costume designer who worked on famous Broadway shows, built the little "castle" in the late 1920s on a 488-acre tract of land deep in the woods in New Hampshire, near Brattleboro Mountain. She and her entourage spent summers there and she would drive up from New York in a 1927 open Packard touring car driven by one handsome young chauffeur or another in riding pants and boots. She and her group scandalized the locals, women in heavy makeup and smoking in public, one or two wearing tuxedos, with thin moustaches painted on, men in God knows what kind of bizarre costumes. The chateau had elaborate stone work, including a Roman arched stairway and ornate interior furnishings, including Belgian tapestries, ancient Chinese porcelain, fourteenth-century Italian pottery, and alabaster and gold Buddhas. But after three decades of joyous summers, Madame Sherri returned in 1959 to find her home completely vandalized. The piano had been axed, vases had been shot and shattered, the tapestries were knifed, and the paintings were shredded in their gilded frames. She never came back; her remaining years she spent in Brattleboro living on welfare, one of the town eccentrics. The building was burned in 1963 and friends of mine in Brattleboro and Bellows Falls refer to the little castle as a "bordello"; I'm sure the less gentle of heart call it a "whorehouse"; the result, I guess, of trying to rationalize—or explain—the destruction. The stupidity drives me crazy.

Anne Marie's poem about the ruin is a kind of elegy to Madame Sherri. I love that she's wearing her new blue dress in the poem, in which she looks so beautiful. I'm done—a long time ago—writing about ruins, at least that kind, but if I did compose something, I guess it would be a love affair between one of the frogs and Madame Sherri. I don't know what Allen would do, if anything. He did ruins different from me. It's too bad he and I couldn't have driven up from the city in the Packard, eating Portuguese sardines and soda crackers, drinking port and dago red, singing some stuff from the 1940s, giving the chauffeur a few orders, talking to Madame Sherri about Paris. We would have both relished that. Now the only living things, besides the weeds and the water lilies, are the frogs. God knows they sing too, though they have no memory of Paris, and they don't eat sardines or drink port, those look-alikes.

CAVES

I TRY TO THINK of my favorite cave. There was one in the cellar of a house I lived in in Philadelphia that you reached by walking through three other cellars and which felt as if you were in the dead center of this glorious existence. And there was one seven flights up in the abominable heaven they call "maids' rooms" in the City of Lights. I moved from that maid's room, that *chambre de bonne*, with its little porthole and its tiny sink, to a very old hotel near the Seine. The room was only one flight up—a kind of miracle among those I knew and loved—and it had huge shutters that completely kept out the light and two giant pillows on the bed and a small carved writing table. It was a cave, though, partly because it was practically surrounded by a large courtyard and partly because, of all the languages spoken up and down those worn stone steps—Polish, Arabic, Greek, French, Romanian—none of them was English. One of my caves was an old lawyers' office in Indiana, Pennsylvania. I treasured it because of its seediness and its former use and its view out the alley and because my landlord, a young millionaire and a patron of the arts who charged me only seven dollars a month rent, came himself in his blue suit and his camel-hair overcoat to bleed the pipes or do whatever other magic was necessary to generate heat out of the inefficient furnace, his mouth open and breathing hard, his eyes half-worried, half-laughing, his hand searching around down there for some knob or other to turn or pull, one way or the other. Another was above an Army-Navy store with a window full of dusty amazingly cheap jackets and shirts and shoes, which I loved to look at. That cave was ruined forever during one long Christmas vacation when the hideous sounds of "Rudolph the Red-Nosed Reindeer" came surging through the cardboard walls without letup, day and night.

One cave, in New Brunswick, New Jersey, was so large I was able to play full-court handball with a friend from Connecticut in one of the three rooms. I loved that place because of the tree in the backyard and because of the fruit market downstairs. There was an electrical fire in the basement one freezing winter night, and I arrived with my eyes bulging and my heart pounding to see my books and papers scattered on the steps and on every inch of available floor space, my poor thoughts and fantasies exposed to the triple hell of smoke and water and ice. I had to fight with the firemen to get in; I had to climb over those frozen hoses and struggle through that black air. I think the building was made over after that into small cheap apartments and that it lasted for another six years or so before Johnson & Johnson tore it down to make room for a large bush or an Italian ice cream parlor for its crazed employees across the way in that glass outhouse designed by Philip Johnson, one of the relatives, I guess. I think it's actually a children's garden, built out of railroad ties and garishly painted pipes. A corner of one of my poems is forcing its way between two bucolically laid bricks on one of the walkways. It takes the place of dandelion or milkweed and is there for the picking. Some hungry child will eat it, or some clean mother will drop it in a wire basket in a sudden lurid fit of citizenship.

Wherever I wander, whether in Pennsylvania or Ohio or Mexico or Greece, I dream about the caves I might have lived in or worked in and compare them to the ones I had. I used to own a small house in Easton, Pennsylvania, with a garret on the third floor and a small back room on the second floor overlooking a patch of garden and a church in the slight distance whose small bell rang on the hour, and both of these rooms moved me to tears, as did the kitchen, a square room with a pine floor and an old cupboard and windows all around. For fifteen years I owned a house on the Delaware River in Raubsville, Pennsylvania, with walls two feet thick and a walk-in fireplace and wide plank floors. That house was *filled* with caves, and was itself a kind of cave. I loved it most the day I bought it, before we converted it. It seemed gigantic then, and primitive, and open. I remember sitting on a cement step on the side porch, with bees attacking me and ivy getting ready to strangle me. I was half-joyous because of the thick lilac trunks and the dark cool interior and the near-silence, and half in despair because of the rotting roofs and the rusty cisterns.

I had another cave across the road overlooking the great river. I constructed it myself from a broken-down three-car garage. I put vertical spruce on the outside and plaster on the inside and raised the roof to accommodate some large windows I had bought for a few dollars from a friend, a penniless painter from Kintnersville, who found them in a junk pile on the side of the road. It was a sharp climb down to the river on a hill covered mostly with maple and black locust. I loved the view best from the river's edge; then it seemed I was looking up into an Arizona or New Mexico apartment complex built a thousand or so years ago. For not only was there the hill itself, but a two-story cement retaining wall on which the low wooden building rode. I stood by the lapping water amazed at the beauty of that building and struck by my handiwork and my skill as a contractor.

My truest of all caves, though, was the New York apartment on Vandam Street. I climbed up five stories to get there, but once I was inside I was overwhelmed by the plaster moldings and the light fixture. I could see the Empire State Building from my chair, beyond the rows of colonial houses in Soho and the darker taller buildings on Fourteenth and Twenty-third Streets. My bed looked onto one of those vertical shafts, and in the spring and summer the wind poured over me, caught in some mad and one-of-a-kind crosscurrent of shaft and window. I lay on my bed face-down, almost dizzy from the slight roar, and happy—if there ever was happiness—from those cold walls rising over me and from the peace and secrecy.

My first cave in Iowa City was at the corner of Van Buren and Ronalds. It was brick and low and completely Dutch in design, standing apart from the rows of white clapboard Victorian houses. It could have been the oldest house in Iowa City, and it was once, I'm told, a nunnery. There was a large oven in the cellar, and three crumbling rooms on the first floor, and a cross between a stepladder and a staircase going up to the second floor, which was one large garret, lying under the roof. My music system was on the second floor; I wrote either there—in bed—or downstairs in the kitchen, at a white wooden table. In fact, I had two rooms too many. I didn't need the living room or the extra bedroom, except perhaps to house my occasional guest or provide floor space for my plants.

I will never be done with caves. They certainly connect with a history not hundreds but thousands of years old, and they are loving reminders of our most delicate and perhaps our happiest time on earth. It is not only out of poverty and melodrama and disgraceful nostalgia that we live our real lives out in caves; we do so because only that way can we decipher the words assigned to us, and stray as we have to. For those who don't, or can't, there is no shame; there is merely no sacred life, and no language. I feel like saying it's the poet's job to remember (and not only the poet's)—that is, to keep the past—but that's not saying it accurately. It's more to the point to say that he can't help doing that, even if he struggles a little against it. It is in the cave that he remembers. Remembering is the art of the cave dweller. And remembering is itself an act of living in the cave. I remember now unashamedly, I even reminisce, I will interrupt myself—or anyone—with a story from my childhood or for that matter from theirs. I am amazed at the joy it brings me, as I am saddened by the ridicule and shocked at what is forgotten or never known.

I don't know what the liberated shadow that Plato held so dearly actually saw when he emerged into the light. Or what he said to the others when he returned to the cave. What the intensity of their vision was on that sheet of wall in front of the flickering fire, what stories they told and dances they did, that Plato doesn't tell us. They must have lived in such ignorance and superstition. Surely they exchanged bones and grunted. And Plato, where had he wandered in Egypt and Sicily? What caves had he seen? I don't for a minute accept the parable as a metaphor for illumination and redemption. That was a cave the philosopher was talking about, and it was a cave he rejected, just as he rejected its poetry. I would have loved to have seen him with one foot out of his own cave, starting his long walk, maybe with his sandals over his shoulder, like Loyola, or Mao Tsetung. What a dream of light! Innocent and brutal.

Zeus himself was born in a cave. His mother had him there to keep him away from his greedy father—that is the official version—but it may also be a subtle reminder that the god of overwhelming power, represented by terrible lightning itself, had his first sensation—his first thoughts—in the secret dark. It wasn't the brilliant light that was under attack in Greece, as it would be hundreds of years later in western Europe and America; it was, as we all learned and taught, human arrogance and self-confidence. After all, the Greeks had more or less invented that light. The dialogue between Dionysus and Pentheus that takes place in *The Bacchic Women* is the best example I know for summing up the conflict between simple wisdom grounded in great complexity, and prejudice grounded in neurotic repression and fear. It is amazing how lucid and light-footed Euripides makes Dionysus, our god of madness. Pentheus, the grandson of Cadmus and ruler of Thebes, actually the cousin of Dionysus, is arrogant and self-important. He refuses to respect, or even recognize, the god; he has enormous faith in his own power; he is a blasphemer; he doesn't listen to counsel. For this, he is finally ridiculed and torn to pieces.

There are many like him among the Greeks. Oedipus, before he is blind. Creon. They are famous. Odysseus, on the other hand, listened carefully to the gods, but there is a pedantry and prudishness about his orthodoxy. Both he and Theseus fought against the cave, and they did so with recklessness and lack of reverence, although the stories that come down to us are only about the overcoming of the monstrous, the crude bull, the one-eyed giant, both of them ignorant and trusting, easy enough to outwit. That Calypso lived in a cave, but she was soft and loving. I don't think she ate human flesh, but the Minotaur did and Polyphemus did and Scylla, with her six dogs' heads. Not to mention the Maenads. Dionysus' cave—it was the right thigh of Zeus, where he was sewn up and nurtured, from which he was finally born, which he always remembered.

It may be that the large number of actual caves in the area of Greek hegemony led to the obsession among Greek philosophers with

the great states of light and dark or—what is the same—the pas-
sion for opposites, including the defining of a thing by its other,
or its naught; or it may be just that caves are perfect locations—
metaphors—for our instinctive, and extreme, philosophical and
poetic states. For me, Plotinus, that wounded Egyptian, is the best
example of this. It may, in fact, have been his only obsession—light
and dark—and all his ethical and metaphysical concerns have to be
considered from that point of view. "The mind gives radiance out
of its own store," he said, in the *Enneads* (VI, 6). It was, at once, the
supreme answer to darkness and the only explanation for transcen-
dence. Sitting there on some shadowy rock or staring wistfully into
some hole in the ground, he may not have been that different from
St. Jerome in his dim grotto or Don Quixote waiting to be lowered
into Montesino's cave. "Call it not Hell," Don Quixote said, "for
it deserves a better name." It was a dream place he visited, "a royal
and sumptuous palace of which the walls and battlements seemed
all of clear and transparent crystal" and an "enchanted solitude"; but
he arrived there by committing himself to the "black and dreadful
abyss," by letting himself down with a rope. One thing produced
the other.

I sit in my chair reading Plotinus and longing to be in Ethio-
pia, in one of the remote churches carved out of solid rock, or in
southern France studying an ochre antler in some hidden recess. It
is my lower faculty, my nature-loving and generative faculty, that
is doing this to me; although Plotinus would say that the material
universe, where the lovely caverns lie, is modeled upon the ideas
laid up within the Divine Mind. I warn myself that it is all right
to read Plotinus but very dangerous to talk about him. He is such
a bad writer, Porphyry tells us, because he not only didn't rewrite
but didn't even read what he had written down. His handwriting

was slovenly; he misjoined his words; he cared nothing about spelling. His one concern was for the idea. If one does nothing else he or she should read Porphyry's biography of Plotinus, at least the first few pages, to see what a great soul did in the third century of our era to escape the pain of existence, besides crawling like a worm across some bloody stone floor and mumbling in lost tongues like a wounded hyena or a stinking fox. "Plotinus, the philosopher our contemporary," Porphyry tells us, "seemed ashamed of being in the body. So deeply rooted was this feeling that he could never be induced to tell of his ancestry, his parentage, or his birthplace." His whole life—from the time he was twenty-eight on—was committed to the understanding of things—i.e., nonthings—so he could live, at the end, in the world—i.e., outside it—in wisdom and purity. At his death, according to Porphyry, he said that he was striving to give back the Divine in himself to the Divine in the All; very Emersonian. It was a philosopher's death pure and simple, concocted or not. Porphyry says a snake crept under the bed in which Plotinus lay and slipped into a hole in the wall at the very moment he died. He is from both worlds, isn't he, that snake? We know him well by now.

It's hard to know what Plotinus actually thought of caves. It depended on whether, at one moment or another, he was thinking of them as places of confinement or places of liberation—Plato or Pythagoras. In the extraordinary section of the *Enneads* where he discusses the descent of the soul into the body, he refers specifically to Empedocles' grotto and Plato's cave, and he says that the function of the soul is to break its chains and rise to the place of intellection (the intelligible world). But at the same time he praises the descent and says—after Timaeus—that the Large Soul was sent into the world and small souls into each of us to make it a rational universe and to make the sense world complete by assuring that it contained as many kinds of organisms as in that revered, intelligible world (place of intellection). Although no soul, he says, not even ours, enters into the body completely. By her higher part the soul always remains united to the upper world—even if the lower part is turned toward the body (every soul has something of the lower on the body side). It is such familiar doctrine after all these centuries, after so many Christians and humanists and Kabbalists have gotten hold of it. My own guess is that Plotinus, more than anybody else, much more than his own beloved Plato, even more than our own Jesus, has given us the modern version of the soul.

Prison poets in particular, they are the cavemen among us, the true Neoplatonists. It is as if they received two sentences—as if they were buried twice. I think of the long and shameful list, and I think of the crude and desperate systems of survival. I close my eyes and try to remember a whole poem by Nazim Hikmet. I know twelve lines of the cucumber poem, but that was written after he had been released from prison and exiled himself from Turkey. I read it aloud all the time, and I lecture my bewildered friends and students on the special function of the cucumber in eastern Europe and western Asia. I talk about its digestive qualities and its mystical history and its glorious associations with different creams and cheeses. He is a classical poet, Hikmet. He spares us the pure horror and lets us concentrate on some joy or some sadness.

> One night of knee-deep snow
> my adventure started—
> pulled from the supper table,
> thrown into a police car,

packed off on a train,
and locked up in a room.
Its ninth year ended three days ago . . .

("One Night of Knee-Deep Snow")

The poverty of Istanbul—they say—defies description,
hunger—they say—has ravaged the people,
TB—they say—is everywhere.
Little girls this high—they say—
              in burned-out buildings, movie theaters . . .

("13 November 1945")

To talk to anyone besides myself
        is forbidden.
So I talk to myself.
But I find my conversation so boring,
    my dear wife, that I sing songs.
And what do you know,
that awful, always off-key voice of mine
    touches me so
        that my heart breaks.

("Letters from a Man in Solitary")

Miguel Hernández is a little more bitter. He came from the bitter side of Europe. It is his last few letters that deal with the actual horror, the rat shit in his hair, the pus in his mouth. In his final poems he reflects, he embodies, the outright battle between light and dark, in which the prison—at Madrid, at Orthuela—is not only the poetic ground for metaphor but the living stage of his vision. The rage and weeping, the cruelty and isolation and boredom, the tenderness and hope, were expressed that way. He came finally to inhabit the same cave as St. John of the Cross; perhaps to fight the very same battle.

> I live in shadow, filled with light. Does day
> exist? Is this a grave or mother's womb? . . .
> Maybe I'm waiting to be born or see
> that I've been always dead. These shadows rule
> me, and if living's this, what can death be?

("I LIVE IN SHADOW, FILLED WITH LIGHT")

I wish I could talk to Etheridge Knight about this. I want to ask him if he began writing before he ended up in the joint. And I want to know if he felt guilty or ashamed because the spirit descended on him and left the others miserable and alone. If he felt more entrapped, or more liberated because he was writing. Who his critics were then. I myself lay once under a bare lightbulb on a terribly uncomfortable army cot, the mattress removed, with forty or so others lined up on either side of me. And I marched to an early breakfast with a number on my back and guards with loaded guns in front and back of me. And I fought with a pig of a provost-sergeant and was threatened with the hole. It feels odd—and alien—to talk about it now, and I feel foolish listing myself this way with the holy ones, for my time there was short, and my cause was absurdly small—compared to theirs. I was twenty years old at the time. I didn't know it then but my soul had descended into that place for the sake of making the universe more complete, and I had lost my way, and I was expiating for my own, or someone else's wrong. I began writing poetry seriously there, weak and humid poetry, and I started to think a little like a poet. That helped me, and the physical labor helped me, and the love of my fellow prisoners. I read the New Testament there for the first time, and I talked to my friends about their terrors. They thought

I was a preacher—because of my reading, I suppose—and I couldn't disenchant them. That provost-sergeant was shot dead one day a few years later in a courtroom by an angry prisoner—or his brother. I know I plotted his death for years and even remembered his name for a month or two. I will not recognize him when he comes on his smoking knees asking for forgiveness.

Radnóti, the Hungarian poet, died sometime after October 31, 1944. Miklós Radnóti. He was shot in the head and buried in a mass grave at Abda, a small village in western Hungary. He had been an inmate, a slave, in a forced labor camp and was executed either by a German or an Hungarian guard. The grave was exhumed on June 23, 1946, and though the corpses were partially decomposed and there were only shreds of clothing, Radnóti's body was discovered there. In the back pocket of his trousers a small notebook was found, soaked in the juices of his body. The notebook was cleaned and dried in the sun. It contained his last poems. It is ironic that his final cave wasn't even a freezing barracks but a hole in the ground, a pit, which he shared with a few hundred other Jews and a few unlucky Christians. Although I don't know if it was a true cave since there was no way out—no light. His last poem was written for a fellow-slave, a violinist named Miklós Lorsi, who died a day or two before him. Here it is:

> I fell beside him, his body turned over,
> already taut, a string about to snap.
> Shot in the neck. You'll be finished like this—
> I muttered to myself—just lie still.
> Patience flowers into death now.
> *Der springt noch auf*, a voice said over me.
> Mud and blood both drying on my ear.

("SZENTKIRALYSZABADJA, 31 OCTOBER 1944")

The string about to snap was a violin string, the heart's blood of that musician. Think of him after a forced march, after a day in the mines or on the roads, trying to remember a note.

The good institutions have been very busy with jailed poets and novelists from all the continents. There is a standard plot. The poet is whisked away in the middle of the night. It might be the only time in his whole life he is given such attention. His trial is held in secret and his lawyer is either not permitted in court or is a spy for the police. The illegal action may have consisted of printing a poem or having a lucid opinion. If there is a charge, it is treason. He is put in prison. As much as possible he is isolated and confronted with ambiguity. Sometimes he is abused—frozen, starved, tortured. That is almost for nostalgia's sake, for it is not needed. It is to remind the brutes they are brutes. The reason he is put in prison is simply to eliminate or reduce his effectiveness, his presence.

The prisoner, the poet, understands this and is determined *not* to permit it to happen. He responds specifically through his poetry. His greatest act of rebellion is to find a medium to express himself in: toilet paper, soap, skin. His great victory is to commit his poems to memory or to communicate them to the world outside the prison. He stays alive by writing.

I knew a young Russian poet who came to America a few years before the Soviet system broke up. She was arrested in 1983 for "oral agitation and propaganda" (writing poetry). Her lawyer was not allowed to attend her trial. Her family and friends were barred. She was sentenced to seven years of hard labor, deported to a corrective labor camp in the swamplands three hundred miles southeast of Moscow, and subjected to physical abuse, harassment, humiliation. She went on a hunger strike to protest the harsh treatment of two other women and was brutally force-fed. She was sent to an isolation cell (the hole) for insulting officials. She edited a communal diary, which was smuggled out to the West. She wrote her poems with a matchstick on slices of soap. She managed to keep her poems alive by reciting and memorizing a certain percentage of them every day. She stored them in her brain. She was able to sneak some of them out. She was told by the officials that she was forgotten, that no one remembered her, that nobody wanted to help her. Her cause was taken up by poets living in the West. She was adopted by Amnesty International. PEN International lobbied for her and her case was brought to the Soviet Writers' Union. She was freed by Mikhail Gorbachev on the eve of the Iceland summit meeting, and she and her husband flew to America.

The cynical and mean-spirited among us insist on pointing out that our writers in the West are not imprisoned because their words are not taken seriously; or they are ignored or drowned out in the general noise; or that writing as such cannot be a rallying point against the government, even though our state has demonstrated with great clarity that when writing is taken seriously—in the case of the blacklisted Hollywood writers, for example—it can move with great speed and ruthlessness, constitutional rights and humane traditions notwithstanding. There is no hole, but that's not necessary. Our poets must actually step on the White House lawn or damage a nose cone to get attention. There is a certain tolerance and freedom of expression and movement in the institutional arrangements that the poet can take advantage of, even if they were not designed in any way for his benefit. Poets know this. They profit from the arrangement, even as they are overcome with guilt and anger. Sometimes they want to know what they would actually have to write down to make the state take offense. In the meantime they are permitted to type and to weep more or less in peace; they are even given a table and a little glass of water and a check. They all end up singing, one way or another. For them it is the notes that count, for they are true troglodytes, those poets. It is a way of out-witting the guards.

I think we are specialists in imprisonment, even if we know very little of liberation and redemption. It is like going from cell to cell. Poe, Melville, Dostoevsky, Dickens, Kafka, Beckett, Rhys, Coetzee. If someone is spending his life staring stubbornly at a brick wall, he is one of us. If someone is being led hopelessly from room to room and building to building, he is too. He who lives in the light has to learn, above all things, he is living in darkness. Someone is finally being visited by his keeper; he asks the questions he has been rehearsing for weeks; he begs for his stub of a pencil back. Someone is bleeding to death from a hole in his stomach; he is covered with flies. Someone is so self-conscious and alone that he is almost burst-ing with regret and sadness.

There are caves where the light comes in on a single brilliant beam for one minute a day, and there are those where it enters only once a year. There is the cistern where Jeremiah ranted and the hole where David cut a corner from Saul's coat. There is the cavity in God's brain where the Virgin lay, and there is the grotto where Alexander Pope chanted. There is the collective unconscious of Jung and the electric corridors of Ludwig II. I open my Virgil to "The World Below" and find myself in sudden full belief, as Aeneas was. I had a Sibyl of my own, although I had no doves to guide me and no ghost to tell my fate and future. She lived in the great black stones of the Carnegie Library, and it was through those books she spoke to me, as she spoke to the Greeks and Italians through bark and leaves. It was a honey-combed cave she lived in, Virgil tells us, and her voice bounded and drummed and hissed as it moved from room to room. Apollo rode her to make her sing. He goaded her as she stormed about her cave, trying to shake his influence from her breast. He tired her mad jaws. In the end the cavern's hundred mouths all of themselves unclosed to let her verses through.

It is not easy to go into the underground. I remember listening to music on Saturday mornings in the Carnegie Library listening rooms. I remember going from shelf to shelf in the poorly lit stacks and sitting cross-legged on the cold floor turning my pages. There was a huge dinosaur there in the great reptile room in the next wing, and there were dozens of marble reproductions in the corridors and recesses on the way over and back. I believed then in dinosaurs, in their pinheads and grinning mouths and giant tails. I believed that the very large ones were vegetarians, the smaller, more agile, meaner ones carnivores. And I believed that Greek men were like their statues, with long thick legs and short muscular torsos, and that Greek women were large and graceful, and always a little bent over so you could catch sight of their stone breasts. The guards who were stationed throughout the enormous building were all old, with white hair and blue eyes and freckled skin. They were thin-lipped and short-tempered, and they all wore black uniforms—suits with gold buttons—and stiff white shirts. In Virgil, the way down was through a wide-mouthed cavern guarded by a dark pool and a gloomy forest, and deathly exhalations rose through the air. Aeneas offered up a fleeced lamb and a sterile cow and entire carcasses of bulls, pouring rich oil over the blazing viscera, and with the golden bough held stiffly in his outstretched hand he followed Sibyl down through all the smells and noises of hell. That I did too, but I had no golden bough, and my path was different. I think, if anything, I went down and back daily since I had my own map. After a while it became easy. The stinking pools and the writhing hands bothered me very little. It is fifty years later, and I look back on that time with love. If I had to, I could find that path again, and sacrifice, and walk through the darkness.

TREE OF LIFE

I HAVE TO TAKE IT AS A SIGN of some kind that the huge arborvitae that leans against my house and practically creates a cave out of half of my front porch was broken in two yesterday by the wind and snow and that a part of it hangs uselessly down exposing raw wood and creating a horror where such loveliness and richness once existed. Two great branches grew from the thick trunk and one of them, really the central stem, split in such a way that half of it, almost to the inch I would suspect, hangs perfectly in the snow, as if it were a skirt just touching the ground. The weight of the snow in the branches produced a third arm—for there was another crack—and another skirt, this one an old-fashioned train, a wedding gown that dragged, unfortunately, with no one to hold it up.

I am ashamed to say it, but I didn't sleep the night of the rupture. I lay there with my heart pounding and thoughts of impending old age. I couldn't stop thinking of that cedar of Lebanon somewhere in Ezekiel, the tree that stood for one of the nations that God was striking down for its pride and arrogance and indifference—Assyria or Egypt. Ezekiel spoke in God's name and with his voice and his power, even if there was some pity in that voice—as there always is in Ezekiel. He compares Assyria, in its greatness, to great Egypt. "Assyria was a cedar in Lebanon," he says, "with beautiful branches and shady thickets of lofty stature." Using lovely desert imagery he

alludes endlessly to the waters that nourished it so that the poem—
·for it is a poem—became a paean to water. At the end he compares
this cedar not only to lesser trees, the planes and cypresses, but
praises it above the cedars in the Garden of God and indeed over all
other trees in Eden. It is a radical vision, and even a little shocking,
as well as being the kind of hyperbole that poets use to upset com-
puter scientists and tree surgeons. And it brings the whole matter
to another state altogether, even as it transports that very cedar into
Eden. Assyria itself was a brutal empire, and nothing should have
made a prophet happier than its decline and overthrow, but there is
sadness in Ezekiel's voice. Assyria was destroyed—we would have
to infer—not because it tortured and enslaved captives or because it
deported whole populations or because it razed cities and brutally
disrupted the peaceful life, but because it lost itself in arrogance,
in forgetfulness. It was more a dirge than a cry of anger. It was a
reminder. The sin was "towering high in stature" and being "arro-
gant in its height." The lesson was for the Jewish nation, belea-
guered as it was at the time. I suspect that the lesson had a double
or triple edge. It was a reminder of what had actually happened to
Israel as a result of her own pride, it was a reminder of the power of
God and how he uses powerful nations—and it was a call for purity
and obedience.

I cringe a little at the connection I am making between Eze-
kiel's tree and my tree. His was not only stately and magnificent
in itself, but it was, in the poem, a great symbol of a gigantic and
brutal empire and its fortune, even as it was a symbol of the fate
of all gigantic and brutal empires. And it became such an effective
and powerful symbol because of the visions, belief, and amazing
poetic skill of that prophet in his poetic, his image-making and
world-sundering mode. Whereas my poor tree was an overgrown

bush planted in the wrong place, caught in a snow-storm; and God knows, it wasn't even a tree I truly loved or felt connected with, except by virtue of its monstrous size, its intrusion into my house, and its name. It was presumptuous or superstitious for me to take its cracking as anything but the normal consequence of age, size, weak wood, posture, and a heavy snowstorm. Was my fate either of such consequence or worthy of such attention? It was silly, although in all fairness it was the natural working out of a metaphor from a metaphor-generating organism who takes all things surrounding it, near or far, as his most reasonable concern. I'm sorry it was that tree, even if I would have been more stricken if it had been my redbud or my willow that had been destroyed. Here in my living room there is a great birch branch leaning against the wall, as part of the Christmas decoration, although in all honesty it's been standing there since Columbus Day. What a lovely tree that is—the birch—and how even more special it is because of the birch tree disease that kills the babies—and makes the survivors so rare—one of the seven plagues that has landed on us for not listening to some Moses or other who came our way to turn our sticks into snakes, a true charmer. The death of that tree—my white birch—would have been, for me, a disaster.

Everyone I talk to has one tree above all others he or she would hate to see destroyed. One person said the yew was the one she most identified with, although since her father grew apples, and she grew up with apples, she felt she should say "apple"; one person said it was the lemon tree because it was a tree of all seasons and a good and useful servant and it was beautiful; one person said it was a toss-up between a certain ancient apple tree in western Massachusetts and a buckeye tree in northern California; one person loved a giant fir in her mother's front yard. Some mentioned particular trees, some the genus. One preferred the eucalyptus because it came from Australia and had shredded bark and sad dangling leaves and seeds like hats. One almost wept over the live oak trees of her youth; one agonized between the dogwood and the magnolia; more than one remembered the honey locust, and one the flowering mimosa. One loved the copper beech because of its leaves, and one the hawthorn because of its thorns and flowers, and one the hemlock because of its kindness. One even loved the ginkgo because its leaves were lemony and they made good tea. No one mentioned the black birch of my fourth decade and the pitch pine of my third; and no one loved the hackberry and the poor mulberry. And no one, surprisingly, mentioned the palm. My own tree—the black locust—blossomed every other year and brought a sweet odor that lasted for weeks in our backyard and along our riverbank. I loved it, in addition, because it was unloved by others, because its limbs broke off in such embarrassing abundance, because it lived such a short life, because it was called ugly when it was so beautiful, because it was the tree of my boyhood—in Pittsburgh—because it was called *acacia* by the naturalists, and because it originated in the Allegheny Mountains, in some little upheaval, three or four million years ago.

Certainly there's a lot of difference between conceiving of a tree as an object of veneration, or even worship, and admiring a tree for its great beauty or size or fecundity, but I think it's true that there are more trees that are worshiped, even today, than we would readily admit. And not only on the part of terrified children or poets. I know a woman who hugged an ancient aspen every day and gave thanks that it was not converted into pulpwood. The tree, in turn, told her when to leave and where to go to start a new life. She said that touching that tree's bark was like touching the cheek of a woman roughened by cold weather. And I know a man who got on his knees to a loblolly pine, but that would only make up for another man I know who cut down all the loblolly pines that surrounded his giant trailer (Caesar cutting down the grove of oaks in Gaul) because they created too much humidity—he said that—there where he lived in southern Louisiana. I think I worshiped a certain black birch that grew in my side yard in Raubsville, Pennsylvania—the black birch of my fourth decade—as much as anything else because it grew so close to my house, and peered inside and always consoled me, and because it gestured for patience and forbearance and pity with a new arm that it bore bravely after the stupid destruction one afternoon of one of its two great limbs, cut down, in my absence, by a hysterical assassin wielding a deadly gasoline-driven saw. I also worshiped a certain sycamore outside my former house in Iowa City because it bent over so daringly, and because it was unbearably beautiful and because it reminded me of my dead sister, Sylvia, for whom I write, because she would have also been tall and she would have bent over that way.

What makes our tree-worship different from that of the Primitives and the Believers is that we are more or less free to create our own ritual and, more importantly, we can pick our own tree, those of us who want to. Which makes tree-worship the same as other kinds of worship. The sacred trees I remember are the palm and the cypress and the pomegranate. And the ash from Norway; and the oak from England. The palm was sacred in Mesopotamia because it abounded there, and because it produced dates in profusion, and possibly because it was bisexual. The cypress was sacred in the north—in Syria—the solemn and lovely cypress, because it grew there, because it dominated, and because of its pyramidal shape, and maybe because its silhouette adapted to phallic symbolism—and maybe because it resembled a flame which, long before Zoroastrianism, had been a cause for contemplation and reverence and absorption, perhaps even adoration. Also the wood was lovely. The pomegranate was probably also sacred because of its wood but mostly, I'm sure, because of the fecundity of its fruit. There is no other fruit like it, not even the small terrible Florida orange that fills your mouth with a whole grove of seeds, not even the sugar-baby, hardly the product of any tree, which is almost more black seed than it is red meat and juice.

It may be that in the worship of individual trees the memory of the great forest is there and that the feelings of awe and fear and elation come partly from a knowledge of what that tree was like in its own community, especially if it were a tree like the oak whose power would be cumulative—that is, it would be more lovely and more awesome in the forest itself. Although it is also true that certain individual trees, because of their size or beauty or even grotesque-ness, might be loved and remembered, or worshiped. I seem to speak too lightly of this, perhaps too unthinkingly, as if those who walk by their old elms or stand in front of the huge spruces or white pines were actually venerating or propitiating a god—as if they believed there was a god in those trees—but it would be more accurate to speak of those trees as "godlike," even as we spoke of the experiences as "religious," with those sad entrapping quotes around the word. Of course, any apologist would explain that the gods are more or less absent everywhere, including in trees. When I stood in front of my black birch, when I stood in front of my arborvitae, I didn't think that tree was truly tenanted by a divine being, but I would have been willing to say a prayer, or sing a song, and I think when I lay down on the ground in the middle of that pitch pine forest in southern New Jersey and listened to the wind I felt hopelessly lost—literally and figuratively—and at the same time, totally secure.

I suppose that to worship a tree—or a woods—is a kind of idolatry, even if you don't think the tree is literally occupied by a divine being or that God is rustling through those leaves. And even if you don't honor the trees with sacrifice and surround them with taboos because of the supernatural power and life that resides in them. Which begs the question of just what it is you're doing when you do worship a tree, besides getting in touch once again with the living world, as the ancients saw it, although that way can also be a diversion, insofar as it creates complacency or puts too nice a face on our terrifying reality. Finally, no matter how symbolic the tree becomes it is the piece of wood itself that is prayed to. I have no problem with that. I would just as soon believe that a god is living in the tree as believe that the memory or idea of a god is there, or that he or she is temporarily there. I think I feel that way about the Host too, although, as a Jew I should probably refrain from commenting. My God, what does it matter if God was in the bush when he talked to Moses, or if he was the bush? Talmudists write—and probably speak—about idolatry as if the mountaintop and the calf and the spring of water and the palm tree loaded with dates and the pillar and the grove were still a threat, as if any minute we would grace a willow and snake and sway in front of it; and reformists—of all ilks—teach and preach that idolatry is not kissing wood but kissing money, or whatever else stands in for the holy. I am on the side of the good reformists even if I am occasionally mean and disrespectful, although I would prefer to believe rather than not believe, so I have spent some time in regret. My true feeling is that I am not unlucky to be living now. I am filled with as much joy—and as much rage—as any foolish believer walking through Toledo in the eleventh century C.E. or Crete in 1500 B.C.E. or Los Angeles in 1936 C.E., my three favorite times and places in history. The sticks in the frozen rivers are holy, and the rust on my rails, and the sleepy spiders behind my toilet—this I know: and if I don't get on my knees to them it's only because I'm a little embarrassed at being seen. I am sad that for the sake of the pure, the impure must be so violently condemned, and I am sad that for the sake of the holy we have created the unholy, and the profane to appease and accommodate the sacred. With all my heart I want to give myself to the unholy. I want to touch it lovingly and not be repulsed. I want to ask its forgiveness—and share my meal with it. I have gone far enough now that I can do that. The unholy is my child; or it is my great-grandfather, who lived differently from me. I hope it loves me.

The sacred tree, the tree of life, whatever it's called, has been imagined and re-imagined—in one way or another—by every one of the hundreds and hundreds of cultures that have appeared and disappeared throughout history. It was for the believer the source of all life and of its periodic renewal. It was an emblem of the whole universe; the trunk was the world, the roots were the abyss below, the branches were the sky, and the fruit the astral bodies. It was a candelabrum and it dripped the oil of mercy. It was a haven for all animals, especially deer and peacocks. It derived its power from the four rivers of paradise. Its roots were sometimes in the sky and its boughs brushed the earth. It had oracular qualities, it whispered and predicted. It gave perfect shade. It was decorated with rags, and painted red, and its roots were watered. It loved bells, and the cooing of pigeons. It was the backbone of Osiris and the cross of Jesus. Its branches covered the whole of paradise and contained 500,000 different varieties of fruit. In the Muslim version its branches could not be circumscribed on the fleetest horse in a hundred years, yet any of its fruits could be picked at will by the boughs spontaneously bending down to the blessed. It was a fig tree, and a black pine, and an oak, and a cypress, and a mulberry. It was the omphalos. It was the first marriage bower and the first church and the first pillar.

Most people, when you ask them about the sacred tree in scriptures, when you make reference to the Garden, they talk about Eve's tree (or the snake's), the tree of knowledge, and they seldom—almost never—refer to the tree of life that stood near it. I have to remind them that there were *two* trees in Eden, although I could never understand—for mythology's or religion's sake—why there had to be two, unless different traditions were being drawn together, or unless that was the only way the writer (or the writers) could conceive it, or—hilariously, astonishingly—unless there actually were two trees. The fact is there was a confounding: though the tree of the knowledge of good and evil is mentioned twice, once to establish its location and once to establish the prohibition, when Eve contends with the serpent she never mentions that tree but only the "tree in the middle of the garden" which is how the tree of life itself, and not the tree of the knowledge of good and evil, is originally described:

> The serpent said, "Did God really say: You shall not eat of any tree of the garden?" The woman replied to the serpent, "We may eat of the fruit of the other trees of the garden. It is only about the fruit of the tree in the middle of the garden that God said, 'You shall not eat of it or touch it, lest you die.'"

It is only later that the function, and purpose, of the tree of life is differentiated from the other tree. It was the tree of immortality, and man would become truly a god "and live forever" if he ate of that tree—not just become "like one of us," knowing good and bad. It was for this reason God banished them and stationed "east of the garden of Eden" both cherubim and a fiery ever-turning sword to keep mankind away, "to guard the way to the tree of life." I am amazed that there was no original prohibition against eating from the tree of life itself, seeing that it bestowed immortality. It is possible that before the tree of knowledge was eaten from, there would have been no concept—perhaps no need—no desire for immortality, given the state of mind—of body—of Adam and Eve, and so the prohibition would have been useless and the tree of life would have assumed its value only when knowledge was arrived at. It could be that the tree of life was originally the center of the myth—before there was a tree of knowledge; it could be that at one time the same tree performed both functions, that it gave knowledge *and* immortality; it could be that one of them was a vine, probably the tree of knowledge, hanging from, say, a fig, or that they grew in some other way symbiotically; it could be that the arrangement as it is— i.e., two trees—was and is the result of some profound mythological or religious insight or the reflection of some condition in human/ godly relations that we have lost knowledge of; or it may simply be that earlier man wasn't interested in an efficient releasing of his mythical resources but was willing to squander them. I think it was simply that mankind, as he lived in the Garden, had no need or interest in immortality since he didn't know death—much as the animals and plants didn't, and it was only knowledge that brought an awareness of death—as it did of shame, sadness, and longing—and it was only this awareness that brought the desire to overcome it, to become immortal, to eat of the other tree. I'm not sure exactly what the serpent promised them, or what they understood. They would become "like divine beings who know good and bad," their "eyes would be opened." Maybe they thought that was enough; maybe they were duped twice; and maybe they couldn't even fully understand the first admonition if they didn't know what death was, nor could they understand what the serpent meant when he said, "You are not going to die." They were perhaps not even being disobedient, just foolish.

My own tree of life has little of knowledge or wisdom about it. And no one guards it with a whirling flaming sword, either in the east or in the west. Maybe if there had been cherubim they would have shaken the tree a few times to loosen the snow and my poor overburdened branch wouldn't have broken. As it is, it stands there hopelessly ruined and there doesn't seem to be anything I can do by way of trimming and shaping to give it an acceptable look. In a few months the raw wood, the part exposed, will get dark and even the joy—and horror—of fresh amputation will be gone. I'll cut it down then, probably in June, a good time for cutting in this case, and I won't grieve too much because there was, after all, something a little grotesque about the tree's size and its location, and it will be a relief to be rid of the gnats and mosquitoes who took refuge in the shade. There is a kind of brownish swamp birch growing just in the right place, dead center of the porch and a foot or two beyond the arborvitae, and I'm going to cultivate that birch with all my heart. It's only about an inch in diameter now—maybe an inch and a quarter—but I have high hopes for it, especially since the birch disease seems confined mostly to white birches. Anyhow, I have good luck with birches and, so far as I know, I have the only full-size white birch within the radius of a couple of miles. Eve's—and Adam's—tree of life may have been a fig or a date tree—I kind of suspect that. If it was fruit I was thinking of, my own would be either an apricot or a grapefruit. If it were an apricot, it would be drenched with sun; if it were a grapefruit, it would be loaded with seed, and juicy beyond compare. Eating it I would live forever, I would become like one of them, singing I guess, dancing, flying about, loving, studying. What would be different, what would be changed? I mean for the mind. I mean aside from an end to the rotting. For how many centuries have we longed to know this, what the mind would do if there were no rotting? What would the mind do?

WHAT I HAVE TO DEFEND,
WHAT I CAN'T BEAR LOSING

I AM THE AGE not only to remember the election of 1936, which gave Franklin D. Roosevelt the kind of mandate he needed to establish his very capitalistic brand of state socialism, but to remember the frightened faces and crowds of men doing nothing in the first months of the third decade of my century, when I was bravely and trustingly going off by myself to taste kindergarten and the first grade in the suburbs of Pittsburgh. I think Pittsburgh placed first, or fifteenth, a few years ago in the annual fake contest of livable cities, but over the years it had ruined the lungs, hearts, and minds of too many not to be held accountable and, worse than that, ridiculous in its fin de siècle self-praise and maudlin ignorance of its own history and nature. I remember listening to the election returns in 1932 in our living room in Beechview and feeling the excitement but not in the least understanding what was going on; and I remember when I first heard the word "cut" and understood, in a trice, that it meant not only less money but more fear and even a kind of hopelessness as one or two youthful dreams of my very youthful parents were slightly shattered and their vision slightly contradicted.

My father was the manager, and buyer, of the men's and boy's clothing department in a moderately large credit store called the

Palace, or the Palace Credit Clothing Company. I don't remember now whether they sold furniture and dry goods too; probably they did since the building was four or five stories and had a large enough force of employees to have annual picnics where dozens of people ate, drank, drowned, played ball, and got into occasional fistfights or debauches. In those decades, the 1920s and '30s, credit stores thrived in the American cities. They were more or less the only places you could buy on time and pay a little later for either the things you needed or the things you were being taught to need. There were charge accounts in the ordinary department stores but you had to be a better risk to get credit there. My guess is that the prices were 10 or 20 percent higher in the credit stores to cover loss and to accommodate helplessness—and my guess is that, though the bottom line was sales, the credit stores thrived, as banks might do, on collections and collection fees, and that most of the customers were permanently indebted to the stores where they made their purchases, a little in the manner of the company store. I remember there was a team of collectors who worked for the Palace, mostly rosy-cheeked overweight bullies, and I remember my father getting into a fistfight with one of them at the annual picnic when the collector Jewed him while under the influence of some Irish or Polish Comfort. My father knocked him out—no hard feelings—with one solid punch to the chin and that ended their rancor.

My grandfather, Jacob Stern, owned a thriving stogie factory and horse-drawn wagons with "Stern's Cigars" painted on the side and back, but he died early and my father had to start working early, when he was twelve, as a messenger boy in the oil fields of northern Pennsylvania.

One of the saddest stories I know is how my father, when he was fourteen and a delivery boy for a small department store, got off a streetcar, with lampshades and buckets and a large wooden swing set he was delivering, to go for a swim in a water hole he saw out of the streetcar window and was fired when his boss learned about his delinquency. I'm sure he saw other children swimming there and half forgot himself. When I read Dickens or Blake on the denial of children their natural joy, or when I think of how *Modern Times* or *À Nous la Liberté* pits the human dream of liberation against greed and exploitation, I think of my father; or I sometimes think of him when I read Eugene Debs or Simone Weil on oppression and liberty. I wish Matthew Arnold had had the opportunity of carrying swing sets on his back when he was fourteen, or balancing a bucket or two on his shoulder. He may then have forgiven my father his lack of correct knowledge and taste, or he might even have acknowledged him as human—and suffering—and looked with something less than horror at the little delivery boy's own desire, wherever and however he learned it, to rise from stiff to Philistine at any cost, though the delivery boy would have called it by another name. Nor would he have had Arnold's moral grandeur to help him understand his dilemma and his responsibilities.

I am probably shifting the burden to that delicate poet and school inspector, for it was I who struggled for ten desperate years to find my own breath, and it was I who riled endlessly against smugness and utilitarianism. We all had crosses, my father, my mother, and I, and we collided in the dark and we almost asked forgiveness. My father was a Truman democrat. He was a manager but he loved unions and always respected working men and women. I never heard him express words of bigotry or racial or religious hatred. He treated his female colleagues with equality, though no one told him to do so. He never belittled anyone. Moreover, he was the best pool player at Schuster's pool hall, he swam like a porpoise, and he consistently drove the ball over the fence at H.B. Davis field when it was his turn at bat. I learned a great deal from him.

My mother, like my father, was born in Europe—Bialystok in her case—was the youngest in her family, and became American with a vengeance. I remember her telling me once about a young man who courted her. He was handsome, rich, intelligent, a man of affairs, and he had a car. But he had an accent—he was a green-horn and nothing, apparently, upset her and her friends more than that. Her closest friend—for almost seventy years—was a woman, a girl, she met the night before her marriage at a mikva. Her friend married a European, a man with a strong Jewish accent. He ended up owning a large supermarket chain and shopping centers in five states, but he always remained—by some common consent—if not less than desirable, at least less than perfect because of that accent. My mother's father was trained as a rabbi in Poland and was a *shoket* and a *cheder* teacher in America. My mother, like my father, was chary of giving up too much information. I don't know whether they didn't consider it important or whether, on some level, it was risky, but there were many things I never learned, though I pestered them for answers.

My maternal grandfather, I learned, was a scholar, and not that interested in religion. His reading and his writing was secular. He read novels, belles lettres, poetry, and philosophy, in German and Russian, and wrote a kind of literary criticism in Yiddish. As far as I can discover, everything he wrote is gone, though I have searched diligently. He was remote and unaffectionate. He used the living room of a three- or four-room apartment for his study; he smoked Russian cigarettes, which my grandmother always hand-rolled for him; he had a delicate stomach; and he dropped his bloody clothes, after the weekly chicken-killing, in the front hallway where his wife would pick them up and wash them by hand. They were a poor family, with an outdoor toilet. Down two flights. One time, my mother told me, he acknowledged a book she was reading, *Anna Karenina*. He was a little surprised, though not necessarily pleased. He had read it in Russian, he told her. When it came time to let my mother's brothers know they had to quit school and go to work—after the eighth grade—it was my Grandmother Libby's job to tell them. The event was vivid in my mother's memory. My grandmother entered their room one morning and said in Yiddish, "Today, you have to go to work, my sons." That was all the preparation. "*Tacha?*" they said. "Truly?" It was a few years into the new century. Their earnings would be needed.

My mother went to commercial high school and until she got married worked as a bookkeeper at Kaufmann's department store, in Pittsburgh, the same Kaufmann whose son commissioned Frank Lloyd Wright to build Fallingwater, in Bear Run. She was always loyal to Kaufmann's and bought all her clothes and furniture there. The one event that stood out in her memory during those years was the time she delivered a package to the owner of the *Pittsburgh Leader* and saw a larger-than-life photograph of Lillian Russell, the owner's wife, on the wall. A half-century later my mother would dress up as Lillian Russell on the last night of a Caribbean cruise—I think in the harbor of Caracas, Venezuela. I have the photograph in my possession. She is wearing a large hat, a picture hat with a pink plume, and she is carrying pink flowers to match; her face is absolutely white with powder—and red with rouge—and she is smiling happily. She won first prize for best costume. How delighted the owner of the *Leader* would be.

I have paid careful attention—I'll put it that way—to the issue of class, and I like to think that Pittsburgh, the city I was born and raised in, had not only a special connection with but a stranglehold on that issue; and that not only were the battles fought there but the city itself, in its physical arrangements, was a kind of stage set for the struggles. You could *see* the classes in terms of the clothes we wore, the kind of air we breathed, where our houses were perched, our proximity to the three rivers, our accents, our food, the degree of anxiety and helplessness we had, where we shopped, where we worshiped. This was certainly true in other industrial cities as well, but nowhere, I believe, as strongly, or clearly, as in Pittsburgh. Probably those of us who were born there at a certain time were geniuses of class; we understood it in a way that no one else could. It would be as if you grew up on a military post or at a religious center and would understand certain things—about war and religion—whether or not you wore one of the two collars, or medals.

I was a good child of the 1930s, and I was one who learned my lesson well, but I did not go to work in the mill when I was sixteen and I did not belong, then, to a union. Like anyone else I had a dozen jobs, from selling shoes to unloading boxcars to nursing juveniles at a settlement house, but that was always to pay for gas or to give me a little pride, and to help pay my tuition when I went on to college. The "natural" sentiment, for me and my friends, was for the left, and the left then meant two things only: a pro-labor stance and an anti-fascist stance. Our position was rather dream-like and sentimental. We hated the bosses, whom we never saw, and we loved the workers, whose children, if we were Jewish, often treated us with contempt, hatred, and violence. I understood the nature of state barbarity and institutionalized Jew-baiting when I was eight, and I knew some songs from the Lincoln Brigade when I was fifteen. I made a kind of package out of my belief in justice, my unspeakable naïveté, and my hope for perfection. By the time

I went to college, World War II was on. The lines were simple and my package was safe. I tried to volunteer when I was seventeen, but I was too blind, they thought, to do much good, or harm. Later they changed their minds, but the war was already over and my package was already a little torn.

My grandfather, on my mother's side, had no middle-class ambitions. He owned no property, he did not—he could not—educate his children, he saved nothing, he had no long-range economic and social plans. Moreover, he was one of the poor, by any standard, yet he read and wrote in at least four languages, was not only respected but revered, according to family myth, and made judgments that amazed his little world. (I can't remember if it was he or his father, also a rabbi, who was carried home on the shoulders of his adorers—like some English athlete—after some wise decision or brilliant interpretation.) In the community he was a kind of aristocrat, even if he shared, as he probably did, the dread of the poor outside the community.

My grandfather on the other side died in his fifties, and though he owned a large house and had servants and twenty or so women rolling beautiful cigars in his small factory while they listened to tragic stories in Yiddish (told by a professional reader according to a labor contract negotiated with Samuel Gompers's union), his store was depleted fast, and his sons and daughters, even if they had the memory of a little wealth, had to go to work early, though there certainly would be power and identity in the memory itself. I grew up, then, the grandson of two petty princes (I have no doubt that Marxists would see them both as petit bourgeois, the enemy) with a lot of pride, a lot of affectionate memory, and a good deal of family mythology. We had a maid, owned our own house, bought a new car every two or three years, saved money, and had some hopeful and vague plans for my future. I think I was supposed to be a lawyer, then a judge. Whatever our political sympathies were, whatever our sense of justice was, whatever identifications we made, as Jews and Americans, we were middle class, whatever that is, and we were that with a vengeance.

I never lost my true loyalties, but for the first few years of my hectic exposure to and indoctrination into books and writing I put "those things" (the way Emily Dickinson did life) on the closet shelf. Politics, which was my passion in high school and my first few years of college, would give way to aesthetics, and I would be consumed with the music of language and the insatiable desire to "know things as they are," as Matthew Arnold, that pious Hellene, would describe in *Culture and Anarchy,* a book I read with pure joy when I was twenty-one and starting to fill up the empty spaces. Arnold, others too, would teach me to adore culture, as he described it, to believe it was beyond and above class, to despise Philistines, to hate machinery (like a good Oxford Englishman), to search for perfection, to assume a certain grandeur, to believe in Greece, to believe in ideas, to believe in light, and to turn a critical eye—and tongue—to whatever was squalid and ungenerous and insensitive in our culture.

I didn't give in completely, but I almost did. It is true that, for Arnold, "culture" was different than it would be for Wilde or Pater or Ruskin or, for that matter, H. L. Mencken. Arnold points out in the very beginning that his motive is not mere curiosity, or exclusiveness and vanity; that culture is not a *badge;* and he insists that it has its origin in, and should have as its purpose, the "love of perfection," that it is motivated not merely, or primarily, by the passion for pure knowledge but also by the moral and social passion for doing good, for "diminishing human error and misery," and for

"clearing human confusion." I'm not sure I was getting that mes-
sage at the time, or that I was not reading Arnold from the point
of view of my own passions, and choosing and selecting what I
wanted to hear. In a certain way, poetry would become a religion
for me and whatever stood in the way of that religion would have
to be either ignored or despised; and in a certain way the "ideas of
perfection" that I had somewhere and somehow gathered together
from reading the prophets and from listening—on various levels—to
the bearers of social justice, the utopianists, of the 1930s, and from
responding, *reacting*—I am sure of this—to the shock and sadness of
my own life—my sister's untimely death, the violent anti-Semitism,
the stupidity—would be transferred from the realm of politics to the
realm of poetry; and I would look for the ideal not only in form,
in language, in beauty itself, but in my statement, my content (my
belief). The truth is I have never lost that belief. The truth is that
the writing of poetry was the way I was able to discover and give
language to that belief.

I had no trouble with Arnold's notion that culture transcended
class—or ignored it. By the late 1940s, in my early twenties, I was
quite at ease as an "alien," the ridiculous term Arnold used to
describe persons who are led not by their "class spirit" but by a
"humane spirit," by the "love of human perfection," although I
think I then perceived artists themselves as a kind of class—in my
innocence—and I had a lingering hatred for the rich and powerful
in my city, and a lingering, if sentimental, attachment to the poor
and powerless and a desire to defend them; in short, an ongoing
love for social justice, even as I had put it on the other burner; and
I had a keen memory, drawn from the details in my own short life,
of the self-absorption and arrogance of one class and the meanness
and selfishness of the other, colored, in both cases, by a pervasive

bigotry, although I was more willing to forgive and understand one and not the other. I may have given myself up to Yeats and Marlowe, but I never forgot the disgusting religious, racial, and ethnic hatred. Maybe "Jew" is my class, and that should be stamped in my passport, as in Mother Russia, although I am as unforgiving of that community—my community—as I am of the others, in its *own* bigotry, shortsightedness, betrayals, and spiritual forgetfulness. I think it is the *idea* of the Jew I cling to—if I can put it that way—and I think *what I have to defend, what I can't bear losing,* is either contained or symbolized, in a significant way, in that idea. I'm not sure if it's a historical presence I'm talking about or a kind of thought. It's probably both, and I feel the need to react, more here than elsewhere, when either the presence *or* the thought is confronted with abuse and ridicule. I felt for a while that this attachment was sentimental, defensive, and nostalgic, but I don't feel so anymore.

I voted for Henry Wallace in 1948 as a protest of sorts against the stupidity of my America, which viewed anything to the left of Harry Truman, the courthouse Democrat, as veering on communism, our obsession then. The Wallace who was vice president under Roosevelt and got passed over when Roosevelt, exhausted from the war, left the picking to the bosses and their friends. I remember the phrase "Check it with Sidney," a reference to Sidney Hillman, a labor executive who headed the Ladies Garment Workers Union. He preferred Harry. To the right of both of them was Thomas A. Dewey, the governor of New York, the little man on the wedding cake, as Harold Ickes called him, a specialist at miscalculation.

Ordinarily I wouldn't have dreamed of voting since none of them was the right one for me. If anyone had asked me where I stood, what I stood for, in 1948, besides creating a new voice for the

sonnet or dreaming or humming till I wept at the sound of Bar-
tók's new concerto—I would have sent a division or two into Spain
to unseat Franco; I would have stopped the runaway inflation by
price control, even if that would have limited greed; I would have
sent federal troops into the South to oversee voter registration; I
would have offered incentives for women to remain in the work-
force; I would have created ten huge national free universities; I
would have made religious and racial quotas in the universities a
federal crime; I would have limited incomes; I would have given
preferential treatment to rebuilding the older cities and limiting the
spread of suburbs; I would have subsidized and encouraged inner-
city transportation systems and, incidentally, held the officers of
General Motors criminally responsible for their collusion with local
officials in the destruction of public transportation systems in such
cities as Los Angeles and Pittsburgh; I would have subsidized sub-
stantial and beautiful public housing; I would have asked Congress
to establish a national health-care system, and I would have insisted
that a poor child in Kentucky or the Bronx get the same care as the
generals did in their version of socialized medicine.

In addition, I would have supported a democratic Indochina
and kicked out the French and English; I would have helped Cen-
tral America establish democracies in spite of the oil and agricul-
tural interests; I would have made Germany morally and financially
responsible for no less than one century for its actions in the 1930s
and '40s; and I would have extended aid to the Soviet Union and
forced an agreement—including arms control—through generosity
and understanding. For starters. Luckily nobody asked me and I was
permitted instead to study Provençal poetry and read James Joyce
and Ovid in the privacy of my New York apartment, for which I
paid seven dollars a week rent.

The aspect of Marx I always admired was his dream of freedom, his yearning for liberty and equality, as it was coupled with his indignation, his idea of social justice. I was never very interested in either his analysis of the economic struggle or the philosophy that underlay or rationalized that struggle, or the mysticism, or the kind of paradise he evidently dreamed of. I suppose I was myself a latter-day utopian socialist; although part of me was a good social democrat—or democratic socialist—and part of me, maybe the clown part, the nihilistic part, was pure anarchist. I always responded *personally,* when I responded at all, to oppression in its two thousand and one forms. I fought, tooth and nail, with three college presidents, with committees, department chairmen, and deans. I lost tenure once and was threatened twice more because of my political activities, the one time over the Asian war and the other over destructive and exploitative educational policies and philosophies. I fought the governor of Pennsylvania—his name was Richard Thornburgh—when he (and Jinny) censored a deeply moving photography exhibition on the walls of the state house in Harrisburg, Pennsylvania; and I fought a dean of men—his name was Carl Grippe—in my days at Temple University when he tried to censor a poem in the student magazine of which I was faculty advisor. (I was the one who made the call to the *Philadelphia Inquirer.*) I organized and led civil rights marches in Indiana, Pennsylvania, I helped desegregate the foolish swimming pool there, through a violent act or two, and I threatened a boycott against a chain of hotels (Holiday Inn) for not putting James Farmer's name (head of CORE) on the marquee in front of the motel the way they put the names of other celebrities: religious leaders, Nazis, newlyweds, and such. I headed a teachers' union in the state of New Jersey. I wrote contracts, I negotiated, and led two strikes. I marched—softly—in New York, Washington, Pittsburgh, Philadelphia, New Brunswick, Indiana, Pennsylvania, and even Iowa City, Iowa. I organized a Writers Against Reagan reading in Iowa against apartheid in South Africa, and wrote a poem for the occasion. (A thousand people showed up and every college in Iowa divested within a week.) I sat at phone banks and stood at mimeo-machines and typed on Underwoods and passed out leaflets. I was never kissed goodbye by Emma Goldman and sent over the Alleghenies to shoot Henry Frick; and I never had my head cracked open by an underpaid guard; but I am moderately content with what I did do—moderately—and I'm grateful that I was where I was at the time.

I think the person I'm closest to now, in her thinking and her analysis, is Simone Weil, though I reject her irrational, and sometimes contrived, conclusions. I like her personal struggle and I am moved by her desperate life. She finally saw so vividly what the nature of oppression was, and the dream of liberty. There were two classes for her, and only two, given the fact that one could be an oppressor in one place and a victim in the other. She claimed that every oppressive society was centered in a religion of force, and that the rulers, whether they are priests, military leaders, kings, or capitalists, always command by divine right; and those who are under them feel themselves crushed by a supernatural power.

I believe she is correct, though I would change "divine right" to "right," and I might change "supernatural" to "overwhelming" or "overpowering," which gives a clearer and perhaps more contemporary idea of the irrationality and madness of those who would lead us, and control us. I also believe she is correct in her notion of the two classes; I think the three-class system, so dear to the heart of feudalists and post-feudalists, obscures and softens the real oppression. Liberty, for her, is a state where movement proceeds from no other source than the mind, one's own mind, as slavery is a state where all movement proceeds from a source other than one's own mind—a philosophical, or mathematical, way of putting it. Man is a limited being, she points out, compared, say, to the God of the theologians, who is the author of his own existence. Freedom, for her, seems akin to wisdom, and true liberty would be defined as a perfect relationship between thought and action. She says that the least evil society is that in which men are most often obliged to think while acting. She wanted labor itself to be so transformed that it would exercise fully all the faculties. She wanted what she called "science" to become concrete, and what she called "labour" to become conscious. It was her own utopia, based on her own sad life. Not only would cooperation and affection be the governing law but Greek geometry would descend upon earth, a wonderful, mad notion.

When I am in an extreme mood, or when I fitfully believe in natural goodness, "original blessing" as one of the theologians calls it, I opt for some form of anarchy and turn to a brief period in Spain, or to the busy head of one of the Italian dreamers, or to some community or other in upstate New York or downstate Arkansas, for my paradigm. That's when I start talking again about René Clair's film *À Nous la Liberté,* the 1930 movie about industrial happiness where the workers dance, the product (radios) is turned out "automatically," and only the janitor who sweeps the floor and changes the colored lightbulbs and the orchestra itself "labors." We hardly know what to imagine when the long night of oppression comes to an end. Me, I will read and write and explain and recollect. And enjoy silence. And plan my disappearance.

For the first hundred years it was a struggle—against ignorance and against injustice. I hated my own ignorance and I hated the world's injustice. Well, there was a third thing, it was arrogance, in the form of snobbery, in the form of rank, in the form of hierarchy. And lying, in its thousand and two forms, political, commercial, historical, religious, professional, personal. I have argued—and raged—against these four things. The forms and the intensities depend on one's own life, on the circumstances. Not everyone slept in a Murphy bed, ate Kellogg's corn flakes and Otto milk every morning, and studied in the living room at a rickety secretary; and not everyone had such faith and innocence that he believed absolutely everything he was told. My chemistry, my mind—my culture—was such that I adored Amos when I read him and later Proudhon when I read him. It was such that I read Amos and Proudhon in the first place, not to mention Zeno and Tolstoy. And it is such that though I once admired Matthew Arnold, I now find him bigoted, mean-spirited, and insular. I guess he reminds me a little too much of my dear enemies in certain rarified sections of the city of bridges I was blessed to grow up in.

There is a large room in the art museum in Pittsburgh that contains work by western Pennsylvanians; and there is a painting in that room by a revered Pittsburgh painter and teacher named Samuel Rosenberg. I recall the date as 1933, and I associate the phrase "American Dream" with that painting, though that may reflect my own bitterness or humor and not be the title. It may be called *Empty Street* or *On the Way to Work*, or it may just be called *Study Number 6*. It shows two figures, separated from each other by twenty feet or so, walking bent over, one behind the other, as if in the wind, or the cold, on a sidewalk beside a wall on an otherwise empty street. There are streetcar tracks but no streetcars in sight. There are neither automobiles nor animals nor stores nor people nor cultural artifacts, just the two men, almost huddled over, their heads bent, carrying—each one of them—a package in his arm, a lunchpail maybe, or clothes. The figures are potato-like, quasi-abstract, monochromatic. The painting is realistic but also expressionistic, and there are memories of early Van Gogh. The sky is yellow, the wall is filthy, the street is laid in cobblestones. There are small crooked telephone poles to add to the ugliness and loneliness. Nothing identifies the country, or the century, but I know it's Second Avenue, in Pittsburgh, and I know that those men are walking home after a long and probably onerous day at Jones and Laughlin Steel Company—J & L—the firm, the family, whose money made it possible for us to enjoy books from New Directions under the wise guardianship of James Laughlin, a guilty son. I still love that painting, though I am probably less critical of it than I would be of James T. Farrell or John Steinbeck or John Dos Passos, not to mention some of the unnamable poets. I knew Sam Rosenberg. He was small and dapper. He always wore a dark-blue suit, a white shirt, and a red tie, even when he taught. Maybe especially when he taught at Carnegie Tech.

As I think of the painting now, I see it is not so much a statement about the Depression or even about the vicissitudes of work, but about human oppression and the eternal forces. Nobody is there with a whip and the men are even free to stop somewhere for a beer, but that is not what they do. I hate to think we're talking about a permanent condition in human history, but at this late date I'm beginning to have my suspicions. If my heart goes out to those men, it is not because they were open-hearth workers or because they were trapped and hoodwinked—not only that; it is because they suffered unduly, and because someone was responsible, and because they had gardens somewhere. I don't mind the sentimentality; and I don't even mind the cynicism and bad logic that points to them as possible bigots and wife-beaters as a way of justification—or perhaps punishment.

I am free of some arguments and I have made some choices. My own poetry embodies everything I have done and everything I believe in—it couldn't be otherwise—including what I haven't consciously thought about, including what I don't know. But it does it in its own way. It would be fascinating to show the relationship between class and form, class and diction, class and image. It should be done, and someone should do it—or has done it. If there is a human voice behind, or a human voice engulfing, the *poetic* voice—the *persona*—it is that voice I am interested in. That is the voice that is like a fingerprint in its uniqueness. That is the voice that explains itself as it instructs us, that laughs and sighs as it loves us. It is the voice I listen to when I read Yeats and Chaucer. It is what the beloved Walt meant when he said, "Missing me one place search another." "Let us stand up, it is time to explain myself," he said. I have never for a second lost sight of my own explanation. It's as if I always knew what I had to do.

RUTH

Ancient snow had fallen there
Its head was crowned with clouds.

FROM THE ALBANIAN ANCIENT EPIC *KENGE KRESHNIKESH*

I WROTE MY POEM about Ruth Middleman on New Year's Eve 2000, and published it in 2002 in a volume titled *American Sonnets*. I knew Ruth in high school, maybe junior high, and though I was only a year or two younger than she, we were worlds apart, and the thought then of dating her, of even having more than a brief awkward conversation with her, was absolutely out of the question. For one thing I and my friends didn't date, nor, I should add, did we use the word as a verb as it now is used. We *went* on dates, that is, some people did. *We* went to bars and picked up girls or we met them Sunday nights at the weddings we crashed in neighborhood synagogues. When I was sixteen, say, I was five foot, ten inches tall and wore a size eleven and a half shoe. But I was still sixteen and spent most of my time playing nine-ball, drawing maps of Europe—to perfection—and running by myself around the Schenley Park oval in Pittsburgh, an abandoned 1920s racetrack. Ruth—her maiden name was Rosenblum—was seventeen and for a while eighteen while I was sixteen. She was, I recall, Miss Pennsylvania and dated men closer in age to twenty-five or thirty. I don't know if I was, as such, in love with her. I guess everyone was. But given our age difference, her beauty and popularity, and my own sense of youthful inadequacy, it would have been absurd to pine after her. It was not even imaginable. Though I thought of her—a lot.

I lost sight of her for maybe six years and when I was twenty-two or so and recently out of the army, she was already twenty-four, a graduate of the University of Pittsburgh School of Social Work and a recreational leader, a group worker, at the Brashear Settlement House in the South Side. I was in between degrees, a starter poet, and making plans to go to Europe as quickly as I could finish my M.A. (at Columbia) and get together some money for boat passage. (Once there I planned on going to school—probably in Paris—on the World War II G.I. Bill.) In the meantime I was also working at the Brashear House, teaching boxing and being an "older brother" to the young Polish and Slovak boys. I spent every day there, from about three till nine or ten at night, and Ruth and I ate supper together in the old kitchen and drove home together in her Mercury coupe. I was no longer an insecure wordless teenager in ridiculous clothes and uncomfortable in my body; and she was no longer as sought after as she had once been. We were equals. One night her older brother discovered us in the small front seat of her Mercury, near her mother's house, in a compromising situation and openly expressed his disgust. To this day I feel her humiliation, as I also felt embarrassed by her mother's overtures, come Friday night, over the candles and the rich dinner. She was a widow, her mother, once wealthy but rather lost now. Certainly she was reaching out, but such a thing as marriage, say, was absolutely the farthest thing from my mind. I understand she periodically sold jewelry and silver for some income. It was the world of Chekhov.

Ruth and I encountered each other eight years or so later, in

Philadelphia, where I was beginning my college teaching—at Temple University—and she was working and teaching, married to an old friend of mine from Pittsburgh, with two small sons. My wife, Patricia Stern, didn't much like her and considered her haughty. That was the word she used. Ruth bore herself like a Russian princess, with her hair pulled back. Pat was particularly bothered that Ruth sat in the front seat of the car—I guess my car—with me, while she was apparently relegated to the back seat. I don't remember that and I don't know where Ruth's husband—Donald—sat, although he was a little meek compared to Ruth and might possibly have also sat in the back.

In the poem I wrote about Ruth I say that my wife hated her because of her "snooty attitude," akin to "haughty," but it was my wife, not I, who used the word, though I would agree to "haughty." Pat—in the poem—also remembered that Ruth's boys threw green apples from one of our trees at each other, but when I think back I realize that, at the time, though we did have an apple tree, we didn't yet own a car, so I don't know whose car it was, or if in fact there was a car and Ruth did sit beside me, and Donald did sit in the rear.

But it was the tire iron, it was the "creasing her head with a tire iron," that was the most shocking piece of information in the poem. We were living and I was teaching (my next job after Temple) at Indiana University of Pennsylvania, about fifty miles east of Pittsburgh, and one day we read in the *Indiana Gazette* that Ruth—my Ruth—was coming home at two, three, in the morning, presumably from an assignation, when the meek one emerged from the shadows and hit her over the head with the blunt piece. It mostly missed, but it led certainly to their divorce. Pat and I were variously horrified, amused, and unbelieving, in our small urban wilderness.

The poem for Ruth is called "Les Neiges d'Antan," the famous refrain of François Villon's poem "Ballade des dames du temps jadis," which, though commonly isolated as a separate poem and even in the 1950s turned into a popular (sort of) song, was really an integral part of *Le Testament* (The Testament), Villon's wild and glorious poem, the very heart of his work. It is actually in the 42nd stanza and at the 330th line that the ballade, as such, begins, and it is 28 lines long and precedes another ballade, 16 lines long—titled, sometimes, the "Ballade des seigneurs du temps jadis"—also an integral part of *The Testament*. More or less confusing. The ballade is mainly of interest (to me) here because of the last line—"ou sont les neiges d'antan"—but also because of the nostalgia as it is realized through the memory, the presence, of snow.

In the Modern Library edition, John Payne titles the poem "Ballad of Old-Time Ladies," and the refrain is "But what is become of last year's snow?" Norman Cameron calls it "Ballad of the Ladies of Bygone Time," and his refrain, echoing Dante Gabriel Rossetti's famous one, is "But where are the snows of yester-year?" Only he leaves out the first word, *But*, and makes the last word a single one instead of hyphenating it. In French, it does say "But," and who knows about yes-ter-year? Galway Kinnell—as literal as possible—translates the line "But where are the snows of last winter?" I always remembered the famous translation as Swinburne's rather than Rossetti's, that mad Algernon who wrote the jeweled lines—and praised Whitman, for a short while—but it was "A Ballad of François Villon" I was thinking of, the poem whose refrain was "Villon, our sad bad glad mad brother's name." Here is my poem:

Les Neiges d'Antan

Where art thou now, thou Ruth whose husband in the snow
creased thy head with a tire iron, thou who wore
ridiculous hats when they were the rage and loved
exotic culture and dances such as the *Haitian
Fling* and the *Portuguese Locomotive*, my wife
hated because of her snooty attitude
or that her hair was swept up and her nose was aquiline
and her two boys raised hell with our green apples
the Sunday they came to visit, she in whose Mercury
we parked for over a year, every night
in front of her mother's house in one of the slightly
genteel streets that led into the park
the other side downhill really from the merry-go-round,
or where is Nancy or who is the Nancy Ezra Pound
located in between his racial diatribes
and dry lyrics three times at least in the *Cantos*,
but tell me where that snow is now and tell me—
as in *where is Tangerine* and *where is Flora*—
how old Ruth is and where does she live and does she
still dance the *Locomotive* and does she bundle.

I think the volta in the poem, for it is a sonnet, albeit somewhat
longer than the customary 14 lines, occurs in line 17: "but tell me
where that snow is now . . ." Suddenly the snow, just as in Villon's
poem, takes on a special quality. It is *laden*, and it is symbolic. And
it is transformative. For from then on, in the few lines remaining
in the poem, the tone is different. It is not only serious but it deals
exclusively with loss—and with yearning, the essence of nostalgia.
Thus the dance called the *Portuguese Locomotive*—in the early part
of the poem—is treated comically, as is the *Haitian Fling,* names
that I'm sure I made up; but when the *Locomotive* appears in the last
line there is nothing of the comic attached to it. Even in the word
"bundle," which refers to the premarital sexual behavior of the

Plain People of Eastern Pennsylvania, there is nothing, or almost nothing, of the comic. Although in context you'd expect it to be amusing, even ridiculous. Is all this engineered by the evocation of the word "snow?" Is that word so powerful and provocative, or is it the way it is used, and where it is used, and the tonal shift, and the sudden slowness of the language and the repetitions and the nature of the information rendered? Though it is not my intention to show the genius of the poem but just to explain how it works—as an illustration to show how poems work—from my hapless point of view. The rest of the poem consists of (engineered) information, some suddenly remembered, some thought through. I have always been struck by the "Nancy" whom Ezra Pound introduced into the *Cantos* maybe three or four times, almost as an interpolation, something *beyond* the poem as a work of art, someone who haunted him and made him stop scratching. She also seems to be an integral part of his nostalgia for the Belle Époque moment just before World War I, England and France during the Rotten Decade.

I can't speak about Villon's nostalgia. I have just reread *The Testament* and have paid close attention to the verses preceding the great ballade—how *that* grew out of those verses—and what the ballade itself, as a seed so to speak, generated in the verses that followed. What strikes me are the stanzas that speak directly about mortality, about death, beginning, in line 300, the verses about the death of his father—to be followed, as the poem says, soon by his mother, and then the son himself. It is not the conventional medieval curtsy to death; it is a painful lament where the connection to life is fierce and death is unredeemable and meaningless. It is specifically the stanza about the "tender bodies of women" entering their agony that brings on the memory of Flora, the beautiful Roman, and the others. Villon's nostalgia is for life itself as once beautifully and vividly

lived, as it is for other lost and disappearing cultures. I am not abso-
lutely sure, but I think the original *ubi sunt* theme, which appears in
culture after culture, even beginning with *Gilgamesh,* is more for
warriors and gods lost than for beautiful women. The dead heroes
were thus honored and the dead women, in Villon, might even
have been a mockery, a comedy, or, at the very least, an odd—even
jarring—imitation of the dead warriors. Later it would be the dead
poets, as in William Dunbar's "Lament for the Makers" or, more
recently, Kenneth Rexroth's and William Merwin's laments. In the
hands of poets it would finally be them. Of course. The stakes, even
if they are sometimes cast in literary and historical terms, are not
light. Death is directly and overwhelming involved.

The question I would ask is what is the connection to snow,
for it is the "snows of yesteryear" (that word) that constitutes the
refrain. Just as it was the unconscious memory of snow in the Vil-
lon poem and even, maybe, in Philadelphia and Pittsburgh, that
generated the first line in "Les Neiges d'Antan." Snow stands for
emptiness, evanescence, forgetfulness, peacefulness, the past, sim-
plicity, a clean slate, a cover-up, an ending, a beginning. In "Les
Neiges" the violent act against Ruth may just have happened *as it
was snowing.* In Villon's ballade it may likewise just be the snowfall
of the past or a specific, or personal, past; but it retains its power, it
is inexhaustible.

In my own life snow was overwhelming. Pittsburgh is a kind
of trap in the mountains and the snow was quite heavy, as snow
always is in one's childhood and youth, as it was most literally then,
compared to now. Moreover, the snow then—in Pittsburgh—had
a certain specific smell and texture, mixed as it was with the soft
coal flecks and with the gaseous odors. I can sometimes all of a sud-
den smell that delicious (and unhealthy) smell when I open a win-

dow and encounter the snow on the windowsill, or when the wind blows through it in a certain way. The book in which "Les Neiges" appears, *American Sonnets*, has about sixty-five poems. At least seven take place in snow, not just in winter, but in *snow*.

For two years now I have been thinking of Ruth and have wanted to find her and talk over this life and read her my poem. I kept looking for her—but unfortunately, I misspelled her last name. I finally found her, in some web or other, but to my sorrow she had died two years ago, from emphysema it turns out. Nor did it have anything to do with snow, or with the melancholy evocation of beautiful and heroic dames of yore. It was stark, brutal, absolute, painful. And it made all the more telling the meditations, confrontations, and realizations—should I say the horrible knowledge itself—of Villon's great poem, just as that poem made her death, in its absoluteness and finality, though I had not seen her in forty-some years, all the more terrible.

Against Whistling

AGAINST WHISTLING

How we walked for an hour hunting for the right wall
and how we kicked our feet at last while singing "Summertime,"
and one of us had a harp and one a black potato
and our feet touched the grass which from the bridge above us
must have looked heavenly which it was all fall and how
we looked like birds perched, as they say, on the wire
only there were fewer of us given our size and species
though we communed and we partook, and there was even
a kind of sound come separately and come randomly
partly from the mouth and partly from the potato
and we took at last to naming the separate grasses
which is the way it is beside walls and under wires
and some of us grew so happy we started to whistle
which is always a bad thing for beaks and for potatoes
given how in abandonment your eyes might be closed
and the horror of eagles might come down upon you.

GERALD STERN

WE SHOULD NEVER WHISTLE, which is a bad thing for beaks—
if we are birds—and for potatoes—if we are playing that gruesome
misshapen little instrument with holes in it, for if we give ourselves
up in abandonment, and close our eyes, a larger bird might descend
upon us, screeching perhaps, but certainly ripping. I call it "the hor-
ror of eagles," but it could be the horror of pelicans, or whatnot.

Anne Marie's son Luke said, of the eagles, that the bald eagle prefers fish but in lieu of that will eat carrion, the dead meat of the highway, and the fields. I knew that already, but it was a pleasure to hear him say it. The golden eagle, we all agreed, doesn't go for watery things but captures and eats small game, rodents and the like, even lambs, even small deer, the spotted things we love to death.

I know a woman who lived in Colorado before she moved to Boston, before she moved to New York. She was having a garden party in her wild extended garden, which merged, as I recall, almost into wilderness itself, but still was controlled and domestic, when suddenly, in the middle of the festivities, the eating and drinking, the flirting, the serious conversation, a tiny meow was heard, and looking up she saw a full grown pussycat being carried off by a golden eagle, his wings noisily flapping, his talons hopelessly penetrating the hair and skin of the cat. I don't remember now if it was my friend's favorite pet and what its name was nor do I want to call her and remind her of her loss. Only that when she told me of the pathetic little sound was I struck by the horror of it, a soft familiar creature, at home under our hand or on the foot of our bed where she leaps up so noiselessly, suddenly in a place she didn't belong, certainly bewildered but maybe not yet absolutely overwhelmed, so quick and unexpectantly did the eagle descend, so quickly and confusedly was the cat rising in the air and looking down on those terrified guests. Nor am I appeased by the fact that the cat herself is as often as not the vile hunter and holds in her paws and penetrates with her own claws and licks with her tongue and chews with her teeth smaller and more helpless victims, the mice and moles of our woods and meadows, and even curls up as if in friendliness, and even closes her eyes as if in love.

I don't know who the "we" were and why we were singing

"Summertime." Let's just finally totally acknowledge that a thing takes over in the writing of a poem, whether it be some odd unconscious—oh, wrong word—or a person, since we personify, we might call the muse, or just *Henry*. (Why not Henry?) And he or she just dictates, and at this late date that is the easiest thing in the world to understand, even if it's only half right. Some poets are more tepid than others, or more or less courageous and daring, imaginative, responsible, and all that. Some speak, or read, French or German and include it in their poetic language. All that; all that. I am a poet of faith. I believe that if I have the right beginning and if I'm in the right state (blessed?) that the right ending will occur. I am also a poet who believes overwhelmingly in endings. I think endings are beginnings. I would even say "new beginnings" but I hate that redundancy. Also I believe that if you wait long enough the ending will come to you. Sometimes it comes in two minutes though sometimes it takes six years. (Why did I say "six" instead of "four"? Dictation!)

So was there a "we"? Was I literally walking with some others—or flying, as the case may be, hunting, indeed, for the right wall? Why not? And why not be kicking our feet out—as you do—and why not be singing that song as well as any other? And what was a "harp," in this case, and, in this case, what was, what is, a black potato? Was it a Jew's harp (jaw's harp)? Was it an ocarina, was it a tooter, a kazoo, an oaten reed, a piece of grass? I know I was—in the poem—in my first city—Pittsburgh—for we were sitting under a bridge, as you always are under or over in that place, and if we looked like birds on a wire it was a great distance to look, some deep hollow or other, or creek or river, and if we were transformed, in a way, into birds (the eye's imaging) there would of course be fewer of us since boys and girls—at least then—didn't run in packs of, say, eighteen or twenty, but typically, three or four or even two. And ah yes, we sang and, ah yes, we had bad voices and little harmony, and ah yes, we called the clumps of grass by strange names and we were happy—most of us—doing nothing, for we had somehow escaped work, which was expected of us, and God knows we began to whistle, though why it is a bad thing for beaks and potatoes to whistle I have no idea, nor do I know why, and how, those words scratched themselves on my tablet, and certainly if you consider how consumed and concentrated you certainly would be in group whistling, and if even your eyes might be closed—as I say, "in abandonment"—then it's little wonder "how eagles might descend upon you"—or even larger boys with pimples on their faces, or cops, or dogs—which ran in frightening packs then—or the owner of the land himself, all of which I never for a second thought of for I thought only of the horror of eagles.

If I say I am against whistling I don't really believe it, nor would any reasonable reader. I am actually *for* whistling and for noise and complaining and singing and most of all harps. Harps of every kind, and since I am a Peruvian, then potatoes of any sort, any color, any shape, any taste, any size. I wasn't against smoking either, for we smoked tobeys, as we later would Camels and, for the proud and pathetically arrogant, Chesterfields.

The question is, "What does this poem sound like—say, to a stranger, that is, a reader of poetry who doesn't know the facts of my life or the sound of my voice or possibly even the nature of my imagination or the limits of my experience or the facts of it?" The writer takes cheap refuge in the notion that it is the reader who creates the poem; that is not what I'm saying. To give the reader latitude, to give him a certain freedom, is to give him freedom in terms of how the writer knows language and its uses and its implications and the degree to which he, the writer, controls—by steering—this language. It is not a sloppy game of picking some words out of a hat and putting them in a certain order, no matter how colorful or grotesque or musical those words might be.

But this still takes us back to the steering and the cultural meaning and even the *intentions of the author* and even pronunciation. A writer must let go of the rope and he must swim in the open, with the reader at his side—a metaphor for which I should be hanged, or at least hung. What I do, more and more, is drop a word, or fiddle with an idea, much as I might let a worm fall from the end of a thread into a river, and let the fish eat what they may. Sort of. And I, as well as the reader, am such a fish. That is, *I have faith*, though sometimes I bluster, and sometimes I rote-ate, and sometimes I delude. I know soon enough. It only takes a year or so, say, for a ten-line poem; though sometimes a day.

I could keep saying this, and in different ways, but I have done it enough. I am describing my present practice, but I'm not doing it entirely, for sometimes I am taken by the full shadow of an experience or a thought, and sometimes it's much more than a shadow. It's a subject! My God, *that* thing! That tried and true. That boring. That cold and clammy. What? Can't I write about Muriel Rukeyser? Eleanor Roosevelt?

I know it's all a question of music, and I should talk (write) only about music and what the music of poetry is compared to the music of sculpture or the music of music. When my friend Karl Stirner, who is a sculptor, talks (he doesn't write) about the vertical and continuous lines in African art, of which he is a devotee and a collector, he refers to music, even as he plays eighteenth- and nineteenth-century German sounds on his Victrola to keep him company as he works. (He works in iron, that drawing in space.) It's the defense of last resort for every artist striving for definition. Music. Except maybe musicians. Musicians use words—of all things! I must admit, though, that I am quite fond of musicians when they do that. There is such freshness, such openness about it all. I'll always treasure how Ken Gabura, who headed the experimental music department at the University of Iowa, during the 1980s, responded to a long poem of mine called *Bread without Sugar* by insisting that it was a piece of music—and experimental to boot, and proved it to me in a series of conversations in his attic and on his front porch. I was totally convinced and enthusiastic. In fact, he arranged for me to talk, at a rather formal meeting, to his graduate students gathered there from twenty states and, I'm sure, six countries, on the music of my poem—not its *musicality* mind you, but its music: harmony, tone, rhythm, melody, movement, dominant whatnots. I may have been hypnotized but I pulled it off; the students were happy, some of the other faculty attending were happy, I was, and most of all Ken. He had discovered in this poor lyrical disheveled ranting scribbler a composer of the first order, nor have I ever been the same after that. I have retrieved both my harmonica and my trombone, given my new occupation, and so far I play two complete tunes on the mouth organ and I can not only find all seven positions on my trombone, but I can perform "Pennies from Heaven" to the most discerning ear.

Gabura was originally from New York, Queens I think, was educated in the 1940s and '50s, had the conversion in the '60s, and moved to San Diego where he distinguished himself in new-ears stuff. He had come to Iowa to transform the music department but they cut the budget under him and he was planning on remaking himself in New Mexico. I remember a piece of music—all talking—based on Ben Franklin's life and writings where the audience was on stage and the performers were in the rows and the aisles. He came to my house for a dinner party one night and when I was passing around seconds on ice cream I tossed him the carton but he missed it and ice cream spread all over his beard and the front of his shirt. We were both shocked. My friends at the table suggested I did it on purpose because he was flirting with my girlfriend but the fact is he couldn't catch. When I saw the magnified eyes behind his thick glasses and the startled, betrayed look I was devastated, for I rather loved him. Less than a year later I ran into him at the university hospital where he had just been told he had cancer and had three, four months to live. He tried vitamin injections in Mexico but ended up in his bedroom, reunited with the children he hadn't seen for twenty or so years. In the early days, he played in a jazz band, a cornet. He knew Fifty-seventh Street well.

It would be interesting to know what music Cage listened to for his own pleasure. What Joyce and Stein read. I don't go so far as to read Kipling whom Eliot loved; but I do—at least I did—enjoy Jeffers, and I'm very fond of D. H. Lawrence. (We're talking poetry.) And not only "Bavarian Gentians" and "Snake," but "How Beastly the Bourgeois Is," a much better poem than I used to think. There is great pleasure in comprehensible subject matter. It's an intriguing idea.

In the meantime I'm listening to Górecki's Third Symphony, Beethoven's Eleventh String Quartet, and learning to sing off key. As far as the poem is concerned, I suppose it's a warning of sorts to be alert to everything from oncoming traffic to poison ivy to death. But, if anything, it's joyous—even though I invoke the cry "against whistling," for the poem is not really against any form of noisemaking and indeed celebrates our long-ago attempts, that squealing and moaning we once called singing.

THE MOROSCO

I

It would be the same now as it was then.

II

Nineteen eighty-two. I was walking down Forty-fifth Street fresh out of the Port Authority when I came upon a small bronze plaque on the front side of an old theater, commemorating the first showing of O'Neill's *Beyond the Horizon*. As I recall, the plaque made allusion to the "first American tragedy," or maybe it was Eugene O'Neill's first tragedy, and the date it was first performed. I think it was 1920. I remember how everything started to work for me all of a sudden, how all the elements started to quickly come together. I thought of the old theater and the sweet plaque and the empty street and my own earnest, almost scholarly manner. I thought of tragedy, and particularly "American" tragedy, and I thought of the quaintness of the theater district as a location for that tragedy and I thought of O'Neill, that fine fatalistic Irishman, and I remembered vaguely that early play and, as I recalled then, its rather lyric and autobiographic quality; and I realized, by the excitement and the concentration, that a poem was in the making—and I reached for my pen and paper among the mass of magazines, socks, hairbrushes, and such I was carrying in my fat black McCarthy briefcase.

I keep changing my method of keeping track of the poems I am working on at any given time. During that time I had moved away from marbleized notebooks and cardboard folders to 8½ × 11 manila envelopes, with the title of the projected poem and a number for reference, which would collate with a numbered list of titles I kept in my "master" notebook or on a piece of paper on my desk or in my wallet. Of course I confess all this with a certain amount of shame—even with scorn—now that I have abandoned that method. In this case I wrote down the first few lines—the real makings of the poem—on the face of the envelope itself. I always think I will return to the original lines in a few days, but as often as not whole months pass, with other poems, and with life itself, intervening. Sometimes the poem is gone, even though the lines are legible; sometimes the lines generate an altogether different poem. I have the manila envelope in front of me now. I note that the number is "4" and that the title is "I Walk Through Piaf Territory," although I note the alternative title, "Beyond the Horizon." The lines I jotted down are "I walk through Piaf territory / past the bronze plaque for Eugene O'Neill on the wall of the Morosco Theatre on 49 St. / That's where tragedy started in 1920." Hardly lines of poetry, though I think I liked the first phrase, and the ironic line about tragedy starting in 1920, with all the possible interplays and over-lays, World War I, America coming of age and such. I had what I thought were the makings.

I remember that it was Bastille Day, July 14, that I came into New York on some business and walked over to Forty-ninth Street (my notes said Forty-ninth Street and not Forty-fifth Street) to look at my site. It took me about fifteen minutes to realize the site was indeed on Forty-fifth Street, and it took me only one slow ago- nized second to realize that the marvelous Morosco Theatre was no longer there, or the Helen Hayes on Forty-sixth Street for that matter, or the little Bijou; that the whole block had been razed, that the workers were retrieving the last few slices of marble from some weary façade, that the plaque had disappeared, that the poem had disappeared, and that this was the place—the very place—that was the center of the great Broadway controversy only a few months earlier; that it was the Morosco Theatre, in addition to the Helen Hayes and the little Jewel, that were quickly, and noisily, knocked down in order that the owners of the soil could extract absolutely maximum profit from the ugly new buildings they were bound to construct there, that I had read for days on end about it in the *Times*, and seen the pictures, and even noted the protests, with all the righteousness—and lying—you usually get in such cases.

I played with the idea of the poem a long time. Clearly I could not re-create the mood. The circumstances were gone, the images were no longer available, the posture was now not only senseless but, more than that, ridiculous. And to change the circumstances, to create another posture, would not only be cheating (I didn't care too much about that), but it just wouldn't work. My poem had been buried in the rubble. Nor could I, in the face of such a direct assault, in the face of political cynicism and aesthetic indifference and short- term greed and long-term idiocy, retreat into nostalgia or bitter irony. The wreckers would just love that. They would themselves preserve my little poem somewhere; maybe they'd put it in a zinc container, or let it flutter down from the belly of an old biplane, or even put it up on some obscure wall of the Koch-Portman, in the waste disposal room maybe, provided they could read.

The protests, I recall, were orderly and cooperative; no one was shot or maimed. I don't remember anyone even being punched. I never managed to get to any of the rallies or gatherings and I had to depend on newspapers and television for my information, but I think the feelings generated were a combination of horror and sadness, horror that the theaters were going to be demolished and sadness that it had to be so. There was, from time to time, a little hope, as judges and politicians showed signs of interfering, but the hope was of the nature we associate with terminal diseases, gestures of decency and kindness, expressions of logic and sanity in a world grown morbid and mad, mere pretenses to control.

As typical in these matters, there was a barrage of statements and counterstatements; there were speeches, visitations, reports, and interviews. It was very much like the dust and smoke you get during a war and, as in a war, there was camouflage, smoke-bombing, propaganda leaflets, heroics, rumors, shortages, anxiety, fake reassurance, distant thunder, and absolute cynicism. Clearly the enemy wanted to move west. It wanted to get away from the congested and expensive East Side, and a most marvelous first target was the decayed Times Square area. And, like good conquerors, it could destroy existing institutions—theaters in this case—in the very name of *saving* them. Side by side, cheek by boring jowl, with reports of the imminent collapse of the Morosco and the Helen Hayes were other, and glowing, reports of the continued development of Theater Row and the earnest revitalization of the whole area. It was a perfectly orchestrated nightmare. It was designed to produce disorientation, torpor, and guilt. People were given little flags so they could wave them like smiling zombies when the wreckers marched in. Famous personalities were involved, actors and producers and playwrights. Joseph Papp's name figured prominently;

so did Arthur Miller's. Helen Hayes said she didn't know whether she would lend her name to the proposed new theater being planned for the Portman Hotel. Tony Randall, José Ferrer, and Madeleine Sherwood, representing the Actors Equity Association, showed up at City Hall to urge the city to halt the demolition of the three theaters. At various times the Morosco Theatre was declared eligible for federal landmark status, the opponents of the Portman Hotel came up with alternative designs for a hotel-and-theater complex, and Supreme Court justice Thurgood Marshall issued a staying order. Russell Baker wrote a wild and bitter article predicting the vacuity that would ensue once the hotel was built and the area was "cleaned up." I knew the jig was up long before when I read that Reagan's top political aide, Lyn Nofziger, as well as Secretary of the Interior Watt himself, were intervening directly to help poor John C. Portman, the beleaguered developer, in the best style of laissez-faire capitalism. Nofziger apparently had "pressured" the Advisory Council on Historic Preservation to permit demolition of the Morosco when there was a threat that it might be designated a landmark, a blatant violation of the National Historic Preservation Act. When the lower federal courts ruled in favor of the Portman group, John C., speaking out of Atlanta, said, in all his wisdom, that he was "heartened and encouraged" by actions of the judicial system and hoped that "this long, tortuous legal journey will be over for us, and we can get on with building this project for the people of the city of New York." It was a "project," not a building. Mr. Papp vowed to move into the Piccadilly Hotel, which was also scheduled to be torn down to make way for the project, and to wage a continuing campaign against those who would destroy the theaters. "We will have an honor guard of fifty people on duty at all times," he said, "so they won't be able to start demolition in the middle of the night."

Actress Tammy Grimes said she was prepared to "stand between the Morosco and the wrecking machines," if need be. New York City, which promised $30 million in tax abatements, didn't blink an eye, although it did shake a little when the Manufacturers Hanover Trust Company and Equitable Life Assurance Society hinted they might back out of the deal, or at least make new demands for their security. When the huge hydraulic backhoe, with the "Godzilla" on its side, finished chewing up the Bijou and started biting into the east wall of the Morosco the crowd shouted. Some openly wept. There was a last picture-taking session inside the Morosco Theatre, arranged by the *New York Times*. The play was over.

III

I stood across the street from the rapidly diminishing façade of the Helen Hayes or walked up and down Seventh Avenue outside the cyclone fence. I observed that *The Pirates of Penzance* was playing nearby, as were *Annie* and *Oh Calcutta!* I was lingering there, somewhere between the Church of Scientology headquarters and the bronze statue of George M. Cohan. 1878–1942. Cane and hat. I was in the midst of Italian ices and Goyim-for-Jesus, across the street from the Calvin Klein ad and the Wienerwald Restaurant. Hard by *Apocalypse Now* and *Rocky III*. Near Howard Johnson's, the Gaiety Male Theater, Burger King, the Swingers' Club, the Playmates' Club, the Hotel Edison. I could smell the old plaster and the bricks. I could feast my eyes on the crushed Budweiser cans and the flattened Burger King cartons. There was a deep hole in the ground where the theaters had been. It really did look as if the proverbial gigantic molar had been extracted. Joseph Papp and Arthur Miller and José Ferrer were nowhere around. Weirdly dressed tourists kept passing by, and I ran into an old friend of mine who was singing and dancing in a nearby show. She had been in on the picture-taking spree in the empty Morosco. Near that old bushel basket. She had wept openly.

IV

I had not given up my own poem completely, of course, only it would have to take quite a different turn than I originally intended. I had to take a step away. I had to become more ghostly, almost disappear. I had to go where I would be less affected by the particulars, where I could not be so madly mauled. Into the unconscious, the dream-space. I would go there not only for relief, but for understanding. I was almost embarrassed by the realization, it seemed like such a monumentally simple and traditional thing to do. And it seemed to smack totally of unconverted Romanticism. Yet within that order, within that disorder, lay the poems, and sometimes the bones, of so many American poets, particularly so many of my very own contemporaries whom I admired so much. Did we all move from disillusion and hopelessness? Were our poems indeed buried in that rubble? Were we ghouls, living off of ash? Did we love it? Were those crocodile tears behind our dreamy incisors? Were we just lemmings, following one another through the decay? What would Hegel say? What would Jefferson?

I think that our very best poets were fated enough—call it lucky, call it unlucky—to make those terrifying links between their personal loss and the great public loss, and that through the memory, through the absolute knowledge of the beautiful first kingdom and its destruction, whatever that kingdom was to each of them, they were able to see, sometimes quite bitterly, the destruction of the second kingdom, the public one. I think that they were moved, out of pain, to engage their loss and go beyond it, and that they used various techniques and philosophies and gestures to do this, although none of these were escapist, in the conventional sense. I think that these poets were overwhelmed by the idea of lost innocence and beloved unity, and that they were attracted to earlier writers who created *their* visions from altogether different cultures, and for different purposes. Jacob Boehme, Christopher Smart, for example. I think that these poets inevitably had to be Romantics, as Romanticism is perceived by critics and scholars, although the posture of individuals among them might be extremely anti-Romantic, whether from the point of view of language or idea, and that, as Romantics, they turned away from the cities, from what used to be called "civilization" (Robinson Jeffers, Gary Snyder, Wendell Berry), or they turned, in the cities, to the poor and hopeless and unacknowledged pockets. I think, first from habit, later from exhaustion, later from terror, they reacted bitterly to technology. I think that technology and the response to technology is at the very heart of the matter, for technology destroyed the past, it ruined continuity, and it didn't give us a chance to learn and develop slowly, even as a mosquito does. I think, moreover, that the issue I am discussing here has peculiar and heartrending significance in America, and therefore for American poets, since the only history we know, aside from fake stone-age memories and alien imports, is deeply connected with technology. It is the very absence of a past, of an ancient and beautiful stubbornness, as Europe conceives it, that made possible the quick development of technology in America. There was nothing to stand in its way. Our nostalgia therefore, except in one or two cases, is always for an earlier stage of technology itself, never for the stage preced-

ing technology, as it often is in Europe, and, at least in the twen-
tieth century, when we imagine "innocence" it is very likely to
involve early junk, even if it does involve childhood (Thomas
Wolfe, Eugene O'Neill).

Moreover, there is a threshold point, and I believe it's 1910,
or as late as 1920, where the feeling of irreparable loss, and
therefore hopeless inability for true renewal, began to domi-
nate. We would have reached that threshold point under any
circumstances, but it was America's entry into World War I,
and the final end of the frontier, and the new immigration
law, and the deliberate imperialization, and the self-conscious
Europeanization, and the total destruction of Native American
cultures and any sustenance we might have derived from them,
and the betrayal of all our trusts, and the leveling process, and
the radical change in our ideals that helped us get there. The
exhaustion of spirit and the termination of belief also helped,
although it is infinitely difficult at so close a distance to pinpoint
loss of will and date it and show how it happened. I believe it
was 1910, no matter what little heroics might occur later on in
the century, and no matter how much our writers themselves
were excited by the prospect of artistic newness, and no matter
how much they, or their critics, confused this with social trans-
formation or connected it with political and moral greatness. It
was no accident therefore that Pound and Eliot and Frost and
Stein did what they did when they did it; and it was no accident
that, in a trice, we became Europe's teachers, its dreaded elders,
rather than its élèves. And it wasn't only because of power and
money. It is quite possible that we missed the opportunity for
greatness altogether because of a few sad facts. It is quite pos-
sible that the near-great poets that we did have, everyone of

them grossly (and beautifully) flawed, Williams, Pound, Frost, Stein, Stevens, Eliot, Crane, were doomed from the start, that they were doomed even as they were lighting up and exploding like great stars, one after another, and it is possible that their great brilliance disguised this. It is more than possible that by 1920, when *Beyond the Horizon* opened up to a curious or indifferent or enthusiastic audience at the old Morosco, certain matters had already been decided and we were now ready at last for tragedy, American style. It is possible that O'Neill already knew it, that drunken Sophocles. We would rise again, of course. We will rise again and again—there are great republics in our future, and hideous ones as well, periods of great darkness and periods of pure sunlight—but we will never be as we once were, in the dreamtime, in our white houses and our green lanes. I must add that I am talking about dreams and their loss, that I am not for a minute overlooking the brutality and ignorance, say, of small-town life, and the dirt and general horror of city slum life, nor the pervasive racism and inhumanity. I come from Pittsburgh!

V

Our loss, the sons and the daughters, is incalculable. Roethke is the oldest of us—although Auden probably belongs—and Kunitz—and it is amazingly accurate that he (Roethke) called his first great poem "The Lost Son." James Wright is a lost son, and Galway Kinnell, and John Berryman and Robert Lowell, and Robert Bly and Philip Levine and Jack Gilbert and C. K. Williams and Allen Ginsberg and Sylvia Plath and Louis Simpson and John Logan and William Merwin. So is David Ignatow. And Muriel Rukeyser. They are lost sons; and daughters. How many poems in James Wright's last book reflect this? How many in Galway's? Who has reread *Avenue C* lately? Who has heard Merwin's poem to his father? Who has heard Ignatow's? Is Stanley Plumly's grief confined only to certain circumstances in Ohio? Is Steven Berg's *Grief* for a particular man with a small-brimmed hat, and that only? Is Paul Zimmer weeping only for Zimmer? Who has read Linda Pastan's lovely poem "I Am Learning to Abandon the World"? Why is it a loss? What has made us so deeply aware of the loss? Why is it that it's more unbearable now than ever before? Who would it be reasonable to blame? Which bastard? Henry Ford? Woodrow Wilson? Stalin? Mussolini? Should we each color in our own bastard? How about a nice orgy of forgiving: no one's to blame; we are all victims; history is running its course; no one could foresee. Here we color in the poet embracing a billionaire, J. Edgar Hoover hugging Martin Luther King Jr., Berkman is bringing Frick an Abe Lincoln rose. He is shooting it out of a toy gun. No one will get hurt! No one will ever get sent back to Russia!

The thought occurs that we have nothing to apologize for, that the great technical breakthrough in art in the first quarter of the twentieth century, and the magnificent poetry that was produced as a result, was made possible not only by great changes in the culture, but (that) the technical was a partial substitute for, or at least a dislocation of, feeling itself; that there didn't seem to be room enough for both. This is probably another way of talking about the modern assault on "excessive" or "false" feeling, and its perceived connection with "outdated" modes of expression. Which often led to a need to conceal feeling. Maybe it's no accident that *our* poetry, beginning with Auden and Roethke, maybe with MacLeish, is elegiac and *theirs* is not; that, except for Pound pitying himself, there are no elegies among them.* My little academic genie cries out that when poetry is in "full-force" and "masculine" and "vigorous," as we used to say, there is no time or occasion for elegy. That we only drop tears in the ruins when there are ruins, or when we perceive the ruins. I wonder how much the will and cunning of just one or two poets prevented a whole generation from seeing those ruins as they actually were. At any rate, those poets who came of age during the Depression, or who first started to write during the second war, or just at the end when we clarified everything with the bomb, saw things in a new light—as did Wilfred Owen at an earlier time, already moved as he was to pity, the last resort. James Wright remembers a mouse taking a nap, for a minute free of the cat. He remembers a stranger reaching his pathetic "trees" out to him in New York City. He remembers that the secret of this journey is "to let the wind / Blow its dust all over your body, / To let it go on blowing, to step lightly, lightly / All the way through your ruins." Philip Levine remembers Old Cherry Dorn, his black head running with gray, bowed in his bib overalls. He remembers "The Conductor of Nothing," the eerie trains "loose, running between grassy slopes / and leaving behind the wounded / wooden rolling stock of another era." He remembers Akron, Ohio, in 1951, and the dew "that won't wait long enough / to stand my little gray wren a drink." Muriel Rukeyser remembers her lonely back tooth; she remembers St. Roach, "Fast as a dancer, light, strange, and lovely to the touch."

---

* Maybe a risky statement. Hart Crane not only was "elegiac," he actually wrote several elegies proper. Jeffers was elegiac, if bitter. It is really a question of who they are. Just as it is a question of who we are—for not all of us live in the same ruins.

VI

It would be the same thing now as it was then, only the poets of the next and the next next must speak for themselves for they have different memories and a different knowledge, even if they all have read Auden and Villon. It could be exactly the same but it's probably altogether different. Or somewhat altogether. I'll know more when we have the conference on ruin. Quite simply, I find, in my eighty-third year, that the theater district is anything but quaint, and the Marquis Theatre, inside the (now) Marriott Hotel, up an escalator, is hideous, as is the hotel itself hideous—in every way conceivable, especially the glass elevator, the endless gloomy dead spaces, and the reception on the seventh floor. I'm not going to start on Disney and its dumb musicals or the general glitz. Or the exhibitionist cowboy in jockey underwear, wearing boots and a hat and strumming a guitar, "older" woman paying to take a picture with him, or pinch his ass. I've gotten particularly to despise the "open-space concept" and "Hollywood Balloons." As far as O'Neill's plaque, I can't find it; it's probably buried in the walls of the Marriott or the ridiculous garage that faces directly on the street. There is a plaque a little westward for one John Golden (1874–1955) "in grateful recognition of his contribution to the welfare of the needy performers in originating and actualizing the annual bread basket drive of the Actors Fund of America." God bless John Golden. And actors—who out-starve poets. Many of the old theaters are still there, waiting for the poets to get to work. Macbeth is at the Lyceum.

VII

It was the same then. I walked up Forty-seventh Street with a ham sandwich and a Pepsi light in a little bag. I sat on the stoop—really it was a kind of concrete abutment—next door to the Maccabeen Restaurant, across from the Rio Hotel. It was starting to rain a little so I had to eat fast. I loved eating a ham sandwich there with the Hasidim walking by me in their heavy clothes, all those layers of holiness. I thought of Edith Piaf again, and I remembered a hotel I stayed at in Paris once that had hallways like paths in a forest and I wondered if the Rio was like that. I vowed I would eventually sleep there and add it to the list of forlorn hotels I have stayed at, for a day, a week, a month—once even for a year. I imagined putting my clothes away, positioning my toothbrush, looking for the Bible and stationery, testing the shower, and lying down, with my shoes off, for my first nap. Listening to music. Sharing a life with the hundreds of others who had been in that same bed. I finished my Pepsi, put it back in the little bag, and stuffed it into my jacket pocket like a good citizen. I passed by the theaters without a second thought and raced toward the Port Authority. My poem was done.

WILLIAM CARLOS WILLIAMS

I

I'LL PROBABLY NOT GET to William Carlos Williams's city again in this life though I don't have much interest, for that matter, in getting back there in the next or even the next next, when I am, alas, a blue jay, or a banana, or a black squirrel, or a yellow Episcopalian. I only went there in the first place (in 1983) because my dear friend Mark Hillringhouse, who was the recently appointed director of the William Carlos Williams Center, invited me—and Diane Freund—to see the newly furbished great theater, originally the Rivoli, and the adjoining lesser rooms and such that constituted the center. There were two thousand seats in the theater but I don't know if it's even altogether finished (even) now—anno 2008. There was an event there—in a much smaller, and newer, space. I know it because the event was the celebration of Williams's one hundredth birthday. In September. It was over one hundred degrees outside and there were seven or eight poets reading, including Ginsberg and Baraka, who came only in time for himself to read, as he always does. Corso, I remember, though not invited, was walking the hall, muttering or reciting. I must add that the town was not Paterson but Rutherford—Williams lived in Rutherford, as did his son after him, also a doctor. Paterson, a city nearby, was the name of his poem, site of silk mills and a waterfall, a Hamiltonian dream.

Diane and I went up to Rutherford from Ocean Grove, where we spent the summer—she was managing a small hotel—a month or so before the event, to meet Mark and to see the great movie house, the new center and Williams's home on 9 Ridge Street—I am a true hound when it comes to these things, and I want to follow the scent again and drag my loose ears along the ground, in search of what I already know. But things could be different the next time, the house might have an addition, or a new garden, or a fence, and the town itself might look smaller than I remember, or more decrepit and the ugly little library might have given way to something more noble, marble this time instead of pastel-colored plastic chairs. Rome had three libraries during Augustus's reign—Rutherford, a mite smaller, deserves at least one good one, if for no other reason than New Jersey's most important poet spent most of his busy life there.

It was a warm and beautiful day—it could have been May, it could have been August. I'll have to check with Mark and see if he remembers. I remember sitting in one of the seats in the huge movie palace and being dragged back to *my* movie palaces in Pittsburgh, the Enright Theater, the Loews Penn, the Stanley, the Fulton, the Warner, the stage shows I saw there, the double features, the Movietone news, the cartoons, the shorts, the special events on certain nights, raffling off dishes and the like and, especially, the sing-alongs—for a quarter, even for a dime. And there might have been a giant entranceway, gorgeous rugs, and chandeliers, not the dead little boxes we sit in now.

Williams's house was on a little knoll, and there was a doctor's sign on the front lawn. What struck me was there wasn't a "grand" entrance to the house, no great wooden or stone staircase, no oak

door, no porch, nothing that was simultaneously inviting and for-
bidding, the way it is elsewhere, almost everywhere. There were
instead, though the house itself was grand enough, two makeshift
side entrances, in two odd corners of the house. And it was right in
town. The library was a block away, the "new" library, built in 1958,
five years before Williams's death. The old library was a converted
or reconstituted church, a few doors from Williams's house.

I had on a straw hat and was smoking a corncob pipe, for that
was my style then. I had bought the hat, as I did all my hats, at
Bergey's Mall, a feed and general store at the corner of Bergerstrasse
and Wassergasse Road, a few miles out of Easton, Pennsylvania, up
and down some steep hills and wild curves, eighteenth-century
stone houses and twentieth-century cows. The store was packed
with merchandise. In addition to barrels and sacks of feed, it fea-
tured jeans, overalls, flannel shirts, candles, apples, knives, candy,
and bacon. And, of course, hats. Len Roberts, the gifted upstate
New York poet, whose skin shone red in the summer sun, lived on
Wassergasse Road. Inside the Rutherford library, a room inside the
room, was Williams's make-believe office, or study, the size, say, of
a large bathroom. There were books, manuscripts, pipes, a hunting
license, a blood-pressure machine, knives, pens, and the famous
straw hat—*his* hat, which sits on his head in the famous photograph
on the cover of one of his *Selected*'s. The hat was on his desk.

With no hesitation, just before we left, I put my own hat on the
desk and Williams's hat on my head. It was a perfect fit, a 7-1/8, a
fine panama reminiscent of the islands and the golden days in Flor-
ida. I certainly tipped the hat to the librarians at the front desk and
it wasn't till we were a good block away that I confessed to Mark
and Diane, who were innocent of the crime. They were amazed
but, as I recall, nonjudgmental, in the good style of 1983. One more

block, almost to the car, the guilt and horror pangs set in. I ran back and, smiling at the librarians, I reentered the office and exchanged hats again. The giving back was the hard part. The librarians were getting suspicious. Imagine going into a bank to return money or a haberdashery to hang up a stolen necktie. Nowadays I get my straw hats in Puerto Rico, real panamas at an amazingly low price. Williams would love the story.

II

I said I probably wouldn't get to William Carlos Williams's city again in this life but I drove up there less than a week after writing that sentence—though I was hardly a yellow Episcopalian. I was going to take a peek at the house, the Williams Center, and the library and see how much the town had changed for good or ill. The Williams Center was more than a little decrepit. Doors were locked. Nobody knew much about it, and when we did get in—I was with the New Jersey poet Peter Waldor—we saw a few old posters and photographs where the reading had been (in 1983), and had a chance to view the old Rivoli from the upper level, probably the former balcony, which was itself now converted to a smaller theater called the Black Box (sideways on the balcony, with bridge chairs). The orchestra seats were in bad repair and the place was dark. Somewhere they show bad movies, either downstairs or upstairs, *Leatherheads*, *Ruins*, *The Forbidden Kingdom*. Someone must go there. Also there seems to be something of a small film festival, though there was no one to get information from. The water fountain was rusty, dirty, and broken—outside a young woman was eating her lunch. She knew nothing about the center.

The house seemed all right—apparently a gynecologist, no relation to Williams, lives there and the town was more thriving, some artists had moved in, there was a Turkish restaurant, and a good shoe store. The library was getting duct work done, so everything was out of place and Williams's study was closed, the items removed. There was, however, a plaque on the outside wall and a red wheelbarrow under the flagpole. The director of the library was a lovely woman who, though she was originally trained in business, had literary interests. She was from Minnesota.

III

I stared at the *Selected* for a long time before I opened it. Williams seemed old to me—he had the old man's chicken neck and I could see his mind, his culture, his pride, his fears, his distance, his attentiveness, in the photograph. The hat somehow looked different from the one I stole in 1983. It seemed less rich, less Panamanian, more Bergerstrassian. I could hear his high voice, which I first encountered at a reading at the University of Pennsylvania in 1959. I thought—sadly, not proudly—of my outrageous behavior and I attributed it to the influence of Georges Bataille—whom I was reading that week—whose selected writings were, after all, called *Visions of Excess*. I even looked him up in my *Cambridge Dictionary of Philosophy* and found a certain degree of legitimacy, and a precedent. It amuses me also that in the adjacent column—on page 73 of the dictionary—is a brief paragraph on Basilides (120–140 C.E.), a Christian Gnostic from Alexandria who built his theory on Valentinus' doctrine of emanations (levels of existence in the Pleroma, the abode of God, pure spirit) and taught, in good Gnostic fashion, that the God of the Jews was a rival to the true father and created the material world. Wherein of course we are locked for a while. In Jew-time.

Jarrell's introduction is as good as I remember it—precise, informed, fair, generous. Although there is a fundamental reservation, and he—Jarrell—doesn't attribute the major status to Williams he would—and did—to Pound and Eliot. He calls Williams good-hearted, sympathetic, spontaneous, open, impulsive, emotional, curious, rash, undignified, experimental, literal, empirical, secular, and democratic. Maybe a little left-handed. I adore, particularly "The Sparrow," "The Dance," "Pastoral," "To Wake an Old Lady," "To Ford Madox Ford in Heaven," "Choral: The Pink Church," "The Bull," "The Trees," "To Elsie," "At the Ball Game," "Spring and All," "The Sea Elephant," "Rain," "Death," "To Daphne and Virginia," "The Terms," "The Locust Tree in Flower," "Raleigh Was Right," "The Last Words of My English Grandmother." The greatest single poem, for me, is "Asphodel, That Greeny Flower," a portion—two portions—of which are in the *Selected*. Auden called it one of the great love poems in the English language and it is that but it is more. It is the absolute confrontation, with almost no mediation, of a human being, a great poet, in the middle of our eventful and horrible last century, with existence itself—what the German metaphysicians dreamed of.

"Asphodel" is essentially a confession, although somewhat veiled, of Williams's infidelities and an appeal to Flossie's understanding and forgiveness. But it is also a celebration of the forces of love and imagination and moves, as Williams's mind does, through the remembered and partly remembered events of his life. The part of the poem I find most moving and mysterious—I would call it the central event of the poem—is the sudden encounter, in a New York subway, with a strange, at once mythical and outlandish, figure sitting opposite him in the car. It is in section III. Williams is on his way "to a meeting," oh, most passive and "interesting" and disgusting and civilized of events. The figure (opposite him) has on a double-breasted black coat, a vest, a heavy and very dirty undershirt, striped trousers, worn shoes, and brown socks about his ankles. He has a gold fountain pen and a mechanical pencil in his breast pocket, and a worn leather zipper case "bulging with its contents" is on the floor beneath him. Williams's face is reflected (from an advertising sign) in such a way that he remembers his own father—"from an old photograph"—fused and *con*fused with the man, for his father wore just such a beard, parted in the middle, and just such a hat and was more or less the same age (in the photograph). Williams describes the "man's brown felt hat" as "lighter than his skin," which is the only mention of race. Finally, the man has a "worn knobbed stick" between his legs, a decoration, a symbol of authority, a mark of dignity, office, or mystery. "I am looking / into my father's / face," Williams says, "speak to him." "He / will know the secret." But he disappears and "with him / went all men." It is a chilling and tremendous moment. It reminds me of that Stetson Eliot encounters in *The Waste Land*— only Stetson is much less interesting, and much less personal. It is hard to imagine Eliot encountering his own father in a subway car; it is doubly hard seeing that father as a black man with a dirty undershirt. He could just as likely be a black-clad Jew with *payes* and *tzitzits*, although that is an interesting thought, Jew-boy Eliot, *père et fils tsuzummen*, as we say, sweating and moaning in the noon-day sun. There are few other events in modern literature to equal it—Hart Crane at the swollen strap, Stevens walking home from the Sorbonne, Paul Goodman on the Hudson, Berryman remembering Delmore, Elizabeth Bishop on the bus. These are the Lear moments in American poetry. And Williams, he of the subway vision, is of the finest.

There is a certain idea—it is more a thought than an idea—of the authoritative figure *behind* a body of poems. He, she, is what we call Hardy or Dickinson, or Browning. The clumsy poet himself, herself, gets to know the authority and more and more imitates him, her. That is one way of talking about it. Another is to talk about the *print*. The soul-print we could call it. Not exactly the persona. Who else could have D. H. Lawrence's print; Wystan's? The less grotesque and peculiar, the better. I came to look for—to honor—to revere that print—Barthes, Foucault, and their dismissal of the author, notwithstanding; it has nothing to do with them. That figure—avatar, spirit, print—in the case of Williams, is delicate, almost fragile, yet overwhelmingly consistent. Insistent is more like it, and lovely beyond words, and decent, and good. One could make distinctions between the figurative one and the biographical one. Between, say, the ghost of the poems and the ghost of the man. The latter may be represented in his autobiography. Reading one (the print), I am totally *engulfed,* I am confronting a presence; the other (the autobiography), I am touched by the quaintness, the particularity. Nor is it a question of prose vs. poetry. It is more the person, on the one hand, and the poet on the other. As to the man, he too is fascinating. Take just his relationship with Pound, through all the years. Or the friendships, such as they were, with the Americans living in New York and Paris. Neither subject is ever reflected, as such, in his poems. Even Ford Madox Ford. Not that it should be. I guess you could make a case that his feeling for Pound—respect, pity, disgust, amusement, embarrassment, loyalty, envy, supreme understanding, is reflected in the way he deals—in his poetry—with any number of poems where the subject is *not* Pound. Perhaps by the verbs and adjectives he uses. He corrects Pound, though not by name and not by number.

One person I talked to said that in borrowing the hat I was borrowing Williams's head—even his mind. He said *mind*, not brain, as if the mind, of all things, could verily be a 7-1/8. Well, "a hat's a hat for aw' that," and before JFK we all wore them, and after some of us stuck to it. And I have even now four or five straws here and there—not to mention the felts and the caps, the greens and grays. The blacks. We called that which we put a hat on a "noodle." Also a bean. Williams would have been delighted—I'm sure of it—by the subject. When the office is put back together, when the vents are straightened out, I know his panama will be back on his desk, or the desk they say is his desk, and I hope to see it there again. And the blood-pressure machine. And the hunting license and alas, a pipe, for that is what the noodle needs most of all, a stinking corn-cob—a rough hewn, hard-smoking, clothes-burning, skin-staining, American pipe. It makes poetry.

IV

I'm a little surprised—though I shouldn't be—at how Williams was received, he who was the *exception* to the others. Would it have been different if he had sat on the sofa pulling his feathers up about him like a peacock or paraded about town like a wobbling pigeon—to speak of only two fellow birds—instead of presenting himself as a listener, a bird in doubt, a dull-dressed doctor in a bow tie, rather amazed at life itself? God, the energy he spent on guilt, in explanation. How much Ezra alone cost Williams by way of excusing his old friend, by way of even listening to him. Didn't Williams even out of respect or affection sometimes half believe the cuckoo economic theories, even as he forgave Pound, because he was insane, because he suffered, because he was passionate? The "Chews" though, that was something else; that truly cost him, he whose (very) grandfather moaned and swayed a little in the ancient manner. Williams's brother Ed, I read in Paul Mariani's biography, was furious when Carlos sometimes more than alluded to a semi-Semitic graft or drift. For Christ's sake, what could we tell the grandchildren? Maybe that explains Williams's raw and vulgar lustiness.

I believe that "Asphodel" is a great poem. It is a poem about hell and about flowers and the despised poem and death and the nature of power and form itself, in art, in nature, in the mind. It is neither optimistic nor pessimistic, but rides the crest and adores the troughs. It is not fragmental—as such—as *The Waste Land* is and much of the *Cantos*, but has both unity and inevitability about it. Not to mention that Williams is able to include personal feelings and real people— while sustaining an objective narrative and a depersonalized form. It is a lucky poem, for it finds its subject and it has a mode and a manner and a style, and it speaks, shall we say, naturally out of an agony of life reflected, no, embodied—destined—in an agony of language. It flirts, it actually *flirts,* with the soft and sentimental. It is the two great principles of life come together. It begins over and over. It is Homer's catalog of ships. It is nervously aware, at all times, of itself, and its purpose and the world out there and the body and the very speculations, the cultural and intellectual accretions, of the busy arguing philosophers and the ranters and warriors and, most of all, the singers. When, in section I, it remembers the sea, it remembers not only a garden, when the sun strikes it, the wild plum, the pink mallow, but a storm "come in over the water," and lightning in the clouds. Though in the midst, it remembers a book he and Flossie read together, a "serious book" he calls it, maybe the *Iliad* ("Helen's public fault"), or the poems of Valéry, whom he quotes ("The sea! The sea!"), out of "Le cimetière marin," that beautiful book- ish masterpiece, which ends with the wind rising and the "vast air" opening and closing his book, as the wind might have William's and Flossie's book, remembered now in Williams's study (so many years later), a poem that ends with a Rilkean shock-statement, "we must try to live"—maybe a little more tired than Rilke. Certainly too tired for Williams, but he—Rilke—the perfect poet for Wil- liams's not-so-secret envy of form—the other side.

Williams used a technique not so much of stream of free asso- ciation but of free thought. "Nothing is free," as Williams said of verse all through his life, certainly meaning more than verse. One thought goes to another and it seems arbitrary or capricious even, but the mind structures it out of a wisdom that the mind alone knows. Did he learn it from Pound? Not to offend, but it seemed more natural to him than to Pound. Nor did he overuse the defi- nite article in the manner that the master did as a means of changing the action, of moving the narrative forward. Where are the critics when we need them? Why it is that in France they anointed Valéry so suddenly, and here, where there was gold, where an unheard of blue shone so as to blind us, there was such slow attention?

And what magic that, in spite of his physical deterioration and emotional upheaval, Williams was able to finish this extraordinary poem, and in spite of his final realizations of the horror, maybe the insanity of history, of existence itself, connected in the poem with the bomb and its worship, it ends in a replication of his and Flossie's marriage ceremony and the celebration of light. Mariani points out that Williams, when he began "Asphodel," thought he was writing his fifth book of *Paterson,* though he soon realized it did not belong with the longer poem. "For all its prolixity," Mariani says, "its sense of rambling" and "nostalgic reminiscence, Williams has created a complex and highly organized design around a handful of symbols that . . . yield up the poem's deeper significance." The subject, as I say, concerns the "long and difficult love affair between Williams and his wife." It is also "the power of Eros over humans." It is also the Cold War and the bomb and McCarthyism and the love of death and the conflict between light and dark. The sole speaker is Williams. Flowers and gardens are everywhere in the poem, but it is the "green and wooden" asphodel that is at the center.

The poem reflects the intense fear, the tightness, and the Manichean vision of that day. Williams wisely settled on "the bomb" as our own horrendous dark god hovering over us and, feeding from our distress and our anxiety, invigorating and destroying us, with its useless power. Williams invokes the flower, which comes "to delect us" in hell's despite, and he invokes love, including his own love, which is also a power. And that is the poem. It's either a sleight-of-hand, or a sentiment, or a true cry. It depends on *language* and its extraordinary use, and it depends on feeling—*authentic* feeling. It is easier to be Augustine—or Eliot. Luckily the poem is *confused*. The "cry" is not just for the presence of love, it is also, in its dramatic personal plea for forgiveness, a moving conflation of the two.

Mariani sees the encounter with the father figure as a symbolic as well as a personal event. It is a journey to the underground—to hell—parallel to Aeneas's visit to his father, Anchises, "amidst the asphodel covered fields of Hades." But it is more ancient, more primitive than that. The man sitting opposite him is a "dark progenitor," "at one with the figure of the unicorn/satyr," the beast/artist, Pan, "confined by the forces of repression to live in this hell." And the knobbed stick, and the case "bulging with its contents between his (father's) legs" is "the huge phallus" of the satyrs. Not too different from D. H. Lawrence's black Pan standing over against "the mechanical, conquered universe of modern humanity." (Only Williams's Pan doesn't have a goat's foot.) My own experience tells me that the events of our poems are almost always literal, amazingly literal, and we draw our mythology out of that—smiling with delight. We *start* with a knobbed stick and a bulging case and a felt hat and a brown skin.

Reading "Asphodel" I realize how, underlying, penetrating, the verse is a rather consistent system of belief, almost a *religious* belief—if such a thing can be both godless and secular; and that that belief is not unlike others in England, America, and the European continent. That it derives from, or is connected with, one way or another, other beliefs, religions, and philosophies, and that Williams came fully to it as he developed his triadic system of versification in the early 1950s, though it was *anticipated;* that it may be called "the religion of the poets," or "modern poets," and that it comes from a complex combination of preceding beliefs, including Zoroastrianism, humanism, deism, Judaism, Christianity, socialism, scientism, Quakerism, Transcendentalism, and Gnosticism; and from St. John of the Cross, Plato, Plotinus, and the language of Williams's contemporaries in France, Spain, England, Germany, and America; that it is dualistic and messianic, and that it centers on light, as a power—or love and goodness—as opposed to darkness and that it emphasizes the affinity between holiness and light. Though it is probably more ancient than all those beliefs by unheard of hundreds of years and comes from the cave and forest and fire and the struggle among the seasons and the struggle between day and night.

"It is all / a celebration of the light," Williams says in the coda—the fourth part of "Asphodel."

Light, the imagination
        and love,
                in our age,
by natural law,
        which we worship,
                maintain
all of a piece
        their dominance.
So let us love
        confident as is the light
                in its struggle with darkness
that there is as much to say
        and more
                for the one side
and that not the darker
        which John Donne
                for instance
among many men
        presents to us.
                In the controversy
touching the younger
        and the older Tolstoy,
                Villon, St. Anthony, Kung,
Rimbaud, Buddha
        and Abraham Lincoln
                the palm goes
always to the light;
        who most shall advance the light—
                call it what you may!
The light
        for all time shall outspeed
                the thunder crack.
Medieval pageantry
        is human and we enjoy
                the rumor of it
as in our world we enjoy
        the reading of Chaucer,

> likewise
> a priest's raiment
> (or that of a savage chieftain).
> It is all
> a celebration of the light.

Williams, like Stevens, says "only the imagination is real." And it is through the imagination, grabbing hold of memory, that love can flower, for "love and the imagination / are of a piece." Indeed "light, the imagination / and love," are "all of a piece" and the *creative urge* is the basis of it all. Though it would be fruitful to examine whether the creation of the bomb was the result of this "urge" or something else.

It is interesting that the bomb immediately entered our poetic imagination, but the inhuman (read "human") destruction and callousness of our time, except in a few cases, took so long. I was there in the early 1950s myself, writing "little aesthetic masterpieces" with no reference to the ugly 1930s and '40s, like so many of the others. The horror—in Europe, in Africa, in Asia, may have been in Williams's mind—it was—but he chose to call it "the bomb." Eliot had already—years earlier—made his comment about how we cannot tolerate too many "secular free-thinking Jews," and expressed his regret over the death of the Confederacy, and Pound was still at it even to his late-late self-serving insane comment (to Ginsberg) that he was guilty of what he called a "suburban prejudice" in his, Pound's, hate-mongering.

All of which may not have a lot to do with my love of Williams and my brief theft of his hat. My gangster cousins kept all their information in, or was it under, their hats and thus managed to stay out of jail for significant periods of time. We poets, though some of us manage to spend a day or two penned up, use our hats for other reasons. Some of us simply want to stay warm, some of us are stylish, some religious, and some depend on the hat to provide us some-how with our music, even, occasionally, our rhyme. It may be the feather, it may be the rim, it may be the ribbon. It may be what's hidden under the lid, parallel to what's inside the shoe. That's why, at the airport, we have to take off our hats *and* shoes. But what do the machines know, in their lust for metal? God pity the hatless and their lack of humility. God bless the very straw, the soft cloth, the colors, the patterns, the indentations, the angles. Most of all, the mystery. I could not steal Williams's mystery.

Acknowledgments and Credits

I want to thank my friends from the past, and the recent past, who have either appeared in these pages or have been helpful to me in their writing: Carol Smith, Richard Hazley, Jack Gilbert, William Kahn, Sidney Santman, Dick Foster, Rosalind Pace, Ira Sadoff, Arthur Vogelsang, Harry Stern, Ida Stern, Ted Solotaroff, Howard Ward, Maryann Kirchwehm, Allen Ginsberg, Andy Warhol, and Pat Stern. Pat, in particular, for remembering certain events and for sharing so many of these things with me. Some of the people are dead, some long dead, but they are all within earshot.

I also want to thank my editor, Barbara Ras, for her faith in me and my work, and my assistant, Stephanie Smith, for her correcting, caring, and contributing.

Finally I want to recognize, and thank, Anne Marie Macari for her faith, encouragement, and inspiration. She has been not only an amazing editor, but also a loving friend and companion. I absolutely could not have written this book without her.

⌣⁀

Lines from "Postcards" in *Clouded Sky* by Miklós Radnóti, translated by Steven Polgar, Stephen Berg, and S. J. Marks. Translation copyright © 1972, 2003 by Mrs. Miklós Radnóti, Steven Polgar, Stephen Berg, and S. J. Marks. Reprinted by permission of Sheep Meadow Press.

Lines from "I Live in Shadow, Filled with Light" by Miguel Hernandez, from *Six Masters of the Spanish Sonnet*, translated by Willis Barnstone. © 1993 by the Board of Trustees, Southern Illinois University Press. Reprinted by permission of the publisher.

Lines from "9–10 P.M. Poems" and "One Night of Knee-Deep Snow" from *Poems of Nazim Hikmet*, translated by Randy Blasing and Mutlu Konuk. Translation copyright © 1994, 2002 by Randy Blasing and Mutlu Konuk. Reprinted by permission of Persea Books, Inc. (New York).

Some of these essays have appeared in the following places: "Vow of Silence" and "Blessed" in *Five Points*; "Bullet in My Neck" in *Georgia Review*; "The Sabbath," "Sundays," "Andy," "Salesman," and "Caves" in *American Poetry Review*; "Charity" in *Organica*; "The Ring" in the *American Scholar*. "Andy" appeared in *Volt* in 2008–09, and "Bullet in My Neck" was selected for *Best American Essays 2004,* edited by Louis Menand, published by Houghton Mifflin. "Some Secrets" was included in *In Praise of What Persists*, edited by Stephen Berg, published by Harper and Row, 1983.

Gerald Stern's recent books of poetry are *Save the Last Dance, Everything Is Burning, American Sonnets, Last Blue, This Time: New and Selected Poems*, which won the National Book Award, *Odd Mercy*, and *Bread without Sugar*. His honors include the Ruth Lilly Prize, four National Endowment for the Arts grants, the Pennsylvania Governor's Award for Excellence in the Arts, and fellowships from the Academy of American Poets, the Guggenheim Foundation, and the Pennsylvania Council on the Arts. In 2005 Stern received the Wallace Stevens Award for mastery in the art of poetry. He is currently a chancellor of the Academy of American Poets. For many years a teacher at the University of Iowa Writers' Workshop, Stern now lives in Lambertville, New Jersey.